Reluctant Heroes

by

Doug Wakeling

Reluctant Heroes

All Rights Reserved

Copyright © 2013 Douglas Wakeling

Reproduction in any manner, in whole or in part,
in English or any other language, or otherwise,
without the written permission of the copyright holder is prohibited

Printed by
Digital Print Australia
135 Gilles Street
Adelaide
SA 5000
Australia

For information address mickiedaltonbooks@lycos.com

First Printing 2013

ISBN: 978-0-9875684-0-3

Published by The Mickie Dalton Foundation
Kempsey, NSW
Australia

www.mickiedaltonfoundation.com

Foreword

Doug Wakeling's family has been part of Australian history since the early convict days when some of his ancestors were transported here from Ireland.

They have been part of the building of the nation, played key roles in many areas and many of them served in the Boer War, WWI and WWII.

His first book, *"Curse the Bells"* was published in 2008. Although a work of fiction, it is also based heavily on the history of the Layburn and Wakeling families.

About the Author

Douglas Wakeling

I hail from Valla Beach on the mid north coast of NSW, Australia. I combine my passion for the written word, history and with my family ancestry. Since the late 1980s, I have pondered over my family lineage, particularly the stories of John Joseph Layburn and James Fines, my great grandfathers and their incredible journeys from England and Ireland to country NSW, Australia.

While writing, *"Curse the Bells"* I lived in Maleny, Queensland, noted for its excellence in the arts, which I put down to the quality of the mountain air in the beautiful Blackall Ranges. I'm a keen rail enthusiast and gardener and my venture into the literary world is sure to continue for years to come.

This book is dedicated to my mother, Marcella Wakeling. She was tragically killed in the main street of Nambucca Heads, New South Wales in 1987.

My mother moved from Dee Why, Sydney to the sleepy village of Nambucca Heads on the mid north coast of NSW to live in a retirement village in 1986. I was having a quiet cup of coffee at home when the phone rang. It was Macksville Hospital and the message was not good. My mother had been hit by a frontend loader in the main street of Nambucca Heads whilst walking over a pedestrian crossing.

I jumped in the car and was at the hospital in twenty minutes.

"Mum what happened?" I said as she lay on a bed in the casualty ward.

She replied, "I don't know. I was crossing the road when this thing hit me." She then hesitated and held my hand.

"Don't talk, save your strength," I said.

"No Doug, I have to tell you about my grandfathers John Joseph Layburn and James Fines."

"Tell me later - just get better," I replied as she lay there gasping for breath.

Then she said, "Doug listen, there is an envelope in the bottom draw in the bedroom, it will tell you everything."

With that she closed her eyes and drifted off to sleep.

The Doctor on duty informed me she had broken both arms and six ribs and would have to go to Coffs Harbour Hospital to be treated in the intensive care unit.

My mother went into a coma and never recovered. Six weeks later she was cremated in the Northern Suburbs Crematorium, Sydney and her remains were placed in the wall next to our Father's who had died in 1961.

Descendants of James Fines and John Layburn in Australia

James Fines born 1799 Kildare Ireland. Transported 1823 on the convict ship *Medina*. He married (11/2/1863) Catherine Disney, born 1817, Sligo, Ireland. James died three weeks after the marriage. She remarried George Cott in 1865. Died 1902 at Bathurst
Children of the marriage.
Mary 1842. Some doubts about the father.
Catherine 1845.
Bridget 1847. Married John Graham 1865, remarried John Ramden 1897
Margaret 1849.
Marsetta (Marcella) born 1850 - married = William Henry Morris born 1837 Warwickshire, England married 1882, Carcoar NSW. Died Bathurst, 1938
Alice 1854.
Jane 1855.
James 1858 died INF.
There were two other boys, both died INF.
Children of the marriage – Marsetta and William Morris
Catherine 1883.
William Henry born 1885 died 1952 Bathurst.
Ellen born 1887 died Sydney 1944
Alice born 1890.
Francis James born 1891.
James Fines 1893 married Ruby May Green 1915 Bathurst.

The Surname Fines, also Foynes, Fyan, Fynes, Fyans derived from Fiennes, thought to be derived from a place in France.
The surname Disney is very rare: Tipperary, English, 17th century from French D'Isigney.

Alfred Layburn. born 1870 = Mary Friend.
Children of the marriage: Florence, born 1895, died Inf.
Gladys. Born 1897 = Keith T Scott. Children of the marriage: Beryl, Elaine and Keith T.
Harold. Born 1899. Married Enid. = Children of the marriage: Owen = Barbara = Heather.

John Joseph born 1876 = Ellen Mary Morris Married 1908.
Children of the marriage:
Marcella, born 1910
Children of the marriage: Peter Oliver, b 1932
John Morris, b 1934
Douglas Andrew, b 1939
Neil William (Bill), b 1943 – his son, Nicholas Wakeling, b 1943

Philomena died Inf.
Enid b 1913. Married James (Jim) Gair
John Joseph (Jack) 1914, died 1969 in Wagga Wagga, NSW, married Joan Boothe
Children of the marriage:
Patricia, b 1939; Helen b 1941
Jack remarried Norma Shultz, 1950
Children of the marriage:
John Douglas, b 1950

William John Alfred Layburn born 1887 in NZ. He served in the Australian forces in WW1 and died in 1918

THE LAYBURN CHRONICLES
PART 1

This story chronicles the life of John Joseph Layburn, from his humble beginnings in the small Hamlet of Otley, where in his youth; he was apprenticed to the famous Chippendale furniture makers, until his death in the new continent sixty years late.

A family tragedy caused him to leave his wife and children in England and set off on a remarkable journey. His adventures took him to the magnificent Niagara Falls of British North America, the historical island of St Helena in the South Atlantic where Napoleon Bonaparte was interned and buried and finally to New South Wales, Australia.

On the way, our traveller was shipwrecked on Flinders Island near Tasmania. John finally settles in the picturesque mid-west NSW town of Carcoar which became his home for twenty years.

Although John does not allow the morality of the day to stop him having what he wanted, he left a legacy of being a loving father whose indomitable spirit meant he was not afraid to take risks. When tragedy strikes, John demonstrates his courage in overcoming adversity and living life to the fullest.

THE LAYBURN CHRONICLES
PART 2

RELUCTANT HEROES

Chapter 1

As the Eighteenth century came to a close in the year of 1799, Michael and Catherine Fines lived in the village of Blessington, County Kildare. The family lived in a neat but simple cottage on a huge estate owned by Sir Patrick Hardy. Sir Patrick owned numerous cotton mills and coal mines in the north of England. The yard was cobblestone and the walls were painted with whitewash. Michael had two girls, and his wife Catherine had lost two other children at childbirth but it was a happy household. They were poor, but contented. Their eldest daughter Rowena, who was twelve years old, was swinging on the half door, when her father came down the boreen.

"Da, do we have a brother or a sister?"

"You have a beautiful baby brother and we are going to call him James. He is going to be able to help me on our tater patch. Ah! It's going to be grand."

"What about Ma? Is she going to be all right?" said the lass.

"Yes, your Ma is fine," said Michael.

Catherine had been visiting her friend in the village when she started to get cramps. The night young James was born it started to rain so Catherine bedded down and stayed the night. It was an easy birth and she was soon asleep. Her good friend, Neve O'Connor, closed the door and left her to recover in peace knowing that being a farmer's wife, life was never dull; up at dawn and slaving away till dark, finding something to feed the family, then, if she was lucky and had an understanding husband, she might fall into bed and go to sleep.

"Da, the gombeen man called. He said we are behind in our rent."

"Ah! Don't be worrying yourself lass, he will get his money."

Next morning Catherine was gently woken by her friend Neve with a cup of broth which she drank, as she had a raging thirst. Finally she dressed. The sun was high in the sky but there had been a light frost, so she wrapped young James and proudly walked down past the lake, then turned up the Boreen to their cottage passing other tenant farms on the estate. Some families had been there a life time and had followed in their fathers' footsteps. Mrs Murphy came out to the fence. She and her family lived next door as Shamus, her husband, also worked in the dairy on the estate.

"Ah! Show me the little darling. Is it a boy or girl?" she said.

Catherine gladly showed Bridget her newborn bairn.

"Ah! What a darlin', doesn't he look like his father Michael?"

Next morning Catherine wanted to take the new born babe out into the field and lay him down naked in the newly ploughed field to ward off evil spirits. It was an old Irish custom but Michael came running over.

"Stop, Catherine please. No, he is our only son and we must be careful that he does not get a chill."

"Ah! Darling Michael, look at the little darling. It will only take a few moments. I will say a prayer to make him safe on his life's journey."

Young James didn't seem to mind as he yawned and stretched his little legs. His mother picked him up and rolled him in his shawl and nestled him to her breast.

Life in county Kildare was hard, but the Fines family had a good roof over their head. Michael had work as a farm labourer working for his landlord Sir Patrick Hardy, who had had business interests in Manchester. One of his servants at the big house let it slip to Catherine that he employed over five hundred people working the cotton mills and the mines. Catherine would work in the manor house from time to time when his Lordship was in residence. He would come over in the spring and stay till late in the summer.

The old century was in its last days when Sir Patrick turned up at his estate. It was small compared to some of the estates in Ireland, only five hundred acres and it had at the last count, about a hundred crofters. Most of the men worked for the landlord in some way or another. Sir Patrick was a kind man and when possible would talk to his tenants and there was always something for each family at Christmas. Sir Patrick had lost his wife and had remarried a much younger lass from Carlisle and she accompanied him on this latest trip.

The landlord pulled up at the Fines cottage one bright summer's morning. Michael came out of the dwelling having only just finished his breakfast.
"Mornin' your Lordship," he said tipping his hat. "It's a fine day Sir, is it not? I was just leaving to go down to the west paddock, Sir."
"That's all right Fines," said Sir Patrick. "I'm just enjoying a morning ride. It looks like a good crop this year. I say Fines, I will get to the point. The staff tells me you have just had a son. Young James I think you have called him?"
"Why yes Sir, would you like to see him?" replied Michael.
"No, no that won't be necessary Fines. Could you bring him up this afternoon? Ah! My wife would like to see him and see if he would be suitable. Ah! Yes, that's the word, suitable, to play with young Horatio, you know, for them to play together when they are older in a couple of years," replied Sir Patrick, having difficulty and being slightly embarrassed. "Bring your wife too, about 4pm, would that be possible Fines?"
Michael thought about the work he had to do for the moment, not only the work for his Lordship but his own patch of taters that was coming along nicely but would have to be hilled up soon if he was to get any sort of crop.
"Yes, your Lordship, we will be there," said Michael.

Chapter 2

Over the next few years, Michael worked between his taters and his illegal still that he and Murphy had going. In the local village of Blessington, near where they lived not far from the Barrow River, they made Poteen and sold it on the black market and so avoided the Tithe Man (Tax Man). The barge men plying their trade up and down the river were always keen to purchase the Barley whiskey and Poteen. They would pull into the river bank late in the night and always at a different place to trick the Garda (Irish police).

When Sir Patrick and his family were over from the old country for their yearly trip, young James would walk down to the Manor house to play with the Lordship's son, Horatio and, at the age of six they played well together. At first, they would run up and down the stairs until the young Master tripped and broke an Italian vase. Sir Patrick was mad and the two young ruffians were banned from the house. Unfortunately the young master, who was spoilt rotten, blamed James for the broken vase. Next morning, when James turned up to play with Horatio, he was politely told to go home.

As young James grew up he tried to go to school, but his father, Michael would keep him home to attend the garden or cut peat from the bog for the fire. As the years progressed, James and Horatio never spoke and there was ill feeling between them. The young master tried to make James' life a misery. Although James liked attending school, after three years he still could not read or write. He was always in trouble with the Nuns, especially Sister Aidan. She would bash the young terror and he was continually on garbage and garden duties. He would, whenever the occasion arose, wag class and spend time down at the creek fishing, but he never missed helping his father as there was always something to do at the cottage such as fixing the thatch or giving the walls their coat of lime wash.

One day the school principal, Father O'Hallaeran, was down telling James's father how the lad was falling behind in his school work. However James had more than school work on his mind. He had fallen in love with Marion O'Connell. They were both in the third grade. Her mother worked in the big house and Marion, at the age of ten, also got her start in the big house.

James had turned sixteen and like his father, went to work for the landlord as a farm labourer. Times were tough and there was never enough to eat. Rowena was now married and was having a baby, and with her husband who was a bargeman, were going to live in the back room. As Michael was working from daylight to dark, his rheumatism got worse and the repairs on the cottage got further and further behind. It soon took on an appearance of what could only be described as a hovel. Gone were the lovely white washed walls and holes started to appear in the roof. That year he couldn't get down to the peat bog so there was never enough heating. It was always cold in the winter time. If they were lucky, they had cabbage leaves and taters for their supper. They were typical tenant farmers. James and his father would eke out a living on the couple of acres and would do mainly ploughing jobs for the landlord. It was a good arrangement though and the family were better off than most.

Chapter 3

The landlord's cotton mills in Manchester now employed nearly a thousand workers and Sir Patrick's trips to the manor house became less and less. Then The Manor House received news that his Lordship had passed away. It was 1819.

James had just turned twenty when the new master arrived to run the estate. He was Sir Patrick's younger brother, Mr David Hardy and all he was interested in was chasing young women around the tavern in the village. He loved his drink and soon found out about Michael's Poteen so, every Friday, he had him bring up a barrel to the big house. Unfortunately David's drunkenness and wild behaviour soon had the local parish priest from the Church talking about his scandalous behaviour. The Priest also made his thoughts known to the village constabulary. There had been an unsavoury incident involving a local young lass. She had turned up at the local inn in a deranged state, ranting and raging about a mad English gent who had taken her down to the marshes and raped her. They all thought it would be best if the good gentleman, Mr David Hardy Esquire, should return to the mainland. There were wild scenes, but his wife Millicent, persuaded him that it would be for the best, otherwise there would be a charge of rape against him. The family of the girl was persuaded to take a sum of money and the matter was dropped. The disgraced Hardy family quickly gathered their things and late at night scurried back to Dublin and caught the next ship to Liverpool. The staff was instructed to place dust sheets on all the furniture and the place would remain vacant until further notice.

Young James' and Marion O'Connell's love blossomed. They had been sweethearts since they first went to school and as they grew older, they would meet down at the river and would find a secluded spot away from prying eyes and lie down in the grass.

"James, how old are you now?" she said with starry eyes. She was touching him and she just could not keep her hands off him.

"Ah! Don't be startin' that love talk again."

"Ah! James me Dar is startin' to say things about needing me room and you do luv me, don't you James?"

"You know I do, but how can we get married? I've no money, and where would we live?"

"Ah! James, couldn't we live at your place?"

James thought for a moment. "There will be a vacant cottage coming up soon. Old Mr Kennedy will be moving out since the death of his wife. He told Da he was movin' to Dublin to be with his daughter."

He tried to manoeuvre his body closer to her and get his arms around her.

"Now, James Fines, what da you think ya doin? There will be none of that till you have me in front of the Priest." With that she jumped up.

James quickly followed and said without thinking, "Marion, me darlin', will you marry me?"

"Ah! James me lad, is that a proposal of marriage?"

"Well, what do you think, my darling?"

"Well the answer will be yes, if me Da suss it's ok."

With that the young couple raced home to her parents to tell them the great news. As they reached the front gate Marion announced, "Da, Da, James has asked me to marry him."

Ammon O'Connell, who was milking the house cow, raised his head and said, "Did he now?"

"Can we Da, please?" asked Marion.

Ammon slowly raised himself from the milking stool, walked the short distance and shook young James by the hand.

"Yes, ye can me darling. You took your time young fella but there will be a year of betrothal and when my Marion turns twenty-one on her next birthday; then we will name the day."

James and Marion announced to the village at the next 'Ceilidh' that they were now betrothed and it was drinks all round that night as they danced an Irish jig. All the girls from Marion's class formed a line and danced the traditional Irish folk dance.

Ammon, a little drunk, said to Michael, "Ah! Don't they make a lovely couple?"

"Ah! That they do," replied Michael.

The Flanagan brothers Patrick, Clancy and Joseph were three lads who played the music at all the church and social functions; they played the fiddle, tin whistle and bodhran. That night they played well into the middle of the night.

Chapter 4

Horatio Hardy, son of the late Sir Patrick Hardy, arrived at the manor house from London late that afternoon. The trip from Dublin was uncomfortable and Horatio complained about everything. Poor Gavin his coach and driver had not arrived on time. Gavin tried to explain but the young master would hear none of it. They finally arrived at the manor house and he roused the cook for something to eat. He had brought his cousin Gaylord with him and was to spend the summer there before going back to enrol at Cambridge. Horatio had failed his last year of his Law degree and his widowed mother had whisked him away for the summer until she could sort something out. His uncle was desperately trying to get the University to arrange a post examination so he could join the family Law firm. Meanwhile he was to take up residence at the manor house. His father had died and his uncle had been hastily returned to London so he was given the responsibility of running the large estate.

It was a cloudless mild summer's night and the two lads decided to venture down to the village when they heard the music drifting over the meadow from the village.

Horatio had instructed the driver to follow the Irish folk music. They turned down the lane and there were about fifty people all enjoying themselves. They instructed the coach to stop and wait.

They both positioned themselves at the makeshift bar. They looked ridiculous in their black bowler hats. Horatio with a keen eye for the girls was feasting on the sight of all the young lasses and then one beautiful young

Irish maiden took his eye. It was young Marion O'Connell. She looked lovely, strutting her stuff. He went to move in on the young lass but Gaylord held him back.

"Don't rush them, old boy. We will take our time and get them later one at a time."

And Gaylord pulled his cousin away.

The lasses were doing an Irish jig which had been banned by the British ruling government. After surveying the scene, some of the local lads quickly formed a barrier, but not a word was said. The two toffs departed the Irish Ceilidh and walked back to the waiting coach telling the driver to move off and drive slowly down through the village. The coach pulled up outside the local tavern. They were looking for young women that were out after the curfew. The village of Blessington was in darkness.

"I say, Gavin, is this the place of ill fame you told me about?"

"Why, yes your Lordship, this is the place 'The Shamrock Inn.'"

Blessington did have a house of ill fame and the Garda usually turned a blind eye to the carryings on at Nelly Shannon's house of pleasure. She always had a few girls imported from the docks of Belfast who would look after the needs of the young bargemen who plied the River Barrow.

Nelly had been having some trouble with the Church lately and would not open the door for just anyone at this time of night. As she peered through her peep hole all she could see were the two toffs. She was tired, it was late and they looked like the law. Horatio got out of the carriage and banged on the door.

"Open up, woman! We have good English money and we want to taste some of your Irish maidens."

Nelly remained silent and had to hush the two girls who were there in the parlour. She was about to call out to the young fellow standing at her door that she would open up.

Nelly said, "How much money would you be talking about? It's late. I would have ta rouse up my girls and they will be sound asleep, looking after their beauty sleep."

Horatio just laughed and said, "Beauty sleep. Don't give us that load of Irish crap. If you don't open this door in two minutes, I will break it down."

Nelly remained silent and looked at the door and had a chuckle to herself. She felt like roaring out that he would need all the king's men to break down this door, but she remained silent.

Soon Horatio lost interest, turned, staggered back and climbed into the cab and told Gavin to "drive on. With a burst of bravado, he shouted out, "Madam! We will be back. You will rue the day when you insulted an English gentleman."

So the coach drove the young English toffs, who had had far too many jars of ale at the Ceilidh, slowly down the country lane into the darkness. They had been driving for some minutes when Horatio was about to instruct the driver to return to the manor house. It had been a long day when Gaylord saw somebody at the side of the road.

"What's that?" he said to Horatio, "In the long grass there?"

"Stop the carriage, driver," said Horatio as he stepped down from the cabin. "Well, what have we here?"

"Please, Sir, we were trying to get home but me shoe broke and I hurt my ankle," replied the young lass.

"Well what are you doing in the long grass?" said Horation.

"Sorry Sir, we thought you were the Garda."

"Well, get into the coach and we will get you home," said Horatio.

"Thank you, Sir, but we live in the next village."

Horatio instructed the driver to return to the Manor and go around the back.

"Yes Sir," replied Gavin.

As the coach turned up the driveway one of the young lasses said, "Where you takin' us, Sir? You not goin' to have your wicked way with us arr you, please? Sir, we will get into trouble fir bean out so late," the lass said with a bit of a giggle. Horatio could not wait as he was trying to undress one of the young ladies. He had practically succeeded, with her protesting profusely but still allowing him to fondle her, when the coach came to a sudden halt at the back door of the manor house.

Cook, who had been woken by the commotion, looked from her room and shut the door.

"Wait here, Gavin. I will get you to take these whores to their village later."

"Yes, Sir," Gavin replied.

Horatio escorted the girls down to the back door. It was two o'clock in the morning and the girls were both giggling as he slapped the one called Colleen across the bottom. He gave them two shillings each and told them to be on their way.

Chapter 5

Rowena was feeding her youngest child in the sun outside the cottage when, from down the road she could see the Gombeen Man coming up the road.

She called out, "Da, it must be Gale day. Here is Mr Flanagan to collect the rent."

Flanagan came through the gate. "Where's your Da, lass?" he said.

Michael came out the door with the hard earned money in his hand.

"Mornin' to you, Fines. Looks like it could rain."

Shamus Flanagan had been collecting the rents from the crofters for as long as Michael could remember.

"I've got some bad news, Michael."

Michael could tell that whenever Shamus called him Michael, the rent was going up.

"Ye see the new landlord, young Mr Horatio Hardy, has said the rents have to go up to double. You have been getting away with cheap rents for too long. I'm sorry Michael."

"Flanagan, we can hardly pay the money now. £3 a year and now you'll want £6. Where will we be finding that sort of money, dear mother of God?"

"I'm sorry Michael, I'm only doing me job. Perhaps your good lady wife Catherine might get a job back at the big house."

That night at the dinner table they discussed the problem. Rowena and her husband who lived in the back room had decided to take the small family to the city where there were better prospects. Rowena didn't want to leave her mother and now her Da was sick, but next morning she packed her things and with three young children, joined her husband on the barge to travel to Dublin. It was nearly impossible for Michael and the family to exist. The potato crop was poor this year and it seemed to be getting worse each year. It was getting harder and harder for his illegal still to make a profit. So James' mother got her old job back up at the big house. This worked well for a while but Michael's illness became worse. Catherine had to return home to attend to her husband. James would work in the fields from daylight to well after dark, sometimes seven days a week.

The new landlord got straight down to work putting off unwanted staff and cutting costs to make sure he could feed his lavish lifestyle. One particular day he was inspecting the cottages and he noticed that the old Kennedy croft was vacant. On closer inspection he asked his head carpenter to estimate the cost of repairs. He was advised it would be cheaper to demolish the structure.

James was in shock as he saw the fire burning and the heap of rubble that was planned to be their new home. He tried to explain to Angus, the carpenter that he would have fixed the place up when his new wife moved in. When this got back to Horatio, he was more determined and pleased that the Kennedy croft had been demolished.

Young Horatio was an obnoxious sod and one day he provoked James, practically running him down. When he was a lad, Horatio had never forgotten James as a playmate and being the spoilt brat that he was had kept a grudge all these years.

Chapter 6

Curfew had been imposed between 1814 and 1818 and was still in force. If persons were caught out at night, they could be transported.

Stories filtered back to Ireland of the penal settlements in New South Wales and the Islands of Norfolk and Van Diemen's Land and were being spread through the local taverns. Although James could not read or write he was able to follow the stories as they were told.

James betrothal to Marion O'Connell was accepted and they would be soon married. Marion had gained employment at the manor house as a maid and was saving her wages and putting together a dowry for her marriage to James. She had been working in the manor house for about six months when Horatio confronted her one day in his typical arrogant English manner.

"Miss O'Connell, my groom tells me you are to be married to young Fines."

"Yes Sir, that's correct. James and I are to be married in March and we were hoping to live in the Kennedy croft," Marion replied.

Horatio just stood there, then said with a sneer. "Look, I am the master of this estate and I've burnt down the old Kennedy croft. I determine who and where my tenants live." With that he just walked off chuckling to himself.

Before young Master Hardy turned up it was a pleasant job working on the estate and there was never any trouble when Sir Hardy was alive. The estate just looked after itself.

James and the family were sitting around the fire trying to keep warm one cold winter's night in January 1822 when there was a loud knock on the door.

"James, James, let me in," Marion cried out.

Catherine opened the door and Marion rushed in.

"James!" she sobbed crying her eyes out, running to James, weeping and placing her arms around his neck. Her dress was ripped down the front exposing her naked breasts.

"What happened?" he said.

Catherine got Marion a drink and quickly covered her nakedness. As she settled down beside the fire, James got her a blanket and placed it around her shoulders. After she had stopped sobbing, she told them how the young Squire had dragged her into the kitchen and was about to have his way with her when the cook came in, and shouting and screaming, separated him from the frightened young girl.

James was furious. His mother tried to calm him down but he stormed out the door and into the driving rain, running the one mile to the main house. He did not care if the Garda caught him but he thought they would not be out on a night like this to catch curfew breakers. Instead they would be at the local tavern. James was more than angry, he was furious. Normally he would never go to the main front door but this night, he walked up to the front door and banged on it, calling out, "Come out, you bastard, come out!"

Lights went on and finally the butler opened the door. James stormed in, calling out, "Where are you, you bastard?" James had fire in his eyes.

The young Squire came to the top of the stairs demanding the butler throw the young rascal out.

"Come down, you bastard," James continued to rant and rave. "I'll get you, you bastard."

Horatio finally turned and returned to his room.

James stormed out and went down to the stables and out of spite stole a horse and bridle. He rode like the wind as fast as he could back to the croft.

The rain on his face had a sobering effect and he thought of how the situation might be interpreted in the morning. He started to laugh and decided to return the horse and bridle the next day. He would tell the young bastard to leave his girl alone and if he did anything like that again he would kill him. So cap in hand he walked back in the morning leading the horse to the Manor House. As he approached the stable, he was met by the Garda and he was arrested for having stolen property in his possession and admitting to being out after dark.

He was arrested along with Patrick Donnelly and Charles Jones. They were sentenced to seven years' transportation to the state of New South Wales. His case was heard at Dublin City, like all the rest. As he was illiterate he did not understand the court procedure and the family could not afford to have representation for him.

Chapter 7

James Fines was given a Convict Indent Number 653 and the charge was given as house breaking.

He and the other convicts were sent to Cork Harbour and imprisoned at Spike Island to await transportation to New South Wales. They were thrown into a cell with about twenty other convicts who were awaiting transportation.

James was described as five foot three inches tall, grey eyes, brown hair with a very much freckled and pockmarked complexion and was declared fit for manual labour. He was to be assigned to a Mr Henry Marr in the Bathurst area west of Sydney.

The conditions in the gaol were sub-standard. The roof leaked and unless you could afford to bribe the guards, you slept on the straw provided on the floor. Rats roamed the dark corridors and the cells were damp and stunk of urine and fouled air from sick convicts who were suffering from most every disease known to man. Each morning, stretcher bearers carried out bodies from the cells.

The first Sunday they were woken early, chained and paraded to the cell yard for religious observance. At first the convicts complained until they realised that it took them up into the daylight and warm sunshine when it was not raining.

On the second Sunday they were introduced to Brother Edmund Rice from the Christian Brothers Society who would lecture them on being good Catholics and he wished them well on their long journey to New South

Wales. He would go on preaching to them how they should say their rosaries and go to mass, keeping away from the evil drink and loose women. He seemed to rant and rave on for hours and hours. The men were starting to get tired and edgy.

He finished off by saying, "Men of Ireland, God will be watching over you every moment when you are not expecting him. So be careful my sons, look after yourselves. Think of your mothers and fathers back here in good old Ireland. They tell me there are snakes that would eat a team of British lords. Yes, me men, do the right thing and good old Ireland will be proud of you. Do your time and if you have to meet the Lord by hanging, then do it like a true Irishman and be greeted at the gates by Saint Peter."

Michael and Catherine were in shock. They had pleaded with the young master at the Manor House to drop the charges against James as he had returned the horse and besides, who would work the fields now? Young Horatio's answer was he would get someone else to take over. There were always plenty of others to work the patch and be thankful for the roof over their heads. Michael was given one month to clear out.

So they packed their meagre belongings and made the trip to the city of Cork and stayed with Michael's brother where they tried in vain to see their son. They were told to come back on the day the ship 'Medina' was to sail (5th September 1823) from the port of Cobh and if they had the right amount of money they might get to see their young son. They did not have any money to spare, so their son sailed off to the Southern Hemisphere never to be seen by them again.

Young Marion turned up with her father the week that the ship sailed but they were also too late - the prisoners had boarded the ship. All they could do was wave the ship goodbye. Even her father had a tear in his eye.

After leaving the prison at Spike Island, in preparation for the journey they were issued two suits of clothing, one pair of shoes, three shirts and a warm jacket. They were also provided bedding and a pillow. Prayer books and bibles were also distributed among the men.

Reluctant Heroes

As James climbed the rope ladder to board the 'Medina' to start his journey to Botany Bay, he looked back over the last three years

Chapter 8

It was Christmas 1821 at Ballbritton. James teamed up with a wild mob that had been tagged the 'White boys.' They terrorized the wealthy neighbourhood, robbing from the rich. He had met up with John Daly from the days when he would hang around the wharf unloading barges. They finally met their match when on 26th December 1821, they were apprehended on the Grand Canal in Kings County. To make matters more serious they had stolen arms from a house owned by Mr J. Cooper.

The two men were sentenced to death in Phillips town under the 'White boys Insurrection Act.' They were tried in the Assizes court on the 20th March 1821.

Seven months later, John Daly, along with 172 men of whom most had been convicted under the same act. John and James sentences had been reduced to transportation for seven years. James escaped and made his way back to his home. He laid low until that night when he was provoked at the big house. If the Guardia only knew that he was a wanted prisoner on the run. No one had twigged that his real name was James Fines. Not James Foynes.[1]

On the night he escaped he was being transported with other prisoners to the jail on Spike Island, Cork. He was in the last wagon and the weather was bad, the wind was howling and lightning lit up the sky. All of a sudden, the wagon tipped when it went into a hole and the wheel snapped. The sergeant

---

Footnote 1 See page 377

and his aide had their hands full as, being the last wagon, they were all alone. The sergeant quickly ordered the prisoners to get down and help with lifting the wheel out of the mud but, to make matters worse, the axle had broken. The twenty prisoners could not move the wheel as it had stuck fast. One of the men shouted out that if they were unmanacled, they could be of more help. Reluctantly the hand cuffs were removed but the wheel still would not budge. The sergeant then ordered a small party of five to fetch a strong limb to lever the wheel out of the mud. The sergeant was not very bright and could not count so six men moved off into the dark night. At the first opportunity, James who was at the back, separated from the group, slipped into the night and hid under some bracken fern. He watched as the men returned with a tree limb and proceeded to the wagon. He did not move as he could hear the men shouting and the sergeant trying to do a head count.

Then he heard in a loud voice, "Fe god's sake, stand still will ye" and finally he heard the command to move off.

For the moment he was free; he wasn't going to Botany Bay. He wanted to get back and marry Marion O'Connell. However he knew his escape was too easy.

Early the next morning, he rose from his camouflage of bracken fern and slowly made his way in a direction that would take him home. It was early spring and there was a heavy fog. Finally he stopped at a crofter's cottage and, knocking on the back door, he asked the lady of the house if he could do some work for a feed.

"Somethin to eat, do you want lad? Well, see that wood heap, start choppin' and I'll see."

It didn't take long for James to chop all the wood.

"Well, let me see. Looks like you running from the Garda. What you do, me lad?" she said as she opened the door to let him in.

James soon demolished the bowl of soup. "Well, thank you me lady. I'll be off now."

"Ar don't be daft! You can't be walking in bright daylight. Go over to the barn and hold up till night time. I'll bring you some supper around dusk and you can tidy up the barn while you wait."

Reluctant Heroes

So this is how he lived for the next few days, travelling mainly at night keeping low until he finally arrived home. His mother cried and thanked the lord for bringing him home.

"Hey, you at the back. Stop daydreaming and get up on deck. This is not a Sunday school picnic."

Chapter 9

As they were not performing any physical work it was more than enough to keep them fit. Four convicts slept on six square feet of space, each having eighteen inches. The ship had scuttle holes along the sides of the vessel to allow fresh air to enter the lower decks. Every effort was made to get the convicts to their destination in as fit condition as possible, unlike earlier voyages. Although the below deck air was putrid from the bilge water, stale and musty clothes and body odour, the convicts had no other choice. As the vessel got into equatorial waters the better behaved convicts were allowed on deck to wash their clothes using coarse soap. Then they would tie them onto a rope and rinse them in the sea and dry them on the ship's railing. As most of the lads had never seen the sea, there was always a fear of drowning but they thought it was better to drown than flounder around in the water and be attacked by a shark.

Life on board the convict ship soon got into a routine and special jobs were allocated to trusted convicts, and as John had been raised on a farm, he was given the task of feeding the two sows that were heavy with litters that were about to drop. The convicts would never see the fresh pork. It would be reserved for the Captain and officers.

The convicts were allowed on deck in the early evening to get some fresh air. There were about twenty convicts allowed at a time. One of his fellow convicts turned to John and said, "Look up there, that's the North

Star; from what I have read we'll soon lose that star as we sail into southern waters."

Some of the lads were grumbling about the lack of variety in the slops that were on offer to eat when one of the lads remarked he had heard tales that on some journeys shipwrecked sailors had resorted to cannibalism. It was called the Custom of the Sea. There was quiet as they pondered over the disgusting thought of eating human flesh then there was laughter and someone remarked, "That was a joke. No one would ever eat another; it was against God's law."

The convicts soon established a pecking order on James' deck. Some of the convicts who had some money could bribe the guards for extra rations, but most of the time they survived on hard tack dipped in tea or if they were lucky, gruel, a hot vegetable soup. The water was putrid. If they were lucky the sailors would add lime juice to it to disperse the taste. If they were extra lucky, they drank beer which had been brewed by an enterprising convict. As most of the boys were from Dublin and surrounding counties, they formed a pack to look out for each other.

The ship's lighting was lanterns that burnt whale oil. When the sea was calm the lanterns would remain still, but when there was a swell they would dance on the rigging and this was always a problems as it could tip over and catch the boat on fire.

Some days they would have the run of the lower decks. If the convicts were lucky they would gather the odd fresh egg to be eaten raw. On some days the boat would only average four to six knots. As none of the convicts had ever sailed further than the estuaries, no-one had the faintest idea how long the voyage was going to take. James was not backward in coming forward. The ship had been sailing for about a week, when the convict next to him pulled a knife on him and demanded his possessions. Some of the convicts had stashed money in all sorts of places - in their shoes, if they were lucky enough to have them. James was quicker than a leprechaun and disarmed the opposing convict of his knife.

Of course James had never seen a leprechaun but on some nights when he had been to the local inn he would swear on the bible he had seen the little fellows down by the bridge on his way home. The trip was uneventful until they crossed the equator and the ship's crew made it a fun day. As all the convicts were sailing to the southern seas they were introduced to 'King Neptune.'

Only the Captain and his officers knew the route the ship was taking. After they had crossed the equator the ship turned to port. Henry who had befriended James took a guess and said "St Helena, I think that's where we are heading, James, me lad."

Sure enough, next morning they were anchored off James Town. The small harbour was full of ships from all over the world. The British navy was well represented. As they passed one old tub that stunk to high heaven, Henry said, "She be a slaver on her way to the Americas - we're lucky we are white."

There was also a French frigate anchored in the bay. There was a truce between France and Great Britain and a French delegation had arrived on the island to negotiate the return of their beloved leader Napoleon's body.

The two convicts had become firm friends but it puzzled James why Henry was sent aboard in Ireland as he was not Irish. Henry later explained how he had been sent to Ireland to retrieve some family debts and he got into further trouble at the card tables. He vowed to James he had given up gambling forever but then he explained to his new-found friend how he started to print his own money.

"You mean forgery?" said James.

"I was pretty good at it you know," said Henry. "I fooled most people until one day I got too brave and tried to fool a bank clerk. You know what James? The ink was still wet on the paper."

They started to laugh and James said, "Well you were a bright one, weren't you?"

They were forever scrubbing down the deck and had lots of opportunities to see the sea life, James, who had never seen the open ocean was fascinated by the dolphins; how they frolicked around the vessel and seemed to keep up with the ship as it ploughed through the waves. The

'Medina' crossed the Southern Atlantic without too much drama. The mountainous seas that they had been warned about did not eventuate and they made their way to the South America continent, stopping briefly at Rio to pick up fresh supplies and water. The Convicts were kept below decks. The captain had on previous trips seen some of the convicts jump ship at Rio, though most would drown or get taken by sharks. Some of the more unruly felons were put in irons. There was all hell to pay late one night when they were woken by the guards dragging one poor fellow to the brig. He had in his possession a file and he was charged with having it in his possession as an implement to assist escape. He was to receive fifty lashes on deck in the morning. It was a gruesome business. All the convicts were shackled and in leg irons and were on deck to witness the punishment. He was from County Derry.

He took it like a true Irishman with never a peep and by the time that they cut him down he was unconscious. The surgeon allowed the seaman to carry him down to the sick bay as he was moaning loudly. All convicts returned to their decks silently as this had been a warning to all of the poor wretches. The ship was fully laden with supplies and the water level was high up the planking to a very dangerous level.

It was a sad occasion as one of their mates, Murphy from Armagh, was found dead. He was aged fifty seven and had been transported for life as he had assaulted an officer of the law. He was committed to the sea. It was a moving ceremony, the parson said some prayers. As soon as it was over, James said to Henry, "There should have been a priest instead of this Proddie parson; he was taller than I thought was our Murphy."

"Ah! James me lad, they tie two cannon balls to his feet to weigh him down so he goes straight to the bottom," said Henry.

The lads were doing their washing one fine morning when James said to Henry, "I say Henry, look at the water. The ship is running low don't you think?"

Henry, being well read said, "Someone should do something about it. There needs to be some sort of line painted on the side of the ship to stop unscrupulous ship owners from overloading."

It would be some sixty years before regulation came in to stop ship owners overloading the ships with cargo. The gentleman's name was Samuel Plimsoll who was born February 1824. This is the same Samuel Plimsoll whose invention of the "Plimsoll Line" gave rise to this regulation.

Chapter 10

The 'Medina' was a day's sailing from Cape Town when James had befriended a young convict from Dublin. He was all of fourteen and had stolen some linen from a gent. He was in agony one morning and was complaining about a rotten tooth. There was always someone who knew a quick way to solve a toothache. They took him down to the infirmary were the young surgeon, using some twine wrapped around the infected tooth gave a mighty yank and the rotten tooth landed on the floor. The young lad was given copious quantities of rum and was sent below to sleep it off.

They were soon on their way again, briefly stopping off at Cape Town at the bottom of South Africa. They travelled onwards into the southern Indian Ocean where the ship was battered by violent winds and mountainous seas of the South Pole. Water came in through the vents and all the convicts on the lower decks were swamped. Their bedding and clothes were soaked took days to dry out. Some of the convicts were violently ill. James seemed to thrive on the trip and except for a heavy head cold, he was fit.

"Land! Land!" Someone shouted. There was a mad rush to the main deck, but there was no land in sight so the convicts returned to their duties. When the cloud lifted they could see land in the distance. The convicts had a glimpse of the great southern land. It was quickly revealed that the sailors could smell land - it had a musty leafy smell.

James and Henry were swabbing the deck when Henry said to James, "I say James old boy, we should try and stick together. Do you know where you are being sent?"

"Well Henry, to a place called Baftus."

"I think the town is called Bathurst and is west of Sydney town," replied Henry. As the coast line passed them by they had the chance to see the barren coast line. Little did the convicts know but they had anchored in a bay that was frequented by whalers. There were three ships in the sheltered bay. The Captain sent a part of the crew to shore to fill water barrels. Henry was telling James where he had read that further up the western coast a Dutch ship, on its way to Batavia ran aground on a reef in 1629 and the captain ordered 125 men, women and children passengers slaughtered. The Commander, a nasty devil by the name of Pelsaert, was taken to Batavia and hanged. It was a terrible business.

"Ah! You two 288 and 642, if I have to tell you again about talking instead of working, it will be lashes me lads. you don't want your pretty backs marked do you?" the guard on deck duty cried out.

The 'Medina' made its way through Bass Strait which separated the mainland from Van Diemen's Land. The seas were calm though it was not uncommon for the wind to change to gale force and many a ship had come to a grizzly end. The weather was kind as they turned and set a course up the east coast of the mainland. As the ship sailed up the New South Wales coast, James and some of the convicts were on duty scrubbing the deck. It was a never ending job and as they entered Port Jackson, they could hear the sound of the waves thundering on the rocks at South Head from a mild swell. James looked up and, for no apparent reason, was reminded of Ireland and the girl he left behind.

Chapter 11

Finally, on 29th December 1823, the 'Medina' sailed up the harbour with 176 male prisoners. What a contrast it was from their old County Kildare of Ireland. The temperature outside was close to 100 degrees Fahrenheit and it appeared to be shaping up to be a hot summer. One of the sailors was telling James and Henry that at the turn of the eighteenth century, Irish convicts had rebelled at a place called Vinegar Hill, west of Sydney. They were rebelling against the laws of the settlement. There had been little or no food and there was a suggestion that the English convicts were being favoured. All Irish convicts had been painted with the same brush as being trouble makers. Before they left the ship the captain came on deck to address the prisoners.

"Men from Ireland, although I personally have not lived here, this is my last trip as I will be returning to England to retire. My advice to you is behave yourselves, serve your time and get your ticket of leave as soon as you can. This is going to be a great country and if I was your age I would be settling here. But let me say this, if you misbehave you will be sent to Van Diemen's Land and I have it on good authority that they are thinking of reopening the Norfolk Island colony to send the worst of you, so look out and the best of luck."

The convicts waited to be led off the ship but the livestock would be first. Although the colony had been in existence for close on forty years, livestock was still in short supply and as soon as it reached the wharf they were snapped up by the few free settlers and some going into the Governor's flock.

There was a government officer at the bottom of the gangplank taking particulars of the convicts. They had records of every character feature including height, approximate weight, hair colour and any other distinguishing features. So with their meagre possessions and in single file, they marched off in leg irons to Hyde Park Barracks. The Barracks was an impressive building designed by a former convict Francis Greenway and was completed in 1819.

The early governors in their wisdom had divided the state of New South Wales into regions; the main ones were west as far as Bathurst, south as far as Goulburn and Newcastle to the north.

Chapter 12

James along with other convicts set out on 6th January 1824 as they were assigned to the government stock establishment at Bathurst. James was assigned as a shepherd at Princess Charlotte's Vale (now near Perthville south of Bathurst). All the convicts who were travelling west were assembled and they set out to walk to Bathurst. They were issued with new boots and convict clothes and a blanket. As they reached Parramatta, most of them were suffering from exhaustion and were glad to have the chance to be in the prison barracks to recover. The convicts cooped up on the 'Medina' for all those months were relieved to be placed in a cell. At least it didn't sway.

James said to Patrick Donnelly, "How much further is this Bathurst do you think Patrick?"

"I don't know James, but me feet are killing me."

The next morning they reached the Nepean River and it was in full flood. The party of fifty convicts just looked and one of them said to the trooper, "I can't swim."

The trooper said, "don't worry Mick, we cross over the river by punt. It's moored around the next bend."

As they rounded the bend in the river the punt stood tied up to the river bank. It had just unloaded a flock of sheep from the other side.

"Sergeant," James said.

"Yes, Mick."

"My name is James, if you don't mind, Sir."

The trooper just looked at James and said, "Look Mick, you Irish are all the same. You will want a feather bed next."

"No Sir. Just call me James. That will be fine."

The trooper thought about it for a moment and his mind went back to the day his father had been transported in 1799 for stealing a damn sheep. His mother and his sister made the long hazardous journey when his father had got his Ticket of Leave. He had served his ten years and had put some money together to bring the rest of his family out from England, so he knew how hard the struggle was going to be for these poor wretches. It was the middle of summer with warm to hot days and relentless flies swarming around, never giving you a moment's peace, but in the winter it was freezing cold, not to mention the snakes, spiders and dingos.

"Pick your feet up there men!" shouted the trooper. "Steady as she goes. Don't make any unnecessary moves on the punt or you might tip it over. James, give your mate a hand and tell him to hang on."

James had a chuckle to himself as he noted the change in the young trooper. *He had called me by my proper name,* he thought.

The punt manoeuvred out into the main stream. The punt man organised some of the convicts to work the ropes and after some effort, got it safely to the opposite bank.

The going became easier after they crossed the grass plains into the small village of Emu Plains. Patrick started to sing, "We're leaving old Ireland forever."

"Ah! Don't start singin' that Patrick, we may get home one day," said James. "What would the stream be called, Sir?" he continued, addressing the trooper.

The trooper replied, "That's the Nepean River."

Patrick, pointing to the west, saw an animal bounding along on the grass plain. "Look James, is that the Kungaroo? It's got two heads."

The trooper had a chuckle to himself.

"Mates, they're called Kangaroos and if you look real close, she has a young baby called a Joey in her pouch. Listen fellows, don't get too excited, there are thousands out where you're going. They're good tucker, too."

That night they camped at the foothills of the Blue Mountains. Most of the men were exhausted and after a quick bite to eat, they were sound asleep.

James was having trouble sleeping that night, thinking of his betrothed back home and how he was robbed of his life with his sweet Marion. He thought, *if I ever got back to Ireland, I will kill young Horatio Harding.*

The next morning they were up bright and early and were on the move, climbing up a well worn track. The bush was alive with birds screeching and the noise was deafening. Later, James was informed that the noise was not only from the birds but insects called Cicadas. There was a great variety and they all had different names. The yellow ones were called Yellow Mondays, the green ones Greengrocers and the big ones were called Flowery Bakers. They all had a chuckle and it was soon revealed that they had a lot to learn about this big wide brown land.

The trooper stopped for a break at a giant tree and one of the convicts asked in a very polished voice, "I say Sergeant, the explorers were Blaxland, Lawson and Wentworth I think. Didn't they first cross here in 1813? I think that's correct."

"Yere! That's right, what's your name?"

"Henry James Howard, Sir, No 642."

"Where did you get that information from?" asked the trooper.

"Oh! In the London Times, Sir," Henry remarked.

"What did you do, 642? You're not our average felon," the trooper remarked.

As the convict party progressed up the track there became a lull as they passed a work gang.

"Look Henry, they're got leg irons," whispered James.

As the party of convicts moved further up the hill, trooper Dan started to tell the men how they would end up on the chain gang if they misbehaved, working on the road gangs with Privates Sudds and Thompson from the 89th Foot. He went on to explain that the pair of overseers were ex-convicts and had a ruthless reputation. "So, fellers, I advise you to keep your nose clean and keep away from the boys from the 89th foot."

"Do you have a name, trooper, Sir? We can't go on calling you trooper," said Henry.

The trooper thought about it for a moment. "Yer, well it's Dan Smith, but don't call me that when my superiors are around. Anyway, what did you do to get transported over here 642?"

Henry had a smile on his face.

"Well, if you ever need some papers signed, I'm your man."

"Forgery, eh?" said Dan. He went on to explain how the track across the mountains was carved out of the bush by 1815, and the distance from Sydney was 141 miles and 101 from Emu Plains. They were making about seven miles a day and they estimated it would take about three weeks.

That evening, Trooper Dan Smith instructed the convicts on how the natives made bark shelters that could be erected in a hurry to keep out the worst of the weather. After six days from the Nepean, they reached the explorer Cox's weatherboard hut, now used as a military post. The group camped there for the night but bright and early the next morning, they moved on through the village of Katoomba. Three more days and they were on the top of Mount Victoria looking down on the Bathurst Plains. They all stopped to take in the spectacular view of the green rolling hills that had so impressed the three explorers Blaxland, Lawson and Wentworth back in 1813.

Trooper Dan gathered the last stragglers around him. "Men, you are looking at the western plains," he said. "It will be your home, so get used to it."

The next day was slow going down a winding track. They finally stopped for the night at a place called Hartley. That night as they lay exhausted, James was woken by a strange noise. He sat up with a start.

"Did you hear that Henry?"

"Hear what James?"

"There it goes again. It sounds like a tiger."

"What's the problem over there?" shouted Trooper Dan.

James jumped out of his blanket and moved over to the fire.

"Dan, I heard a noise over there and it sounded like a tiger."

"Ah! James, me lad. If I knew better, I would say you've been drinking."

Dan and James walked over to where the growl had come from, Dan was in the lead.

"Over there, Dan, look, the eyes." Said James.

GROWL!!

"Holy Mother of God, Dan, what is it?" James shouted.

"Ah! It's just a Moggy gone wild, that's all. It's a big one though," replied the trooper.

The animal growled again and scurried off into the night.

"What's a moggy, Dan?" said James.

"Stray cats that have escaped from Sydney town, that's all," said Dan. He later told the men that it was believed that early explorers, the Portuguese, came down the East Coast of Terra Australis in the 1600s and had left animals; cats, goats and others. Only cats survived and they were sighted by the early explorers as they crossed the mountains.

Next morning, they moved down the hill and came to a river named after William Cox, the explorer. The water was shallow and made a soft gentle noise as it caressed the water-washed river stones. As they crossed the shallow stream, a flock of beautiful blue birds swooped down and appeared to be feeding on insects on the water. As James crossed the shallow river, he was taken in by the river stones. They seemed to shine. He picked up one and put it in his pocket. He was later told that if any convict was suspected of carrying gold, there was a heavy fine and punishment, so James kept his stone that he thought was gold, well hidden. The authorities were keeping the lid on any gold discoveries; true or false, to discourage mad stampedes.

Finally after twenty-one days the group of convicts trudged the last few miles into Bathurst. The men were hot and exhausted as they crossed over the Macquarie River. Trooper Dan turned a blind eye and allowed them to drench themselves in the cool refreshing pools.

"I say, Dan, is this a river? It's nothing more than a series of water holes," said Henry.

"You wait. When it rains, you could be flooded in for weeks," remarked Dan.

Like drowned rats, they arrived in Bathurst. They were escorted to the barracks, given a meal and locked in the compound. Next morning James, along with all the other convicts was told to line up on the parade ground. They were given another pair of boots made from hessian and three suits of slop clothing and another blanket. The Officer in Charge came out and addressed the new batch of convicts.

Chapter 13

"Men, you have been transported to Bathurst to do a job. If you behave yourself, everything will be fine. For those who think this is a holiday, well forget it, if you misbehave, you will be sent to Norfolk Island, so do your job and we will get on just fine."

He then read out a list of convicts to issue them with a new number.

"Convict 288, James Fines."

"Here, Sir."

"293, Patrick Donnelly."

"Here, Sir."

"233, Thomas Johnston."

"Here, Sir."

"432, Charles Jones."

"Here, Sir."

"642, Henry Howard."

In a very polished English voice Henry responded, "Here, Sir."

"234, Thomas Moray."

"Here, Sir."

Trooper Dan took the opportunity to say a few words to the lads and wished them well. They were all marched down to the barber shop for a convict cut (short back and sides) and reissued with convict garb.

"Now you lot have been assigned to Mr Henry Marr and you will proceed to Princess Charlotte Vale where you will obey him and do your work, but let me warn you, misbehave and you will be flogged. For those repeat offenders, I am warning you, you will be sent to Norfolk Island."

They were escorted by three troopers out to Princess Charlotte's Vale. This was located at the southern end of the town.

As they were trudging along the road, James said to Henry, "I don't like the sound of this Norfolk Island, Henry."

"Ah! Don't worries, James. Just do as they ask and the time will fly by."

James pointed out the gallows to Henry.

"They don't muck around here, they mean business," Henry replied.

Mr Henry Marr was an overseer working under Mr John Maxwell who was the Superintendent of Government Stock for the Wellington Valley. He was in control of over 100,000 acres.

They moved off towards the stock yards at Sandy Creek. The six new convicts were divided into two groups and were instructed to go with the experienced men who had been serving their time. Some of the convicts were finishing their term and were receiving Tickets of Leave. Some would stay, and were granted up to twelve hectares of land for their good behaviour. Some would be employed in positions of responsibility as clerks or overseers. A lot would squander their grant, sell to wealthy land owners and just melt into the landscape.

James was under the direction of a Ticket of Leave man, Arthur Thompson, who had been in the colony since the beginning.

James, Henry, Patrick and Charlie, with two other shepherds were assigned to look after a flock of about a thousand sheep. They were about twenty miles from the stockyards. The landscape was totally opposite to the lush green meadows of County Kildare and it was hot. Dan had warned them about the flies but they had never experienced anything like it. They were in their eyes and hair. James felt dejected and miserable and his thoughts turned to Marion. *What was she doing?* he thought. He loved her.

On James' first night under the stars he was looking up into the sky. He had not taken much notice of the brilliant southern sky. Henry, who was somewhat of an expert on everything, pointed out the main constellations, especially the Southern Cross. There were no fences, shackles or guards to keep the convicts locked up. They were on their honour not to run off. Most convicts obeyed the rules, as they were just too damned frightened not to, mainly because of the blacks and snakes but most of all they were terrified of the dark. The flies were a constant curse.

One day Henry rigged some bits of wood from string attached to his hat to keep the flies away. James had his first experience with a dingo. He thought it was nothing more than a dog, but Arthur, the older shepherd warned him they could give you a nasty bite. Then there were snakes. They came in all sorts of colours and sizes to frighten the life out of a young Irish lad.

The convicts lived in a hut divided into two compartments. The flock was divided into two sections and it was the responsibility of two convicts to look after the sheep in the day, then they would bring them back at night to be penned. The convict who was assigned to looking after the camp in the day, would then have the job to keep an eye on the flock at night.

The dingoes would howl a piercing cry and the new lads would huddle together. At first they were scared of the blacks until they realised, if they kept away from them they were no trouble. The convicts from Ireland were frightened of snakes as they had no snakes back home. There were deadly ones in the bush - King Browns and Tiger snakes. One of James' mates had already been bitten and died.

Most of the convicts adapted to the work. It was hard but rewarding. There were always a few bad apples in the barrel, but they were soon sorted out and were punished. Some made the journey back to Sydney and others were transported to Norfolk. Some were strung up at the Barracks in Bathurst.

Some of the convicts had been assigned to look after flocks that were so far out that some of them died of starvation. James had been lucky. Henry had quickly realised that if they were to survive, they would have to eat some of the food the Blacks ate. They finally tasted Kangaroo. They would cook up the tails and make a good soup once a fortnight. The base camp would bring out provisions, which consisted of five kilos of wheat, three kilos of

Reluctant Heroes

mutton or beef or two kilos of salt pork, fifty-six grams of salt and fifty-six grams of soap per week. There were never any vegetables so they would eat grass. They were never allowed to kill a sheep to eat, but if one died or if it had been mauled by a dingo, it had to be reported to the Government Officer and then they would be allowed to dress it and they would eat well for a few days.

Each year they were entitled to two jackets, three shirts, two pairs of trousers and three pairs of shoes made from hessian as well as a hat or cap. If they were lucky, their supplies were supplemented with tea, sugar and tobacco. These luxuries were granted for good behaviour. They were paid no wage. Mail was rare. There was never any from home but occasionally something came from the government.

At least James was lucky as he had arrived in the colony with the mates he was convicted with. Patrick Donnelly and Charles Jones were at this lonely outpost too. Charlie had brought his fiddle and on balmy summer's nights, he would play and the others would sing along and do a jig. An Aboriginal family that lived down by the river would join them. They would sit around and occasionally join in the dancing. It was rare that drink was available but sometimes renegade convicts would tempt them with cheap alcohol. They never had any money so they would trade goods after a drinking session. One night as they were all sitting around the camp fire, Arthur finally revealed how he came to be in Sydney town. He explained how he was a lad of fourteen in 1780 and had been put into gaol for stealing a loaf of bread. He explained how, like a lot of his fellow convicts he was starving and the loaf would feed him and his widowed mother for a few days.

Henry said, "Where was this, Arthur?"

Arthur went on to explain his time at the docks on the Thames. He was up before the 'beak' and sentenced to be transported to America but at first he was taken to the hulks on the Thames to await the next available ship. They waited and waited then something strange happened. A ship arrived and the convicts were unloaded from the ship into the hulk alongside them. Then it stopped. Nothing happened for well over a year. They then found out that there had been a revolt in America and the convicts were to be sent to

Van Diemen's Land somewhere at the bottom of the world. They were told Captain Cook had found it for the Crown, some time ago. It was even reported that they were going to send the convicts to Africa.

"Just 'magine, fellars, we would be eaten by all those cannibals. At least here we are pratie right as long as we don't interfere with the blacks."

Then Henry said, "Lads, have you got near them? They smell to high heaven."

Arthur related the story of when the fleet arrived. He had been assigned with other convicts to cut rushes in a bay not far from what is called Farm Cove. Anyway, it was soon obvious they were being watched by a group of blacks. Our overseer had told them to remain friendly and not cause any friction. Then out of the blue, one of the black women came up to one of our fellows and started fondling his trousers. There was much laughter and merriment. Then Lieutenant King directed one of the guards to drop his trousers and reveal himself. This caused much laughter from the blacks.

"Mind you, the guard wasn't laughing," said Arthur. "He told us they didn't like the way we smelt either. The blacks then disappeared as quickly as they'd arrived. Ah! Henry, me lad. They rub animal fat all over them to keep them warm and keep the midges away."

"We could learn a lot from them," chimed in James.

"Finally, we were addressed by some official," continued Arthur, "and told that we were to be sent to this far-off place and we were going to be on the ship for over a year. I can tell you when we arrived in Sydney, there was nothing, little food and no shelter. I was granted my Ticket of Leave in 1806. You see, I kept out of trouble and got my pardon. I got a job looking after this gent's horses. He was a bit of a lad. He went on to cross the Blue Mountains with two other gents called Blaxland and Lawson. He was a descendent from a convict. I like anything to do with animals. Mr Wentworth told me of the land over the mountains of beautiful rolling hills, so with his advice, I crossed the mountain range in 1817 and I've worked for Mr Marr ever since. The government gave me thirty acres and when I have enough money, I will farm it and take a wife."

James chimed in. "You could have ended up in the place called America and been a free man."

Arthur replied, "James, you are never free but I can tell you this. Keep your nose clean and avoid getting into trouble and you'll do all right."

James and Henry were patrolling a creek bed late one afternoon where two young wethers had got tangled in the briars. There was a howling westerly wind blowing the dust and you could hardly see your hand in front of your face. They put a piece of rag over their mouths to stop the flies and dust. As the sun went down over the horizon, the wind died down. Henry was discussing a letter he had just received from his solicitor in regards to some family problem.

"Were you married James?" asked Henry.

James, hanging onto the sheep, trying to pull it free, finally said, "No! Henry, we was engaged, but the Squire, the yang basted..." He went on to explain the story.

"Simply bad luck, old man. I've had my fill of women," said Henry.

Just then a black and white bird swooped down and knocked James's hat off his head.

"Mother of God, what was that?" cried James.

They both looked in the big gum nearby and there were two of them carolling at the top of their voices. James ripped off a branch and was going to throw it at the birds then thought better of it. "I say, Henry, smell these leaves off the gum tree," he said.

Henry crushed some leaves, smelled the aroma and said, "Magpie, James. I once read that when they are nesting, they are very territorial. All they are doing is guarding their nest."

After that, James kept a close eye on them Magpies.

Chapter 14

They had been out on the land for about two years when they were given orders to report back to the stock yards at Charlotte Vale homestead. It was twenty miles back to the main camp. When they arrived back at the stockyards, five new convicts had arrived from Sydney Town and the old hands showed the new chums who, were straight off the boat, how to look after the flock. Henry was to escort the new convicts back. As the old chums gathered around the main gate, they said farewell to the four lads. No one knew whether they would see each other again.

The head superintendent gave them their orders. They were to take a mob of sheep down to the big smoke to Rooty Hill near Parramatta. The journey would take about three weeks. The Western plains had been sending stock down to Sydney for over twelve months. With every consignment, there were problems, mainly with stock running off or being attacked by native dogs, so the convict's superiors pointed out to the lads that their mob would be counted and there would be trouble if there were any losses. James, along with three of his shepherd mates, Patrick, Thomas and Charlie set out pushing the wheel barrows which carried all their supplies. The sheep moved at a slow pace, eating grass as they went.

On the first day they were to make for Sidmouth Valley, which had become a regular coach stop and resting paddock. On the second day, they made for the Cox's River, while resting the sheep before the steep journey up the mountain. James had remembered the stone he had found, so while the other convicts were boiling the billy, he went fossicking along the creek bed. One of the convicts had mentioned that this river looked like it could have traces of gold.

James did not have a clue what he was looking for, but there in the sand, something sparkled in the afternoon light. He scooped it up and wrapped it in a piece of rag and placed it his pocket. The next part of the journey was the steep climb up through Hartley where they passed a party of new convicts heading west. They had a chance to reacquaint themselves with Trooper Dan Smith. It gave the parties a chance to stop for a rest, boil the billy, light up a pipe and exchange news from home. After a short spell they were on their way again.

A rider came up through the clearing. It was James's mate Trooper Dan.

"What's up Dan, did you lose something?" said James.

"Look James, there has been a lot of bushranger activity down on the lower slopes. Wait for us at the Weatherboard Gate. I won't be long and my platoon will escort you down to Rooty Hill."

"Why thanks Dan, but we will need something to show we were held up to take back to our boss."

"Don't you worry about that James. I'll get a message through to your superintendent that you may be delayed. I am sure when he is told of the problem he will thank us for our help. Don't forget, wait for us at Weatherboard."

It was slow progress as the party of convicts herded the mob of sheep up the track, passing lonely homesteads that were starting to spring up in the hills. As they reached the top of the pass at a place called Victoria, it was getting late so they quickly erected the temporary fence. There was a cruel wind blowing up from the southern plains but the lads soon put together a log fire. Music drifted over the misty paddocks from a tavern but the lads were forbidden to even enter it. Even if they could, they had no money. They soon organised themselves into a roster to watch the mob while some got some sleep. As the morning light filtered through the trees, Charlie was first to stir and soon had the fire blazing and the billy boiling.

"Not oatmeal cakes again!" cried Thomas.

"Ah! Think you selves lucky me lads. Can't you remember back on the 'Medina?' Mushy stale pea soup and those stale biscuits that would break your teeth?"

The convicts soon had the sheep on the move. They meet up with other travellers all making their way west, young families travelling in groups for protection, all saying the same warning, be aware of bushrangers. Late in the afternoon when they made their way into the hut at Weatherboard, the guards on duty allowed the convicts to pen the stock for the night. The clouds had covered the moon and the lads huddled in a group around the fire. James who had elected himself as spokesperson told the officer in charge of Trooper Dan Smith's proposal to return and guide them down to Rooty Hill.

The next day was spent around the camp fire singing old Irish songs and dreaming of the future. One of the men at the hut got talking to the lads and told them about his time since obtaining his Ticket of Leave. He had been granted thirty acres of land on the river at Windsor. He was returning down the mountain and agreed to wait for the trooper and help them with the mob. He was explaining to James how the solution of keeping the sheep in some sort of order was using a working dog.
Patrick said, "Dogs, herding sheep, what sort of dogs?"
Bill Peters, their new found friend responded, "Well they're a new breed of Collie dog crossed with a Kelpie dog and they're now being marked as a sheep dog that can do wonders with all kinds of stock."

True to his word, Trooper Dan turned up the next morning and they were soon on the way through the village of Springwood. The work load was now easier with Billy, Dan and his men to help with the stock.
They were making their way down the mountain and were about to pass over the upper reaches of the Nepean River. The lads were humming and singing away when it happened. Shots were fired from a rocky ridge and Billy went down. Thomas rushed to his side and shouted out that it was only a flesh wound to his arm. Dan and his men returned fire, cries were heard and the noise of men scattering every which way. The sheep went in all directions.
"It's going to be a long day before we can get the sheep under control," James said to himself. He and his boys stayed with Billy, comforting him as best as they could. Patrick, Charlie and Thomas made an attempt to start

rounding up the mob and, by late that afternoon they had all the sheep back and penned. Dan and his men finally turned up and told James they had pursued the three runaway convicts to the river and three of his men would continue to follow them to Emu Plains.

Some of the sheep were delivered to Mr Kinghorn at Emu Plains. The rest were delivered to the stock agent, Mr Blackett over the punt at the Nepean River.

"All present and accounted for. Well done lads," said the stock agent.

They had also been given orders to bring back a mob of Timor ponies for Captain Steel, who had three hundred acres in Bathurst at a property called Belleview. (They had been imported into the colony from an island off Timor near Batavia – probably Portugal). They were also to bring twenty cows for Captain Thomas Raine. It was their job to herd them back to Bathurst.

The convicts had a couple of days to fill in and they would be given a letter to take back to their supervisor for their delay. On the day the ponies arrived at the stock yard, James was worried how they would get them back. They were wild as could be, but one of the free convicts Billy, introduced them to two dogs that had been bred to round up stock and, before long, the beasts were as quiet as lambs. James noticed small burrs around the matted tails of the ponies. He tried to pull them out but gave up.

When they returned to Bathurst the superintendent was so impressed with the way the lads had handled the cattle, he recommended their early release however it still took some time. James, because of his good behaviour, was finally to be given his Ticket of Leave No 29/627.

One of the last jobs given to James Fines No. 288 was on the King's Birthday 1829. The Government handed out woollen blankets to all the blacks. In the two tribes, 'Binjung' and the 'Boogan,' there were only a hundred and eighteen natives accounted for. James had got to know one of the blacks called 'Ogle Eye Jacky.' He would turn up at the Shepherd's Hut and for the first twelve months there was no communication between the native and the 'whites.' Jacky would bring a kangaroo he had speared. Then one day, Jacky brought his lubra and three piccaninnies. Jacky was carrying one of the youngsters who looked sick and was burning up.

Henry said, "Look chaps, I'm not a doctor but I think the child has a fever. He's burning up."

Reluctantly Jacky carried the child into the Shepherd's Hut and laid him down on the bed.

"What are we going to do, Henry?" said James

"Well, old chap, we are going to try and get his temperature down."

So over the next twenty-four hours James and Henry applied cold presses to the child's head. They also noticed pink spots on the lad's body. Finally in the early hours of the morning the lad broke into a sweat. His parents, all this time were sitting outside the hut chanting in "mumbo jumbo." When the sun came up, James took Jacky by the hand and they entered the hut. The lad was sitting up smiling. He mumbled something to his father and climbed off the bed and the family left without a word. Next morning outside the hut was a giant, dead kangaroo.

After that, Jacky would come up to the hut and sit around the campfire until late in the night. They were good mates, although neither could understand the other. Slowly they picked up words and meanings and Jacky would point up into the sky trying to explain the movement of the stars and moon.

"Moonah Kardara!" cried Jacky. Jacky was tugging on James' coat, coaxing him to follow. He moved a short distance to see a giant lizard up a gum tree and so James learnt his first words of Aborigine.

Then Jacky said "good tucker." He had a grin from ear to ear displaying his gapped tooth that had been knocked out in an initiation ceremony. Then as quick as a flash, Jacky let fly with a curved stick. It was a full moon and a clear sky. James was mesmerised as the stick gained altitude spinning in an arc, then it quickly came to earth and brought down a kangaroo. The three men raced over to the stunned animal and Jacky quickly put it out of its misery. With a grin from ear to ear he told the two lads "Boomerang."

Late one afternoon, Jacky summoned James and Henry to visit the natives' camp that night. When they arrived there was a giant fire blazing. The men in the group were painted with white mud and had unusual head gear covered with feathers. Mud, grease and ochre also covered their bodies. Jacky later explained that the fat they covered their bodies with kept out the cold and insects. They danced stamping their feet, then the women joined in. They were stark naked, their bodies shining with grease. Some of the natives were playing music or strange sounds from a log they were blowing into at one end.

Henry again explained to James he had heard the instrument was called a Didgeridoo. The haunting music seemed to put the two white men into a trance. The dancers were gyrating and the two white men were mesmerised as they watched the performance. The blacks were dancing around the fire as slowly, couples would disappear into the night. Finally James and Henry returned to the hut exhausted as if they had performed. Then the next day the natives disappeared.

Arthur, who was a lifer, said "Ah! They're gone walkabout. One minute they're here, next day they're gone. They may come back one day."

Chapter 15

Jacky's age was about thirty summers. When he was a small lad back in 1815, he witnessed the white man first entering the Bathurst area. He had been standing on the elevated hill south of the river where his family observed a strange happening that would change the western plains forever. They watched as a party of white men travelled down through the valley, finally setting up camp on the banks of the stream. They could tell by their camp fires how many there were in the party and the strange animals they brought. Jacky's aborigine name was *'Windradyne.'* He belonged to the local tribe of the plains area. His father was the tribe leader and their numbers were in total about 3,000. They had lived happily in the Wellington Valley since time began, in harmony with nature, living off the land, never taking any more than they needed.

The Aborigines watched always from a distance and observed the strangers. Then, one day, the white men packed up and left. The Government surveyors had done their job and were to report back to the Governor regarding future settlement of the Western Plains.

The tribe's medicine man could tell there was something bad going to happen. He was given the task of going down to the white man's camp fire and discover what had brought the strange pale men to the valley. The tribe leaders called a council meeting to discuss the happenings. Some members of the tribe had just returned from the coastal plains and reported strange things going on; new people building strange huts, burning land, running animals that they had never seen before. So members of the tribe would stand guard all the way back to the big mountain and would signal any movements of the strange tribe. They would use a bullroarer which, when spun around, give a loud roaring noise and would alert the next signal post. Young Jacky who now had been initiated as an adult was ordered to patrol and stand guard down by the river. He was alerted by the noise of horse and cart that the white men were coming. Jacky was ever alert and wishing to impress his elders.

One morning he spotted two white men on strange animals ride into the creek, stirring up the mud. Jacky yelled at the top of his voice that it was not right, it would kill the fish but the men just stared at him and rode on through the creek. Before long there were more settlers and more strange animals that had long hair, and made funny sounds. Then came bigger animals with long horns. The tribes came together once more to discuss the strange deaths of some of their people - they would get hot and they would go off into the bush and die.

Jacky had reached the age when he could go off with his bride. He told his mother and father he would go as far away as possible, away from the white invaders that some of his fellow tribesmen had run afoul of. They had speared a sheep and they were fired on with a magic stick.

Jacky had been away with his lubra for many summers and when he returned, he had two bright young piccaninnies and his lubra was heavy with another child. They searched in all the areas that his family had camped but found no signs, then after they had been back a couple of days, he came across an old lubra sitting on the bank of a creek. She told Jacky how the tribe were all gone, scattered to the four winds. The ones that were left were in the town called *'Baftus.'* She smelt strange; she had a strange bright container and she offered Jacky some of the strange liquid to drink. He raised the bottle and allowed the liquid to filter into his mouth. He reacted and spat it out shouting back at the lubra. Jacky was so outraged he grabbed her by the hair and dragged her off into the bush. Narjella, Jacky's woman came running to see what all the fuss was about. She helped her husband get the drunken lubra down into the bark shelter he had rigged up.

Next morning, when she had slept it off, she explained to Jacky how the tribe had, in the few short years he had been away, been taken over by the white man. Jackie's woman quickly stripped the rags off her and dragged her down to the water and scrubbed her. They fashioned some proper women's apparel, a lap apron that covered her lower parts. All afternoon she let out moans, but Jacky didn't realise that she was in denial of the dreaded liquor. That night she slipped away. She had mumbled to Jacky how she needed some more grog.

Chapter 16

George McKenzie had arrived on the 'Minstrel' in 1825 and had been working with James near Bathurst tending the sheep. He was a Highland Scot who could read and write and had petitioned His Excellency, Lieutenant General and Governor in Chief of the Territory of New South Wales for him to be reunited with his wife who had been transported about twelve months earlier and was in service in Sydney. They had only just got married before he had been transported.

"What's bothering you, George?" said James.

"Ah! James, lad, I am so excited I could cry. I have been granted leave to go to Sydney and pick up me darlin' Margaret from the Female Factory and bring her back here. I sent off the letter months ago and I really didn't expect to ever get a reply, but Mr Maxwell said because of my conduct, he would put in a good word for me."

On returning to Bathurst, George with his bride Margaret, obtained work at the Inn at Kelso and later opened a small store on the Limekiln Bathurst road.

James, on recommendation of the Bathurst bench, was granted his Ticket of Leave on the condition that he remained in the district of Bathurst. This would give him the right to employ himself for his own benefit and he was encouraged to acquire property. He was to present himself and produce his Ticket before the Magistrate at the period prescribed by the regulation, and to attend worship weekly, if performed within a reasonable distance. The Ticket could be resumed at any time at the pleasure of the Governor. James had been granted his Ticket of Leave in 1829, 29/627 but on 25th November 1829, his ticket was surrendered after the magistrate on the Bench at Bathurst convicted him of Drunkenness, Rioting on the Sabbath and not attending Church muster.

The Colonial Governor Darling, proclaimed on 30th September 1829, that all foreign currencies would be recalled in exchange for English silver coins. They replaced Spanish holey dollars and dumps. James could not read or write but he knew the value of money. He had acquired a collection of Spanish, Portuguese and Dutch coinage. He had buried them in a metal box out near the stockyard, and reckoned one day he would dig it up and cash it in. James was unaware that the Governor had only allowed the foreign currency two years, to be handed in.

He finally was granted his freedom No 30/288 on 11th May 1830. James decided to stay in the Bathurst area. The Magistrate disallowed James any grant of land and after some months, he went to work for a retired English Sea Captain who had been involved in the Peninsular Wars, Captain Thomas Raine.

It was a fine spring morning with a light frost on the ground as James rounded up the twenty-two new convicts assigned to Captain Raine. James had been looked upon favourably and had been given responsibility. He had been given special mention for his handling of the cattle he had driven back from Rooty Hill. He was now a free man and he was going to keep out of trouble. There was dust on the road as four riders came up the main driveway to the Captain's house. James recognized one of the riders as trooper Dan Smith.

"What's up Dan?" called James.

At first Dan did not recognize James. It had been some time since their chance meeting on the mountain back in 1825.

"James Fines, how are you, me lad?"

"I'm well. I am a free man now. Got me freedom in May. What's the trouble Dan?"

"Ah! James lad, there's a band of convicts gone amuck. They have shot an overseer on Lieutenant Evernden's farm and the culprits, led by a Ralph Entwhistle are trying to round up supporters and start a civil war, so keep your men in their quarters until this is over. I'll find Captain Raine and tell him the news." [2]

Captain Walpole and a detachment from the 39th Regiment, along with volunteer citizens, rounded up the remnants of the mob numbering about ten at the Abercrombie Caves. They were brought back to Bathurst, tried and were hanged. The whole town was talking about the trial and the hanging. When the town folk were told the story of how incident started, the good citizens of Bathurst were not impressed. Two bullock drivers stopped at the Macquarie River and had shed their clothes to have a swim and cool off. This displeased Governor Darling who happened to be passing and one of his staff, Lieutenant Evernden decided that the Governor should not have to see a naked display like this.

Captain Raine had given James the job of head stockman. James considered the work was no different than when he was a convict, except now he had a room, bed, food and payment for his labour. Captain Raine had brought with him cuttings of Salix Babylonica, the common English Willow. He had the convicts plant the cuttings along the road into the Vale and the property at the lagoons on the river banks. James with some of the new convicts took some and planted them along the creek. Captain Raine told him they would be good to stop the soil along the banks of the creek from washed away. James also noticed strange looking plants growing around the place with attractive mauve flowers but with savage prickles. They soon became known as 'Bathurst Burrs.' He then remembered the burr seeds on the horses' tails.

James planted willow plants - he had collected them on one of the journeys on the convict transport ship 'Surrey.' It was revealed they had

---

[2] Captain Raine. See page 377

come from the grave of Napoleon Bonaparte on the Island of St. Helena and it became a talking point around town. The plants grew without any trouble. The sheep loved the young shoots and they soon put guards around them to stop the stock from eating them in dry times. James was enjoying life as a free man in the state of New South Wales.

Governor Darling had gained a reputation for brutality over the last few years of his stay and he was replaced by Governor Richard Bourke in 1831.

James had seen a young lady, a fiery red head, who had been sent out from Ireland and was assigned as a servant to a Mr Robert Arkel from Rockley Station. All he knew was that her name was Catherine and she was assigned to work for two years. He had briefly seen her when she was passing through with a group of convicts to Rockley.

By now James was being paid, and in 1836 had been working for Captain Thomas Raine for four years.

One hot, windy summer's day, as he walked out to the stockyard, he was determined he would venture out and make his own way in life. He dug up his nest egg and went into the bank and cashed it in. Reluctantly, the bank teller exchanged it. Michael, the son of his old boss Henry Marr, had told him they were going to open up land in the Limekiln area twelve miles out of Bathurst, so with the bit of money he had saved, he purchased a horse and ten sheep at the inflated cost of £3 each. With his swag he travelled out to Limekiln.

James could not have picked a worse time to try and set up a small farm. The Bathurst area was going into its worst drought in its short history. The drought would last four years. The price of sheep dropped to four shillings a head. He selected some land on Palmers Oakey Road not far from the turn off. He just squatted on a piece of land. His old mate, Henry, had told him that if he marked out the boundaries and constructed a dwelling, he could call it home and claim the title. He had selected a site off the road back in the bush in the foothills of Mount Horrible. There was even a dry creek bed and with his time with the natives, he spotted plants that were reeds and he knew that there would be water underneath. James erected a fence, using materials from the property to try to keep his flock in. Henry had advised him that this was important if he were to try and get the deeds to the land. He could not see the sense in going to all that trouble, but he would think about it.

Chapter 17

Catherine Disney was born in the town of Taunagh on the west coast of Ireland in the County of Sligo in 1817, nine miles from Boyle near the Arrow River. Her father Daniel was a weaver and her mother's name was Mary Campbell. In the year of 1835 the English Government were looking for single Irish women to go to New South Wales to marry Irish convicts who had been granted their Ticket of Leave. When Catherine told her parents of her decision to leave, they were not happy. The scheme was created by the Irish lass called Caroline Chisholm who, on migrating to Sydney in 1838 with her army husband Archie, was shocked to find single girls from good Catholic families with no food, no shelter and this had caused some to turn to prostitution. So she set up a refuge in the Sydney area and set out to find work for the girls. At first the girls were apprehensive, but a trickle of girls leaving for work soon became a flood. Catherine and Archie set up refuges in Parramatta. She became a champion of them and there was a steady stream of girls coming and going.

Since she left school Catherine had been working as a pantry maid for the Fitzgerald family. She never really learnt anything from the nuns, she was always in trouble and would end up doing all the cleaning jobs around the convent instead of being in class. The mother superior told Catherine's mother that cleaning pots and pans was her best subject. She also told Mrs Disney "Your daughter is hopeless. She daydreams in class, doesn't know her catechism and when the class are saying the rosaries, what does Catherine do? She gazes out the window. I am sorry Mrs Disney but she is a lost cause. The sisters have belted her and nothing seems to work, but when Sister Amelia asks for someone to work in the kitchen or the garden, your

Catherine is the first to put up her hand. She is good at cleaning and working in the kitchen."

Patrick Fitzgerald had been in Catherine's class and was in love with her so he pleaded with his mother to give her a job in the kitchen. The job was live-in and she had a room to herself.

One morning, Mrs Fitzgerald came in with a small bundle.

"Catherine!" she said. "Something for you!"

Catherine curiously unwrapped the bundle and squealed with delight.

"Shoes! Mrs Fitzgerald. I've never worn shoes in me life. Mar never owned a pair. Oh! Thank you, me lady. Thank you."

"Well, young lady, you must wear them in the house. We have a high standard here. When you go home on your days off, you must leave them in your room, said the lady of the house."

One night, after the family banquet to celebrate the family's oldest member, Mrs Maud Fitzgerald's eightieth birthday, Catherine was making her way up the stairs to her room when she opened the door and there was Patrick. She had no sooner closed the door when he pounced on her, and wrestled her to the bed but Catherine soon had his measure and had his arms pinned to the bed.

"Oh, Catherine I love you, I love your fiery spirit, you got spirit and I want to marry you. Will you be me wife?"

"Patrick Fitzgerald, what do you think you doin? Get out of me room before I call you father."

"I'm sorry Catherine. I can't sleep at night. You are on my mind all the time. I can't work, I am in love with you, oh please marry me, Catherine, I worship the ground you walk on."

With that she pushed him out the door, saying, "Patrick, we will talk about this in the morning."

Next morning she was up bright and early and confronted Mrs Fitzgerald in the kitchen. She had forgotten all about her romp with Patrick but she came straight and told her that she would be finishing up at the end of the month. She explained that she had heard of a plan to get good Irish girls to go to this place on the other side of the world and going she was. She was going to take up an offer to travel to the state of New South Wales with a good Irish lady; Caroline Chisholm.

Mrs Fitzgerald was in shock.

"But Catherine, me dear, that's on the other side of the world and we will never see you again."

Daniel loved his daughter and deep down he knew she would be all right. She was a fighter with that red hair. She also had the lads bluffed at the Convent many a night. She would arrive home from school with a black eye.

The village had been devastated with the potato blight, and families were starving. Daniel's weaving had kept the family with food to eat and a roof over their heads. Young Catherine had broken all the hearts of the young men in their village but her mind was made up. She was nearly twenty years of age with a feisty Irish temper and fiery red hair. She had been promised some money on arrival in Sydney and a job as a cook's assistant. To leave Ireland she was to journey to Galway where she was to wait for her passage to the new land of New South Wales.

It was a sad day as all her family and friends gathered around her on the wharf on the River Erne. Lasses she went to school with were around her trying to persuade her to stay. There were the O'Dowds, the McDougals and the Fitzgeralds.

"Ah! Lass we're going to miss you," cried Mrs Fitzgerald.

The Fitzgerald's were the direct descendants from Maurice Fitzgerald who was granted land after the Norman invasion back in 1235. Catherine's mother, Mary with her younger sister Briny, started to cry as the small craft moved away from the wharf that would take her daughter away to a distant land. As the craft moved off into the mist, a small boat came alongside.

"Catherine, don't go, me darling, I love you, I will miss you. We could be married and have lots of lovely, bonny children," cried out Patrick.

As quick as a flash Catherine returned with, "Ah! Be off with you, Patrick me lad, you only wanted one thing, Marriage! I don't think so."

Catherine's mother had packed a parcel tied with string. It contained a bible, linen underwear and an apron that had belonged to her mother. She could still hear her mother saying to her, "Always have clean underwear."

Through the mist her family were just visible on the wharf.

"Look after you self, Catherine, me darlin' lass," cried out her father as a fog descended over the river and the craft moved away and was swallowed up in the mist. Daniel and Mary realised that they would never see their daughter again. She was lucky to have an aunt in Galway which gave her somewhere to stay whilst waiting for the boat.

On the morning the ship departed, her Aunt Mary on the dock started to cry.

"Now girl, remember what I tell you. Say your rosary, morning and night prayers, look after the bible and, want not."

Catherine kissed her aunt and walked up the gang plank. The ship was the 'Neptune.' It was bursting at the seams with convicts being transported to New South Wales with other passengers in steerage. Catherine had teamed up with three lasses all heading to New South Wales. The first mate ushered the four lasses down below deck.

"Here we are me lasses, you'll be right in here."

As he kicked the door, a putrid smell wafted out into the passage way and then giant rats scurried out between the girls' legs.

"Ah! Come now lasses, they be good eat'n," said the first mate. "I remember back in a voyage in '17, the hard tack had run out and we all lived on the juicy little devils. Drank the blood, too."

One of the girls Betsey screamed out and was sick all over the passageway and the first mate. As Catherine moved forward to take control, she said, "We weren't expecting the Ritz but we aren't staying in there."

The door opened wider and the girls peered into the darkness.

"Ah! Girls leave it with me and I will see what I can do," said the first mate.

Finally he told them, "Well there is always the deck, and I can rig up a bit of canvas to keep out the worst of the cold and rain."

As the girls followed him up onto the deck, a sudden thunderstorm broke, showering them with rain.

"Ah! We'll have to find you somewhere else," said the first mate. "This will never do."

He finally found them a corner down with all the other passengers travelling in steerage. So there they were, sharing a space with dozens of other girls all travelling to the land down under.

It was 'Rafferty's rules' on board. All bound for Sydney, none of them had the faintest idea what they were letting themself in for. As the voyage progressed down the Atlantic and the weather turned warmer, they would often spend time on the deck and the crew would bring out a musical instrument and there would be a sing-a-long. They were constantly on guard with the crew pestering them nonstop. Catherine was a feisty lass with a lovely slim figure and long, fiery red hair. She had few possessions but in her baggage was a family bible given to her by her mother. She guarded it with her life; her mother had told her to record all her children's birthdays and christenings in it.

Ireland's potato crop had failed and the people were starving in the streets. There were families emigrating to America but they had to have hard cash to get there, so the promise of a job in New South Wales, sounded a better proposition. Catherine had gone through a strict medical examination by the authorities and when she boarded the transport she was given a clean bill of health.

The ship called into Cape Town, on the tip of South Africa and they were allowed to go ashore. The girls had no money but were glad to be given the chance to stroll around the docks and visit the markets. One of the girls called Sally brought a gaily coloured shawl. She said the money had been hidden deep inside her person, but later, Catherine got it out of her that she had given the young lad a 'quickie' down the back lane.

When the ship finally got under way on the last leg of the journey, it travelled down into the Antarctic waters, the weather turned bitterly cold and the wind picked up. There were girls sick, not wanting to go on.

"Turn the ship around," said young Colleen.

"Ah! Now don't be talking like that, me love," said one of the officers. "We are going to New South Wales. It'll be alright."

The ship ploughed on. Some days, in the distance you could see huge icebergs, whales and giant sea birds. One of the sailors said they were 'Albatrosses.'

Catherine said, "I have been told that they can bring you luck."

The young sailor then explained how the birds would follow the ship for hundreds of miles. He went on to explain that they have been shot by stupid but hungry sailors who then went on to have bad luck.

The 'Neptune' had been at sea for three days making steady progress when it was hit by gale force winds. It was more like a cyclone, the craft was out of control but the sailors did everything in their power to keep the ship afloat. They were sailing with storm sails, but even they got ripped to shreds. Everyone was seasick, even the first class passengers. Catherine tried to keep some sort of control but she was starting to say her prayers. She was on her knees.

"Oh Mother of God, help us in our hour of need. I promise that I will keep these girls on the straight and narrow and when we get to this place called New South Wales. We will all attend mass every day."

As she was kneeling, water was flowing around her and the floor was awash. She quickly gathered her thoughts and then climbed up to get out of the water. They would have to return to Cape Town for repairs and new sails, but they were being blown way off course. Catherine overheard one of the sailors say, "If this keeps up we will be in Rio, South America."

There was nothing they could do but see it out, when all of a sudden out of the clouds, land was sighted. It was an island. They were able to manoeuvre 'Neptune' through the heavy swell into the lee side and were protected from the storm. A small boat was launched and it made for the island. It returned that afternoon. They were accompanied by a strange craft with four crew pulling at the oars. Two men came on board seeking medical attention. They thought the weather was quite normal. It was later revealed that they were from the island of Tristan da Cunha. Situated at the bottom of the Atlantic, it was one of the loneliest islands on Earth. One of the crew later explained that the island was halfway to South America.

Then all of a sudden it went quiet, the sea was like a mill pond. After the Doctor had seen to the two men from the island, 'Neptune' limped off, back in the direction of the Cape.

As the sun crept over the horizon the next morning the Neptune was underway, finally making it into port at the tip of Southern Africa. Some of the girls wanted to leave the ship but the crew persuaded them to stay for the remainder of the journey. Catherine noted that there was love in the air for two of her fellow travellers. The lads explained to the girls that the worst of the trip was behind them. So they gingerly boarded to continue on their way to the land down under. As 'Neptune' made its way out of the harbour it made a magnificent spectacle with its crisp new white sails. It was again speeding across the southern ocean, now with the roaring forties behind them. They made good time with no more dramas, finally crossing the Indian Ocean and entering Bass Strait.

Chapter 18

The 'Neptune' manoeuvred into Port Phillip Bay and docked at the port of Melbourne. Some of the girls were leaving the ship at this port to start their lives in the southern new state of Victoria. There was much carrying on and tears as they said their goodbyes. One of the girls, who had formed a relationship with one of the sailors, decided to stay on board and take her chances in Sydney.

"Come down and visit us," called out one of the girls as they walked down the gang plank. Little did they know of the vast size of this new continent.

The ship left Port Philip Bay and travelled onto Sydney, hugging the coast line. The girls were at the ship's rail as they entered the beautiful harbour of Sydney. It was a warm summer's day and it was a magnificent sight. There were sea gulls swooping down onto the waves, diving into the water to catch small fish. Catherine said to her friends that she had a warm feeling about their new home of New South Wales. All the girls had positions to go to, mainly servant duties, but there was an air of adventure in this new land.

When Catherine's ship docked in Sydney, the four Irish lasses stuck together. They reported to the Government office at Circular Quay and found the Caroline Chisholm refuge centre where they were given a bed for the night. Early next morning she reported to the Matron in charge. She had been assigned as a cook's assistant to a Mr Robert Argyle in a place called Rockley, in the Bathurst area. Catherine could hardly sign her name but the Bathurst area sounded just like home. They mentioned a place called

Blayney, which she thought was Blarney, and sounded Irish, so with her £2 firmly planted on her person, she set out to cross the Blue Mountains.

There was a party of convicts and free people all journeying out over the mountains. There was safety in numbers and they were accompanied by soldiers. They travelled through the outskirts of Sydney Town. The girls with all their possessions travelled on a flat dray pulled by two horses that had seen better days. The convicts walked alongside. Catherine started to have a conversation with one of the lads named Bryan. He was from Dublin and by the time they had reached the bottom of the Blue Mountains, they were having a great chat about their lives back in Ireland.

The girls were hot and exhausted from just hanging on and as they crossed the Nepean River, the terrain changed. In the distance they could see grasslands, farms and the hills. The party stopped at a place called Emu Plains. Tents were hastily erected for the females but the convicts had to sleep rough under blankets. Luckily it was a warm night and was not raining. As they climbed up the pass mapped out by the three explorers Blaxland, Lawson and Wentworth in 1813, the weather changed and it became cooler, a pleasant change from the heat of the plains. They finally reached a place called Weatherboard where they had some shelter for the night.

There was a changing of the guard and a new party of troopers came to take them through the mountains and down onto the Western Plains. The party of convicts, free settlers and the girls from the Caroline Chisholm hostel travelled across the mountain track and got their first look at the Western Plains, a place from where most of them would never leave.

Finally after seven weeks travelling, they descended down across the Cox's River and the exhausted party arrived in Bathurst. The single girls went to a safe house for the night. Next morning, bright and early, Catherine and the other girls assembled at the coach station. She was to be picked up and taken out to 'The Rockley', a sheep station. Someone had told her the farms out there were that big you could ride a horse and by the end of the day you would still be on the same property.

It seemed like she had been waiting for hours when this young fella called out to her, "Would you be goin' my way, me darlin Colleen?" said he.

Catherine recognised the Irish brogue and said, "I would be doin' nothing of the sort. What sort of a girl do you take me for anyway? Me name is Catherine."

James looked her over. It had been years since he had seen such a lovely young thing, though he had had a few floozies over the last couple of years since he had gained his freedom. She was a fine young Irish lass with fiery red hair and a temper to match.

"Well! It's Catherine, is it? And where are you goin to, Catherine?" said James.

She dropped her guard. She had promised herself she would not have anything more to do with men.

"I'm off to Rockley Station," she said. "They will be wanting me for me cooking skills, if you mind and I'll be there for some time."

Finally the coach pulled up and, as she climbed on to the coach, James said, "I'll wait fo' yer, Catherine."

He smiled to himself as the coach drifted up the dusty road then he shouted out, "It's a long way to Tipperary, me darling."

As the coach reached the rise, she turned around and waved.

Chapter 19

When the trap stopped at Rockley junction, she was met by one of the stockman who was there to meet the coach and pick up the weekly supplies and mail. She climbed up on to the station's buggy and they were off. It was getting late in the afternoon as the wagon made its way through the bush. Catherine was fascinated by the giant trees that towered over the track, and the animals, kangaroos, giant lizards, and birds of all colours. In the seven week journey over the mountains she had been introduced to all the Australian animals and then she saw what was the most wonderful sight, what turned out to be a Koala.

"Look driver! A Koala Bear," she called out.

The driver, sat there smoking a pipe. He never said a word. Finally he broke the silence and said, "It's a Koala. It's not a bear. You Irish Lass, what part are you from?" he continued. He spoke in a Scottish brogue.

Catherine told him where she had come from.

The sun was just setting in the western sky. It had taken a while but he finally divulged his name. He was a freeman from Aberdeen, Scotland and he had done his time.

"How much further, Jimmy lad? We seem to be heading back to Sydney Town?" said Catherine.

"Just over the next hill lass, you will see the homestead of Rockley Downs.

As the wagon reached the top of the rise and they looked down into the valley, smoke was rising from one of the dwellings. The wagon made its way down into the valley, finally stopping. As she stepped down from the wagon, Catherine said "Jimmy, I've seen pigsties better than this back home."

Robert Argyle was single and had been involved in a nasty incident in Sydney. His parents had sent him out into the unknown. He had twenty-five convicts under his control. There were three other girls working on the station, all had been assigned to work there for two years. As soon as their time was up they would be off.

Catherine was ushered into the kitchen which was nothing more than a shed made from slabs of timber with a bark roof.

"Catherine is it?" said the lady, who turned out to be Florence, the head cook.

"Yes, ma'am," Catherine replied and curtsied.

"There will be none of that here, lass. Do your job, keep out of trouble and you'll be fine. Gabriel, take Catherine over and show her where to bunk down."

Catherine had very few possessions so it did not take her long to stow them away. Her bed was in a room with the other girls. They all had bunk beds. The blanket looked like it had never been washed. She took it out and shook it. It was crawling with bed bugs and dust. One of the other girls who was having a quiet snooze was woken by the blanket being bashed and said "Smoke will do the trick, love."

Catherine said "What did you mean, smoke it?"

Wiping the sleep from her eyes the other girl said, "Well love, we place it over a slow fire so as not to burn it and smoke the hell out of them."

Catherine did not know whether to believe her or not but anything was better than nothing.

The other young lass introduced herself as Gabrielle. "But everyone calls me Gabby," she said.

"Do we get into Bathurst often?" Catherine asked. She was thinking of that young fella she had met briefly at the coach station.

"Darlin', I have been here twelve months and never left the property," said Gabby. "Have you met the boss yet? Watch him. He has wandering hands, our Mr Argyle. The girls have christened him, Slimy."

Catherine was a virgin, never having had any serious boy friend's back in Ireland although many a lad had tried to get her to come across down behind the barn. And then there was Patrick. She had a chuckle to herself. She was going to end up with the fella she wanted. Someone with a bit of spunk like young Patrick.

"I'll kill him if he tries anything on me," said Catherine.

She went to work in the kitchen as assistant cook, helping with getting the shepherds' and stockmen's meals. Catherine had worked back home as a servant and had some experience working as a kitchen maid, but she was not prepared for the bush kitchen with a dirt floor. Some days the smoke would linger and her eyes were always red. As the roof at Rockley was bark, there was always the risk of it catching on fire. She would cry herself to sleep each night and promised herself that as soon as she could, she would make a run for it, but like most girls from Ireland, she was scared of the dark and the trip back to Bathurst was a problem. She couldn't remember the way.

When she had the chance, she talked to Jimmy about the times he went into town, but he told her that it would be another month before the next trip. Some of the shepherds only came in once a month to pick up fresh supplies. They would sit around the camp fire on the Saturday night with the rest of the roust-abouts singing ballads. One of the lads had a fiddle and someone fashioned a drum out of some pig skin. The boss turned a blind eye to the liquor. One of the lads had rigged up a still down behind the feed shed in the bush. The boss reasoned that it would keep them from running off.

It was not unusual for some local Aboriginals to turn up at the kitchen door. At first, Catherine was frightened out of her mind but she soon got used to them. All they wanted was something to eat. One of the lubras turned up with a piccaninny feeding from her breast. The baby was very white and Gabby quickly explained to her that it was the boss's. Over the following weeks, Catherine got to know the young girl and was saddened by what would happen to the young baby.

Catherine had been there eighteen months, when one night in the middle of winter, she was coming back from the kitchen area when the boss grabbed her and pushed her into a shed.

"Come on me darlin' Catherine, you want me, don't you?" the boss said as he tried to kiss her.

All Catherine could smell was his revolting breath and, with a burst of energy, she kneed him in the groin and he released her yelling and screaming as his hands went down to his crotch.

"You mongrel thing. I should report you to the authorities. You have no right to do that," said she.

Next morning she decided that she would leave Rockley. She still had six months of her term to go, but she had had enough. She stormed over to his poor excuse for an office, pulled the door open and barged straight in.

"I'm leav'n, I've done me time, so don't try to stop me."

He picked his head up and said, "You can't leave. You still have six months to serve."

Catherine banged her fist down on the rickety table.

"I'm leav'n and don't try to stop me. If you do, I'll report to the Government Agent back in Bathurst that you tried to rape me." Catherine towered over him as she stared him in the face. "Back in Ireland, my father would have had you tied up and flogged," she continued.

He was starting to sweat and his balls ached.

"Ah! Be off with you, there will be no pay as you are leaving before the allocated time, all right?" he shouted. Young Robert Argyle thought about it for a moment and with a rare smile opened the drawer, unlocked a small tin safe and gave her a pound. In the next breath, he said "No hard feelings love, but if you wait a day, we have a party going into Bathurst to pick up supplies."

"Thanks, but I will take me chances, all the same."

That afternoon Catherine set out and started to walk up the steep track out of the station. She had got some provisions from the kitchen. As night started to fall, she became terrified. There was no moon. There was a slight breeze which rustled the gum leaves and then the bush noises started. She was terrified, but she kept going. Catherine had wandered off the track she squatted down behind a tree to relive herself and she started to cry, when she got up and turned around the forest was all around her.

"God I am lost," she cried. Then she remembered something about the stars and what the seaman had told her about the southern sky. That's right the Southern Cross. She started to search but at first she couldn't see anything, then there it was. She thought there was something about the two stars next to it but she couldn't remember whether it was left or right, but there they were. She remembered, draw a line down from the cross and the two stars and then take it down to the horizon and that would be South, simple so she then turned and pointed in a northerly direction, she knew Bathurst was North of Rockley Station and she started to walk, she soon was back on the track and was pleased with her deduction.

Finally, late in the night she stopped under a giant tree and broke off some bread, exhausted, she pulled up the blanket and fell into a deep sleep. She was woken in the early hours of the morning by a strange noise.

"Holy Mother of God!" she gasped. There were shadows in the bushes but she closed her eyes, pulled the blanket over her head and tried to go to sleep. There was a small kangaroo eating grass just near her. At first she was terrified, but soon realised, that as long as she did not harm it, it would soon hop away. She had half dozed back to sleep when she heard it, the sound of a lone horse coming along the track.

To her horror, she saw it was Robert Argyle.

"Thought you would escape me, you bitch?" he shouted. "Oh! I am going to rape you. Don't scream as there is no one who is going to hear you or come to your rescue."

Catherine struggled and tried to bite his hand. Finally she succeeded, which only made him madder. He slapped her across the face and ripped off her britches and under-garments. Catherine struggled, but he was too strong.

He had his wicked way with her and lay there on top of her with a satisfied grin all over his face. As quick as it started, it was over.

He stood up and pulled up his pants and said, "Don't get any ideas about reporting this to the officials in Bathurst as I will deny it and advise the police that I was in Sydney."

With that, he mounted his horse and rode off. Catherine was in shock and it took a few minutes for it to register. Then she burst into tears.

As the first light filtered through the trees, the birds she had heard the men back at the camp call Kookaburras, were in full song, breaking in the new day.

Catherine was relieved. She had been terrified of the dark, but she had made it through the night. Then she relived the shocking ordeal and at first she thought it was a dream. Slowly she pulled herself together and picked up her belongings. There was blood on the ground and lifting her dress and saw her underwear was spotted with blood. As she slowly picked herself up, shaking the leaves off her dress, she noticed there was a piece of bark with a bone on it on the ground near where she had laid. For some reason, she picked it up and placed it with her belongings not knowing its significance.

She slowly followed the track hoping that it led onto Bathurst. She was sobbing and thinking of all the things she was going to do to that bastard Mr Robert Argyle. Then she simmered down, thinking he was not all that tough. She had been on the station about 1eighteen months. She wasn't sure but she started to count back and it would be, she thought, around 1840. She was frightened of the stories the lads told her about snakes, the black natives and wild dogs. Also she was terrified of moonless nights but now, was she going to have a baby? She could hear horses coming along the track. At first she reacted by scurrying off into the scrub and hiding. It was a cart. She contemplated what she would do now, she only had £2/7/6 to her name.

"Woo!" said the driver as she slowly came out of the scrub into the path of the cart. "Well, lassie, what are you doing way out here hiding amongst the trees?"

At first, Catherine looked the old fellow up and down and finally said, "I am going into Bathurst."

"Well climb up here or do you want to walk? My name's Bluey."

She climbed on board the dray and explained to the driver called Bluey, where she had been.

"You worked for that mongrel?" said Bluey.

With that she started to cry and explained her ordeal.

"Ah! Me lassie, he is 'the law' around here. He'll have a water tight alibi, mark my words. Thank your lucky stars you are still in one piece, or are you?"

"No, the bastard stole me virginity."

The driver silently continued on the journey until he stopped outside the pub and said, "Catherine, if you are looking for work, try here. They're always looking for good help. Tell the boss you were talking to Bluey. Better still, what am I thinking? I need a drink?"

As bold as brass they walked in. It only took a few minutes and a word from Bluey to the publican and Catherine had work in the Black Bull Inn in William Street. The Inn keeper asked her about the red mark on her face. She explained that she walked from Rockley Station and walked into a bush when it was dark.

He looked at her and did not know what to believe. "Look we run a tidy and clean place here," he said. "It gets a bit wild now and then, but the first sign of trouble and you're out."

He took her out the back of the inn. It wasn't much, but the door had a lock and the roof did not leak. He had rooms to rent for travelling salesmen and stockmen who were in town after bringing in a consignment of livestock.

She had been there for three months keeping out of trouble. There were plenty of suitors, when one day, this fancy man told her she was being wasted out here. She would make twice what she was now earning, back in Sydney.

"What sort of work would I be doin', Charlie?" she asked.

He just looked her up and down. "With that flaming red hair and that body, darling, we will make a fortune," he said.

"If you think I'm that sort of girl, you must mistaken, now be off with you." Catherine did have red hair, but now it was on fire and when she got excited, all hell broke loose.

Charlie quickly left the pub never to return. Catherine had never had any instruction on babies from her mother or the nuns at the convent. She learnt more in an afternoon with Marion, one of the barmaids, than in her twenty one years of life. She explained to Marion that the bastard from Rockley had raped her and she could be having a baby.

"Well, Catherine you may be pregnant, or maybe not," said Marion. "We will just have to wait and see.

One quiet afternoon she broke down and cried on the boss's shoulder. She told him the story and he believed her but he agreed there was nothing he or she could do.

"Ah! Lass just let it rest and get on with your life, but let this be a lesson."

Then one day, she heard that the owner of Rockley Station had been found dead with a spear in his back. That night she wondered about the bone she had found. Did the aborigines have anything to do with it?

Chapter 20

James had the luck of the Irish. He had tried his luck out at Limekiln, but all his sheep had died. He had built a wattle and daub hut with a bark roof. He had slaved away digging a well, had gone down ten feet and thankfully found good drinking water. In the end the isolation was too much for him so he decided to ride back into Bathurst and go and see his old boss for a job. As James rode in across the river, storm clouds, big black cumulus clouds, were gathering on the western horizon but he knew they had formed before and never come to anything. There were lightning strikes and claps of thunder. James had always been observant about plants and birds. A flock of black cockatoos came from nowhere. There must have been about a hundred of them. His Aboriginal mate had told him that they were a good sign of rain. He noticed as he crossed the dry river bed that the ants were nesting way up the bank. He had observed this back in the late Twenties when there was flooding out on the plains. James was about to turn around and go back to his small holding but he had no money to restock and besides he was just plain lonely.

Captain Raine gave him a job. James even had a room to himself. He had convinced the Captain that the drought was about to break. The Captain had been feeding his flock on the willow branches. James had only been there three days and down came the rain. The Macquarie River broke its banks and the town was flooded in. Finally the river level subsided.

James on his days off would drift into town and have a drink. He had got used to meeting up with three of his old convict mates who had been transported with him on the 'Medina.' John Riley was now working as a gardener handyman at the court house. They used to joke with him that he would not have far to go if he got into trouble. Robert Roach was getting work as a labourer and Robert Lestrange was gainfully employed as a wheelwright. His good friend, Henry, had made it back to Sydney and had opened a printing shop. They all wondered what sort of printing old Henry was getting into.

One afternoon while waiting for his mates to join him at the Black Bull Inn, there she was, this new girl working behind the bar with flowing red hair.

Catherine did not recognise him at first. "What will you be drinking, sir?" she asked.

"Sir, now is it? Catherine, me lovely, three pints of your best ginners please," said James.

"Where do you think you are, in Dublin?" Catherine said.

James just laughed.

Catherine looked and then knew there was something about his eyes.

James said, "You been out to Rockley Station? You said it would be for two years."

At first, Catherine treated him like all the other drinkers, but one day after she had been there for a few weeks, he brought her in a bunch of flowers.

"Why, thank you James and what will you be want'n in return, you Irish rascal?" said she.

"Well, now that you ask, there is a bush dance. You know, a Ceilidh this Saturday night, if you would accompany me. The colony is celebrating fifty four years.

"I'd love to, James me lad," said Catherine without much thought.

As James walked out the door, he said, "I'll pick you up at around 5pm."

Catherine was six months pregnant but being slim, it did not show.

True to his word James spruced himself up, had a haircut, shaved, bought a new shirt and new boots with the new high heel currently in fashion. It gave him an extra inch and if he stretched his neck he was about five feet six inches. He was forever looking in his cracked mirror. His complexion was now a sunburnt brown. He looked quite dapper as he arrived to pick up young Catherine.

"My, you do look smart, James," said Catherine. As they walked down to the park he held her hand and like young lovers they joined the crowd all looking forward to having a good time.

The Governor decided to declare a holiday. It was 26th January 1842 and the day was to be called Foundation Day. The colony was fifty-four years old. The celebrations had been delayed four years because of the drought. All the shops in the village closed their doors in the afternoon and everyone assembled in the park at the Dennison Bridge. There was quite a gathering. The troopers were there in their red coats and they even had a pipe band. They had roped off a bare piece of ground for dancing, and there were girls doing Irish gigs and Scottish reels as well as a group of Morris dancers. Some of the crowd formed into squares and did the Quadrilles. This form of dancing was totally foreign to James. He, with Catherine, joined in and after a few mistakes such as going the wrong way, he soon got into the rhythm of it.

"Ah! James, you can dance," said Catherine.

James was out of breath but didn't want to spoil the occasion. He said, "Ah! I am out of practice. I miss the good old Irish jigs."

At six pm, the crowd was addressed by the Government officer. The bar tent was doing a roaring trade and James and Catherine were having a grand time dancing the night away.

James said, "It's a Ceilidh. Ah! It brings back memories, me darlin.'"

"Yes! James it's a Ceilidh."

James looked into her eyes and said "Catherine, well you be me girl?"

"Ah! you must be drunk and you holding me too damn close and you've got wandering hands. Where would you be from, me Irish lad?" she said.

"I'm from County Kildare, me darlin' and where might you be from?"

"County Sligo, I be from, James me boy."

That night, as he walked her back to her room at the back of the Black Bull Hotel, he explained how he had been sent out in 1823 as a convict to

Sydney to serve seven years for house breaking, and now had his Ticket of Freedom. He went to pull it out of his coat pocket

"Ah! Don't be worrin' me about that, James lad, I have had me eye on you and you look genuine to me."

James stopped and put his arms around her and without a word being spoken, she let him kiss her.

"Oh! Catherine, I luvs yu," said he.

Then after a moment she said, "James, there is something I have to tell yu, I think I'm having a baby. I was raped by the owner at Rockley Station. Marion at the Black Bull has helped me over the months. He was a scoundrel. So you see, James, I come to you not as a virgin. Will you still want me, James?"

Catherine broke into tears. James took her in his arms and said, "I will protect you and love you and I would have loved you even if you were having his bastard and loved it as if it was me own."

When Catherine finished, sobbing, she said, "Oh! James, we are going to have lots of lovely babies."

As Catherine and James were good Catholics and went to Mass every Sunday, Father O'Brien would lecture them on getting married but Catherine kept saying no. Catherine was in an advanced state of pregnancy and she still would relive that night on the Rockley track and wake in a sweat. She would snuggle into James and thank the good lord she had found her man.

In 1842, young Mary Anne was born to Catherine in the small Bathurst Hospital. When she brought the baby home, Catherine and James were living as man and wife. No amount of talking by Father O'Brien could change their minds. He tried his best to get them to the altar. He put his foot down and used every trick that he carried in his Catholic case. He showed them his Crucifix, even putting on his Chasuble but whatever he said or did, he could not persuade James and Catherine to get married, so he told Catherine that her beautiful daughter, young Mary would go to Purgatory. All the explaining in the world by the good Father O'Brien, that the fellow that raped her could not have been the young Mary's father achieved nothing.

James, being a stubborn old fool just said no, and that was that. He said to the good Father, "We will get around to it one day."

James was not all that well up on babies either. He was pretty sure that Catherine had been faithful as they had been inseparable since the Celebration Day festivities so he quickly accepted young Mary as his own.

Then in March 1845, young Catherine was born. The couple were now living in a semi detached house in Busby St, Bathurst. There was a new priest in town, Father McNally and after a drinking session he assured James he would baptise the new baby. Catherine was baptised on 13th April 1846, but shortly after, the good Father was sent back to Sydney with no reason given by the church.

James was keen to get back to Limekiln to try his hand at farming again. The drought had broken and the price of wool was climbing. The wool from the colony of New South Wales was now in demand in the woollen mills in England and on the Continent. Ships could not get it there fast enough, so he packed up his young family and in 1846, made the trip out to Limekiln. James was ever the handy man. He knocked up furniture and was always scrounging things that 'fell off' the back of drays or where he could find them. Sometimes things would appear. He was a master at fashioning things out of kerosene tins and the odd wooden box. Catherine's belongings were a few bits and pieces, but her family Bible took pride of place on the kitchen table. Although she still could not read it, she kept telling James it reminded her of the rolling green hills of Sligo back in Ireland and her desire to return some day. James reminded her of the potato famine and all the thousands of people who had died and how better off they were in the colony.

"No, me darlin', we are better off here. There might be a few snakes and wild dogs and it might get hot in summer but I like it here. Ah! It's going to be a great place to raise our family."

James packed all their belongings on his cart and trudged out to Limekiln. The hut he had erected back in 1838 was still standing 'in a fashion.' It was made out of wattle and daub, and the floor was packed ant bed. The bark roof had fallen in, so he quickly cut some shingles and was lucky enough to scrounge some iron to put on the roof. He assured Catherine she would get a front door before the summer. As for the time being, he nailed a piece of hessian across the opening and kept it wet. This had the effect of keeping the room cool in the summer.

He went about patching up the cracks with more mud. James was a master of scrounging and before long he had built an outdoor oven out of mud and bricks. He also carried home on his cart a drum to catch rain water off the rusty roof, all the way from Wattle Flat.

Chapter 21

The village of Limekiln had got its name from the deposits of lime that had been found there.

When Maurice Walsh served his time and was granted his Ticket of Leave in 1828, he was commissioned to go to Limekiln by the government authorities in Bathurst. He was granted thirty acres of good arable land and was also responsible for three ex-convicts who also had been granted their tickets. He was to start production of lime burning for the expanding building trade. He had two labourers, James Croft and James Wilson who were to work in the lime quarry and he had hired the service of Elizabeth Patfield as a house keeper. Maurice also ran a herd of cattle and he employed William Palmer to assist in running the cattle. William, while rounding up some strays, came across some stone. When he showed his boss, he identified it as good quality marble. He soon had his men cutting the stone and selling it in Bathurst. Maurice was expanding and he employed local men. They would not last long as the work was so darn hard. James Fines started working part time for Maurice Walsh to supplement his income while he was getting his own sheep farm up and running. James and John Tobin found themselves working together, digging lime out of the ground and then heating it in the kiln. James did not understand the chemical reaction that took place. All he knew was that it could now be used for a combining agent for mortar and plasters that were used in the construction of buildings. It was hard work and James would return home at night, put his feet up and fall asleep.

James now had a new flock of sheep. He replaced the fence that had fallen down and soon realised that he could not build a stone fence like he had back in Ireland, though he had got used to the post and rail fence that he had used back at Princess Charlotte Vale. Once he got the hang of making it, he found it easy to build, so James ran the small flock in his paddock. He would stand on the fence and gaze at his beloved sheep and would dream of one day having thousands of sheep grazing on hundreds of acres. James and John soon became great mates. John Tobin had been a model prisoner and was granted thirty acres. James, at the appropriate time, would take his sheep down to Tobin's flock and let the ram do his tupping. Now and again the odd horse would turn up in the village of Limekiln and find its way into James' small holding yard.

James had retrieved some fine young lambs from the big Dulcin property over near Wattle Flat. It was over a thousand acres and James worked on the principle that they would not miss a few lambs. If there was one thing that James knew about, it was sheep. From his years spent as a shepherd tending the government's flock, he knew all the tricks on how to husband them and keep them in good condition, but it was now time to get the wool off them which was becoming a problem. Bold as brass, he approached Tobin and they struck a deal that they would shear James' few sheep in exchange for some help with Tobin's bigger flock. So early one spring morning with the help of his young daughters, they set out to herd the small flock down the road to Tobin's property. As they moved the small flock down the road, some of the rebel sheep would wander off into the scrub.

"Damn sheep! Mary, watch them. Don't let them wander off if you can help it," called James. "Ah! We need a good dog." But he knew they were hard to come by.

There was a breed of dog now becoming popular for sheep herding. They could do the work of two shepherds, or in some cases if you got a good one, three shepherds but they cost money and they were as scarce as hen's teeth. John Tobin had arranged for a gang of three shearers to shear his mob as well as James' small flock. As the wool was dirty it had to be washed and set out to dry on slabs of bark. When it was dry, it was packed into bales with a wool press. James and John estimated that James had about one third of a bale which was marked and numbered so it could be identified at a later date after they had finished. At the completion of the job, the shearing gang with John and James trooped off to the wine bar for a drink. Later that night James weaved his way up the bush track. He was whistling one of his favourite Irish songs, 'I'll, take you home again, Kathleen.'

As he pushed through the hessian door he planted a kiss on Catherine and said "We have sold our first wool clip. We're going to be rich."

Catherine just looked at him and said, "Well, James me lad, show me the money."

James tried to explain that he might get some money but it would be paid in things for the house, the fence and the garden, such as sheets of tin, nails and other essential supplies.

One night at the tavern, John and James were talking. They were always talking about making more money and the subject came up about wool spinning.

"Me Da was a weaver back in the old country," said James.

The next day, James came up the track with a spinning wheel and a sack of wool. He explained to Catherine how easy it was to use.

"Don't tell me how to spin wool, James, me lad. My parents worked in a cotton mill."

"Well, my love, we are going to be rich. You and the girls, you can knit woollen jumpers and we can sell them in Bafust."

"Ah! Yes, James this will be another one of your get rich schemes. You will leave us with all the work and if you make any money, I know where it will end up, down at that 'watering hole.' Who is going to supply all these magic things? There are no Leprechauns in the bottom of our paddock."

With that, Catherine stormed off and got into bed with the girls. "Oh! By the way husband, I heard from our neighbour that the tallyman is due to call. I hope we don't have to pay anything. I suppose he will be like the Gombeen man who used to collect the rent back home."

James, as they say had the luck of the Irish, when not long after the sheep were shorn, tragedy struck. One by one the sheep just up and died. They had the fluke worm. As the price of wool that year was very low, most of the sheep in the area were boiled down that year for the fat that was sold for a range of uses.

Catherine was going to get old Mr Tobin to write young Mary's name and birth date in the Bible. It was in 1842, December or was it November? She had lost track of time, but she remembered young Catherine's, it was 13th March 1845. James had not been back to the town of Limekiln since 1838. The place had changed, and now there was a wine bar and a general store which sold all sorts of goods, sugar, tea, string, flour, cockie's joy. New products were being added to the list all the time. Homemade jams and sweets for the kids, you could not keep James' girls out of the shop.

One morning Sean Murphy came running up the Fines track calling out to James.

"Mr Fines, Da said there is a letter for you, looks port-ant," so James trotted back with young Murphy.

Chapter 22

The store was run by the Murphy's. Everything that the Fines family purchased was on tick. Above the counter hung all sorts of goodies, onions tied by a piece of string, on the counter, blocks of cheese, loaves of freshly baked bread and jars of lollies. Mrs Murphy ran the shop. No nonsense was tolerated from the children but she always rewarded well-mannered children with a sweet. Just as they arrived at the store, the Tinker pulled up outside. He sold all sorts of things that you could not buy at the shop but under the wagon this day was a dog. It came running out and jumped up on James and licked his face.

Old Joseph called out, "Fines, would you like a dog? He is a good ratter and a work dog."

"I don't know. How much are you askin'?" said James, knowing the old scoundrel never gave anything away?

"Nah! James, I am trying to give him a good home, just take him. He is a blasted nuisance and he cost me an arm an' a leg to feed. I don't need him anymore."

"Ah! I'll being taking him off your hands, I have no sheep now but it will be good company for the girls."

As James walked back up the track, he was looking at a piece of paper, old Joseph had given him. It was a map.

"Not much good to me, I can't read," he muttered to himself.

Catherine was forever complaining about the need for a more permanent place for the family to do their ablutions. She was sick of going out in the night to find a place to relieve herself and so she went on and on till finally James, with the help of John Tobin dug a hole in the ground, downwind from their dwelling. They finally finished when they reached a depth of six feet. They put in a wooden floor and a platform with a lid. He put up the walls, (sheets of bark) and a tin roof plus a hessian material door. He was so proud of what he had done, especially when Catherine gave it her seal of approval. On the first night she used it, not liking to venture out after dark, she carried a candle in a jam tin. James was wakened with screaming coming from the back yard. He raced out to find Catherine jumping up and down and pointing into the loo. Finally after she had simmered down, James peered into the dunny to find the biggest frog he had ever seen. Carrying it out into the scrub he casually said, "It looks like it could rain" and walked back into the house and climbed into bed.

After James was no longer running sheep, he looked at his bit of ground. He reckoned he had about an acre that had been worked over, so with a bit of effort and his trusty hoe, he set out to plant a crop of corn. It was bringing six bob a bushel. He had been working flat out all morning when Catherine came out with some lemonade.

"Ah! Darlin' it's too darn hard, 'n me hoe is blunt. I must get one of those file things but I am going to ask Tobin for a loan of his harrow."

His work mate, John Tobin, helped him carry the implement up to the plot. With John's help, they harnessed James' old horse and with a new set of winkers and reins they turned over the ground. The two lads were exhausted when Catherine arrived with a well earned drink of lemonade. James thought for a moment and said "John, can you read?"

"Well, James I can a bit. Not too good though. Why do you ask?"

James dragged out of his pocket the slip of paper that old Joseph the tinker had given him.

"Take a look at this John, what you make of it?"

"Well, it's a map of the Turon River."

After closer inspection it was revealed it was a map of a gold prospector's camp not that far up the river.

"But look, James, I think it's all in Chinese."

"Do we know who might be a able to translate it?"

"Look, I'll talk to a mate of mine in Wattle Flat. His housekeeper is Chinese. She may be able to tell us what it means. Did you say old Joseph gave it to you James?"

The poor old horse had never worked so hard. Still James was not happy. He yelled out to John, "We need a furrow horse, but I guess this will have to do."

The girls were laughing as their father rode the plough as if he was breaking in a wild brumby. Finally, the paddock was ploughed and it was all hands on deck to help with seed planting. Even the girls lent a hand, shooing the Galahs who constantly swooped down to steal the seed as quick as it was being planted.

The day after the corn seed was planted, it started to rain and rain. Little rivers started to drain off his acre but when the sun finally started to shine most of the seed had sprung up. James had never worked so hard. He was down at the paddock from daylight to dark shooing the Galahs away. He would get down on his hands and knees and he would look like he was praying. He told Catherine he was just urging the young suckers on, but deep down he was praying for a good harvest. One morning, to James horror, there was a piebald horse munching away on the green leaves of the corn. James worked on the theory that the horse was trespassing on his property so he tethered it up behind the shed. There were no markings on it, so he claimed it. He now had two horses.

To James' surprise, it was a great crop over seven feet tall and loaded with fat corn cobs. His young family helped him carry the crop of corn up to the shed and they all helped in shucking the corn off the cobs. James was as proud as punch. He collected four bags and wheeled his barrow down to Murphy's who would sell it on commission. He was thinking it would help keep the wolf away from the door but there were no wolves here, well, Dingos maybe. James and Murphy weighed it and the scales topped fifteen bushels. The next time Catherine was in Murphy's store, she collected the payment for the corn crop in goods. She arrived home loaded with fruit and dry goods and five yards of calico. And she informed James that there was a bag of flour to be picked up at the store.

"Look James, apples, and oranges," she said. "And look, I brought two quinces and a pear tree to plant."

James was not impressed as he was expecting a big cheque.

Catherine announced to James that she was expecting again. He loved his wife and two daughters but it was getting harder to put food on the table. Another mouth to feed, he thought! So he set off to the wine bar on the Limekiln road to drown his sorrows. He met up with John who ushered James out the back; all very hush, hush.

"What's up, John?"

"Well mate, remember that piece of paper you gave me? Well my mate Daniel from Wattle Flats, his partner, she's a chink. Well, she reckons it's a map describing the last details of a Wi Lu, a Chinese gentleman who died and left his plot without rescuing his gold to take back to China. What do you think? Do we go out and have a look? We can saddle up the two horses. It's not far. We will take the trail around the mountain and up the valley. She also said 'bad medicine.' It belongs to Wi Lu, and his family would come back and retrieve the gold if any had been left."

Early one morning, the two lads left Limekiln with their swags and James told Catherine they would be back within a week. He gave her a list of jobs.

"I'll give you jobs, James!" she snapped as she swung a broom vigorously at the back mat. "If you not back, me and the girls are off."

As the two lads drifted off to the shed to saddle up the horses they could hear Catherine's booming voice carrying on a treat.

"James, rushing off on some wild goose adventure! You get you self back here in no longer than a week you hear, or I tell you James Fines, we will skedaddle back to Bathurst."

John let it pass but they had only gone a few hundred yards when he chuckled to himself.

"Gee, James, she will have our guts for garters if we are not back."

Reluctant Heroes

It didn't take long for them to reach the Turon River. It was just a trickle but it could be a raging torrent in flood time. They camped the first night and rolled out their swags, and fed and hobbled the horses. Next morning, after something to eat, they were on their way.

"God, it's peaceful out here John," remarked James.

They had been walking alongside the river and in the distance they could see smoke. They trod carefully and, as they rounded the next bend, they spotted a group of Aborigines. When the aboriginals sighted the two white men they melted into the scrub, all accept one, who boldly walked up to James and said, "Moonah Kadara, Moonah Kadara."

James looked closely at the blackfella. There was something familiar about him. Then he recognised him.

"Jacky, old fellow," he said.

A smile spread over Jacky's face. "Yes, goanna up a gum tree," he said.

James tried to explain to John about his time back at the Wellington Valley and his experience with the blacks. The two lads kept walking and as soon as they had passed the camp fire a spear landed in the river bank just a few yards from them. James reckoned they were just letting them know they were trespassing and it would be good if they moved on. Late that afternoon they found the abandoned Chinese camp. There found evidence of a well and sluice box.

In the early 1850s, the Chinese gold diggers invaded the rivers on the western slopes over the Blue Mountains especially the Cox and the Turon rivers. They turned over every stone looking for gold. They turned up in New South Wales after exhausting the gold in California. The gold fever had gripped the both countries. As the hordes of miners arrived in Sydney, the knowledge of further finds in the wilds of Alaska spread, but it was a steady stream of prospectors that travelled over the Blue Mountains searching for gold.

The two lads searched the area all morning without much luck. They found what they thought was the remains of a temple. The canvas sides were in tatters and the wooden structure had a lean and was about to fall apart. They built a fire, boiled a billy and made a damper for lunch.

"I don't know, John. If there was anything here, it's been long gone," said James.

After lunch the lads scavenged the area more closely, especially the remains of the temple.

"Bring the shovel over here, James," called John.

It didn't take long before they had a hole a couple of feet down, when they struck something solid. It was a tin. They hauled it to the surface and with their hands shaking, they prised the lid open. It contained a calico bag; they were silent for a few moments, then John said "This bag is very heavy." As he weighed the bag they slowly opened it. In the bottom was gold dust.

As they filled the hole in and surveyed the creek bed, John said, "Don't even think about it, James. We are out of here as soon as you have finished that cuppa tea."

It was not uncommon for bush rangers and robbers to be lurking around, so as the sun was in its last quarter for the day, they set off with a spring in their step to link up with the Palmers Oakey road. It was after dark when they trudged their way through the bush and reached the main road to Oakey. Although it was a main thoroughfare used by the mail coach through to Sofala, the lads knew the coach would not pass till the next morning.

Around eleven pm they pulled off the road, hobbled the horses and rolled out their swags and tried to sleep. All night James dreamed of the gold. What would it be worth? They were up at sunrise and were on their way. It was not all that far down the Mountain into Limekiln. They had only gone about four miles when out of the blue, three horses came out of nowhere. James looked at John and said "Don't worry, cobber, they won't find the gold. I hid it in the horses' feed bag."

The lead horse rider produced a gun and said, "Where are you blokes off to?"

James elected to do the talking. "We're on our way back to Limekiln," he said. "What it is to you?"

"Look fellars, a smart Mick. You has been out long?"

James could see this line of talk would not get them home so he told the bush rangers he came out on the 'Medina' in '23 and they were both Ticket of Leave men.

"Ah! Be off with you then," said one, and they were detained no longer.

"Gee James, you talked you way out of that," muttered John in admiration.

As they rounded the last hill they could see the plains in the distance.

"Look James, mum's the word," said John. "We have to keep this to ourselves. If word gets out, God knows what might happen. I think we have to dispose of it in small lots to avoid suspicion. It won't take long for the drinkers at the pub to put two and two together. We have been away for four days and you know what they're like, a pack of old women. We shouldn't even tell the missus but if they ever find out we would get skinned alive."

As John had access to scales, he weighed the gold and it came in around 42 ounces. "Look James, I'll check with my friend. He'll know what to do but I'll have to be discreet. You only have to mention gold and they think you've found an Eldorado."

It was three days later when John casually walked up the bush track to James and Catherine's plot. He passed the corn crop that had been harvested. The old horse was munching on the stubble. "Well John, what did you find out?" he asked, as they walked down to James' shed.

"Well, there was good news and bad news. The price of gold is £2-15-00 per ounce."

"Well, is that the good or the bad news, John?"

"That's the good news. The bad news is we only had 39 ounces."

James didn't have a head for facts and figures and thought that can't be too bad anyway. They both laughed their heads off at their good fortune.

"Well, what is that lot worth, me lad," said James.

John drew out a piece of paper which wrapped with a wad of notes. "Don't you worry about that, me lad. I've got it in English pounds. We're rich, over £40 each."

They divided the cash into two equal amounts and James hid his in a kero tin and buried it in the barn.

James and Catherine could hardly write their names nor read. A letter had arrived for them. It had come that morning on the mail coach from a Matthew Marr Esq. who had established himself as a buyer and seller of all fine goods. Matthew was the son of Henry Marr, the Government overseer to whom James had first been assigned as a convict. Shamus handed James the letter and James was dumbfounded as he had never received any mail.

"Could you open it for me Shamus?" he asked.

Shamus could hardly read himself, but he finally figured it out. Attached to the letter was a cheque for £4/7/6 for wool sold.

"Ah! James you're a Cocky and an Irish Cocky at that," said Shamus. They all laughed,

"Ah! Keep it Shamus; the good wife will spend it I'm sure." James was forever dreaming of owning a plough but the money wasn't enough. There was never enough. He was rich with his share of the gold money but he decided to leave it aside for a rainy day, so Shamus tucked the cheque into his pocket. As James left the general store he was glad to be done with the sheep. They had been nothing but trouble since he had nicked them from the Dulcin Vale station and the Sheep Scab Board were coming back to investigate his ownership of the flock. Anyway the rest of the flock had died. But then he remembered tied to the post was the dog. Oh well, another mouth to feed. He undid the lead and James and his dog walked up the track to the house. There were crows in a gum tree. Caw, Caw, Caw. They seemed to be laughing at James. He stopped and was going to say something but shook his fist and continued to walk on. Wafting out of the kitchen he could smell freshly baked damper that Catherine had cooked. He was greeted at the front door by his daughters who, straight away fell all over the dog. The girls named him Kanga.

The village of Limekiln was in the foothills of Mt. Horrible on the main road between Bathurst, Kelso, Palmers Oakey, Wattle Flat and Sofala.

In the year 1847, Catherine and James had another daughter and they called her Bridget, born 7th March, but she wasn't baptised until November.

Chapter 23

One afternoon while James was testing the spirits at the wine bar, a stranger entered the saloon. He did not recognise Patrick, at first.

"Oh! I was told I would find you here." Patrick was in a suit made of fine English wool with a bowler hat to match. He looked like real country squatter gent and a wealthy one to boot.

"Well, I'll be darned. What brings you out here Patrick? It looks like you are doing well," remarked James.

"Well, strange as this may seem, James you know after I got my Ticket of leave I struck it rich and gee it was back in '28. I got into a card game at the Black Bull in Bathurst and went to Sydney, got married to a nice girl and now we own a spread out on the plains. While we were in Sydney, I met up with Henry, you know he was going into printing trade. Your name came up and he wanted to catch up with you about doing some sketches for him .But that was, I don't know, about fifteen years ago He gave me five quid to give you so here it is, get drawing.

"God, Patrick, how did you find me out here?" asked James.

"Well, James me lad, I bumped into some of our mates from Charlotte Vale and they said you were now a farmer out here, so I hired a trap and here I am."

"Gee! You know I can hardly write my name," said James.

"Well, that may be so, but I remember back at the hut how you could draw birds, animals and the natives, using only charcoal. The natives also showed us how to draw on the bark."

Patrick showed James a book of some early drawings of the landscapes and the natives he had found in a book shop in Bathurst.

"I say old chap, look at these," said James. "They look ridiculous. This native looks like a black white man."

Patrick asked James as they walked to the farm, "Did you ever take Henry's advice, James old fella, and get the deeds to this place?"

James just looked at Patrick and said, "Na, too darn hard. Maybe next year!"

So after they had a cup of tea and some of Catherine's damper, Patrick left the sleepy village of Limekilns and returned to his spread. James was dumfounded. He never considered he had any talents and for drawing? He thought to himself he could do with some extra money. That was when he cashed in his stash of coins he had been saving, and what did he do with that? He drank and gambled it away. He told Catherine this was going to be different. He still had his nest egg stashed away in the ground of the shed and now every chance he had he would be off into the bush, drawing birds and the animals. He soon became a local authority on the different types of birds. His favourite was the Jackass, except in the mornings, when he was hung over from too much liquor and they would start their early morning call as the sun came over the hills.

James had heard of a gathering of natives that were camped down near Paling Creek not far from the village. He had been trying to saddle up his horse but this morning, he was puffed out trying to catch him.

"Come here you bugger!" he yelled.

Catherine, called out from the house, "James, you silly bugger, the time you spent catching the nag, you could have been there and back."

Although his enthusiasm was a bit jaded, he finally caught him, saddled up and set out. It was a bright sunny morning. With pencils and paper in a folder, he felt like a real artist and would boast to his drinking mates back at the pub how he was going to be famous. As he ventured down the gully and crossed the dry creek bed, he disturbed a goanna and it quickly scampered up the nearest tree. He hitched the horse to a tree close by. He could hear black cockatoos screeching and displaying their red fan tails. He quickly sketched them before they flew off and then, a group of large red kangaroos scampered past, bounding across the dry gully. He walked over the rise, and saw smoke billowing from a camp fire in the distance. He could hear shouting and screaming as he rounded the bend and there he saw them, a group of Aborigines had erected a lean-to shelter out of some bark.

At first he just stood back, he was in shock. The natives he knew back when he was a convict, were a proud people. There were about fifteen in this group, they were all shabbily dressed in white man's hand-me-downs and they were passing around a bottle of plonk. One of the men approached James, screaming out loud. When he finally worked out what he was saying, it was that he wanted him to lie with his lubra. James slowly backed off, ascended the gully and just looked back at the scene. It was a sad situation and he thought that the black man was doomed. How could this happen in such a short time?

As he walked back down the track he could sense someone following him. He turned around and he saw this young black lass standing naked.

"Please mister don't you want a nice young black gin?" she said.

Poor James just turned around and kept walking. He had never strayed from his Catherine and he was not about to start now. Some of his drinking mates had told him about the black velvet you could get for the price of a cheap bottle of plonk. He unhitched the horse and moved back down the track to the main road. It was times like this he started to think of home, good old Erin and the green rolling hills. Then he was jolted back to life as a flock of screeching cockatoos flew overhead. They seemed to be laughing at him. He sadly returned home, told Catherine what had happened and how shocked he was at the state of the once proud tribe that had roamed the Wellington Valley. He could not remember, but it must have been a long time ago. He started to reminisce about his girl, Marion. She probably had a tribe of kids by now.

James had nearly forgotten all about Henry, when one day out of the blue, Henry turned up. He shouted James lunch and a pint of the best at the local hotel and went on his merry way with James' latest drawings, leaving him with a new lot of paper and another crisp ten pound note. Sadly Henry never came back, so after all the paper was used up, it was relegated to the top shelf in the kitchen.

Catherine came running down to James who was working in his shed, "James, there is a black man sitting on the ground at our front door."

As James reached the back door to their dwelling there, large as life, sitting on the ground was Jacky. As soon as Jacky recognised James, he jumped up and said, "Boss, you give me some flour and baccy?"

James went into the house and re-emerged with a small sugarbag containing some flour and tobacco. Jacky left, thanking him, jabbering away in his lingo with a smile all over his face.

Catherine was pregnant again but after six months at Limekiln, she lost the baby, a little boy. They called him Daniel. James, bundled up the small one and buried him up the back, away from the house. James covered the little grave with stones to stop the dingoes digging up the body. He slowly walked back down the track towards the hut. Things just couldn't get any worse. He was close to tears. He could smell smoke. A bushfire had started somewhere in the valley and he could see it quickly spreading through the grassland. Then he could hear Catherine's voice calling out, "FIRE! FIRE!" as she raced up the track holding young Mary's hand. "It's the hut James, it's on fire, she called."

James was able to salvage most of the furniture and their belongings before the fire took hold of the house. It did not take long for the neighbours to rally around and before long they had a tent and tarpaulin rigged up.

With the help of Tobin and some of his drinking mates, they quickly got together to construct a fine new dwelling. It still had slab sides but now had a proper chimney made out of stone from the quarry and an ant nest floor. It even had a dividing wall to give James and Catherine some privacy, something they never had before. One of his drinking mates even arrived with some grape vine and honey suckle cuttings.

One afternoon, when James was walking up the track to their new residence he was met by young Mary.

"Da! I think Ma is sick," the young lass said.

When James entered the home, he found his wife lying on the bed and burning up with fever. "Mary keep this cloth wet and keep it on your Ma's forehead. I'll go down to the village and get Mrs Tobin to come up and look at Ma."

James, after chasing his horse around the paddock gave up, swearing away at the beast and finally walked the mile down through the scrub to the road and on to the general store. Mrs Tobin was a generous person and she dropped what she was doing and they hurriedly walked back to the hut.

"James, get your wife to take these, they should relieve the fever." Mrs Tobin handed James a small box of pills.

James spent a restless night as he sat by his wife before finally falling asleep in the early hours of the morning. Eventually the fever broke and Catherine drifted off into a sound sleep. She miscarried during the night so James wrapped the small body in a blanket and buried his son. It would have been his second son so he buried him under a big gum tree next to his first son. Once again he placed stones over the grave to stop the dingoes digging up the body and erected a simple cross.

James would trap possums, kangaroos and koalas and use the skins to keep them warm in winter. He was getting a lot of skins and once a fortnight he arranged to have them taken into Bathurst where they were sold by an animal skins merchant. In the winter, he could not keep up the demand, it was such a good little money earner. From kangaroo greenhide he also made reins. He had learnt the skill from his Aboriginal mates, back in his convict days.

James Tobin, who had been granted his Ticket of Leave and was now a free man, was working a marble quarry down on the creek and gave James some part time work. They were working for Maurice Walsh, splitting marble into workable slabs and, as the marble was of a high quality, it was being used in some of the government buildings in Bathurst. The slabs were very heavy and had to be first manhandled onto a dray and transported into Bathurst. It was hard thirsty work.

James was now getting on to fifty and much to Catherine's surprise, he had kept out of trouble. He had stopped regular drinking and only drank on Saturdays and then only when he had any money, which was only after working with Tobin. James had mainly worked with sheep since he had arrived in the Colony. The stone work was starting to tell on his back.

Catherine woke one Sunday morning. She had had a dream, her mother was calling her, "Catherine," she called.

"It's me, Ma."

"Why aren't you married?" her mother cried out in the dream and was urging Catherine to seek out some peace with the Church.

Catherine continually pestered James that they should be married. Deep down she was a good Catholic and started at every opportunity to seek comfort at Mass in the make-shift church in Limekiln. James would usually make the effort to attend with his family, (anything for a quite life) and every Sunday morning, rain, hail or shine in their Sunday best, the family would trudge down Paling Yard Creek Road to the church. As much as Catherine pestered James, he always had an excuse and kept putting off marriage.

Father Kelly was the new priest for the area. Once a month he would make the journey to Limekiln, stay at the Inn and on Sunday morning he would very often turn up late to conduct the service, and James reckoned that like his mate, the publican, he liked the taste of the amber fluid. Catherine would have none of it. She thought young Father Kelly was a fine example of an Irishman devoted to the cloth and she loved her church. There was talk of setting up a building fund to erect a permanent church and the land had been set aside. Father Kelly had, one Sunday morning, laid the foundation stone. The community was poor, no one had any money so the land for the new church sat there, weed infested and they continued to hold the regular services in the temporary church.

James was now working for Maurice Walsh on a regular basis at the Limekiln pits and Marble works. The little village started to grow and by 1849 there were nine families and thirty-six children. Catherine was pregnant once again and, on 31 January 1849, a new baby was born, a girl they called Margaret.

James' family was growing and a new priest, Father Antonio Bourgeois, all the way from Calabria in Italy, performed the baptism. He never once mentioned their marital status.

All the talk about the rhythm method had no effect and Catherine was soon pregnant again – now four daughters and no sons. On 16th May 1850 another girl Marsetta was born. James was celebrating down at the shanty wine bar one day and said to his drinking partner, "I want a son, someone to carry on the fine Fines' name and all I've got is another damn girl! It's going to cost me a fortune to marry them off. That's five - or is it four girls?"

Chapter 24

Catherine was down in the village at the store one day when a coach pulled up from Bathurst and a woman jumped down and raced down the road calling out, "Catherine! Catherine! It's me, your sister Briny."

Catherine turned and, at first she thought she must be seeing things. She had not seen her sister for twelve or more years.

"Briny, what are you doin' out here?"

"I've come to see you, that's what."

So arm in arm, they walked up the bush track to the wattle and daub house James and Catherine called home. Catherine put the billy on and they caught up with old times. She explained how the family was devastated when Catherine left and, to make matters worse, Da and Ma both died of consumption in the winter of '38. Mother cried and before she passed on, the last words she spoke were, "Oh, Catherine."

Briny was only a youngin' when Catherine left Sligo all those years ago. Briny had brought presents for them. She did not know what to bring as there had been no word from her sister since she had left Ireland. She had explained how she was going back to Sydney. She had a friend there and they were going into business together at a place called Woolloomooloo.

"Catherine, do you remember our cousin, Walter? Well, he sent me a letter before I left Dublin. He went to America, you see, and he got involved with some sort of amusement park over there and he wants me to join him. He gave me ten pounds to go towards me fare to California. It's a long way to America and I don't know if I need more than that to get me there. My friend in Sydney and I think we might give it a go down there for awhile."

All of a sudden, Catherine became the elder sister who was concerned for her younger sister's morals.

"Be careful, sis," she said. "This fancy man, is you sleeping with him?"

"Are don't you worry about my man," replied Briny. "Catherine, I can look after me self."

Then young Mary chimed in.

"Ma and Da aren't married yet, Aunt Briny.'

The two sisters looked at each other and laughed. So the happy group set off to meet the Sofala coach in which she had come. It would pick her up late in the afternoon on her return journey to Sydney. As the two sisters moved down the bush track, Briny shrieked out, "Mother of God, corr blimey, what was that?"

Catherine replied, "Damn Mopoke, that's what it is, Briny."

The two sisters finally emerged onto the road. In the distance they could see the billowing dust from the coach as the driver approached and came to a sudden stop.

"Yu going to Baftus, love?" asked the driver.

The two sisters held each other and started crying.

"Look after yu'self, me young sister and be careful," said Catherine. "I have been told Sydney is a sinful place. Ah! That it is."

With tears streaming down her face, Briny boarded the coach. The driver called out to his chargers and they were off. Catherine with tears in her eyes waved to her sister. Somehow they knew they would never see each other again. Catherine was in a daze as she never really found out how her sister knew where to find her.

James was spending more time down at the old Limekiln inn when he ran into an old mate from his time spent at Charlotte Vale. He was heading out to Hill End. He had heard a rumour that Gold had been discovered at a place called Ophir out from Orange. He had a newspaper; *"The Bathurst Free Press."* Neither George nor James could read, but the front page headline said **GOLD** and they both knew what that meant. They got the owner of the store to read the article for them. It went on to say that the whole area had gold bearing quartz and all you had to do was pick it up off the ground.

All of a sudden, the road out through Limekiln was filled with prospectors all heading for the Turon River. They came in their thousands, walking, riding horses or pushing a barrow.

It was an early autumn morning when James and Catherine returned from the store, loaded with supplies of flour, sugar, salted meat, tea and a bag of boiled lollies for the kids. As they were about to turn up the track leading to their patch, a young girl came out of the bush.

"Please sir can you help me?" she said. "I have nowhere to sleep and I have not had anything to eat for days."

Although James had little money, they soon took the young waif by the hand and the threesome walked up the bush track to the humble shack that was their home. They soon had her at the table with a slice of bread and lard and a cup of tea. Catherine quickly had the girl covered with a shawl her to help keep her warm.

They soon had the truth out of her. She had run off from the orphanage at Bathurst and was on her way to Hill End to work in a hotel. She divulged that her name was Sherborn and she was twelve. James and Catherine were at sixes and sevens on knowing what to do with her. Finally, Catherine talked to the priest at Sunday mass and, it was decided that the young lass would return to Bathurst. Sherborn only agreed to return when James assured her that she was welcome to return to Limekiln at the end of the year.

James shuffled off to the pub and regretted making the promise, as they only had a two room wattle and daub hut with a veranda. All the girls slept in a bed under the sleep-out in the summer and in the winter, they all huddled in the one room.

He thought, "I'll have to add another room."

But James had a heart of gold and could not turn anyone away.

The new coach line, Cobb and Co, soon had coaches running from Bathurst through Limekiln, Wattle Flat, and Sofala and on to Hill End. Plans were also on the drawing board to construct a new hotel on the Bathurst-Limekiln Road.

George was itching for James to go with him gold prospecting, but James's health was starting to let him down, possibly from too much late night drinking. His back and knees ached from all the lifting and cutting of the stone. He had worked and slaved away digging lime out of the quarry. He was first and foremost a family man, and all his girls were growing up. He had to feed them and get them off to school.

"George, I'm getting too old for all this activity," he said. "You go and I hope you bring back a big nugget."

As he waved George off, he muttered to himself, "Ah! I must look for those stones I found crossing the Blue Mountains all those years ago."

George had only been away for six months when he turned up one day at the inn with a grin from ear to ear.

"James, it's up there," he said. "The gold is just lying on the ground and in the creek beds."

That night Catherine, James and George celebrated with a bottle of wine and they caught and roasted a chicken. George was heading into Bathurst to deposit the gold in his banking account and return again to the gold fields.

"James," he said. "I heard a whisper there has been traces of gold out around Hill End."

After George drifted back towards the gold fields, life returned to something like normal. Then one day out of the blue, George turned up with a covered wagon. He took the dray around the back and stabled the draught horse in James' shed. After dark, he took James out, with a lantern and revealed to James what was under the canvas.

James just looked and said, "Well, mate what is it? It just looks like a pile of junk to me."

"James," replied George, "with all these prospectors travelling out to the gold fields, we can sell the grog and make a fortune."

"But it's illegal, isn't it?" said James.

"Ah! James lad, who will ever know out here?" said George.

They unloaded all the equipment for operating the still. An old beer barrel and copper pipe, George had thought of everything. He had also picked up barley, wheat and seed potatoes.

George was heading back to the Turon River to prospect for more gold and left James to prepare the ground to plant the crops he needed for the still in the spring. He had even brought some grape vine cuttings off a travelling salesman who had got them off a friend who worked for a winery down near the Penrith River.

"They're supposed to be from a top growing Sauterne wine, which won first prize in the Sydney Easter show," he said.

At first Catherine was suspicious of all this sudden interest in growing plants and she insisted he plant some flowers. One night on his way home from the pub, drunk as a skunk, he picked some nasturtiums out of the garden behind the hotel. Catherine just looked at them and chucked them out the window. Next morning, James rescued them and planted them.

That spring he had a good crop of potatoes as there had been good late winter rain. Catherine became curious and kept saying,

"When are you going to dig those taters, James?"

"Soon, me darlin' soon."

It was well into September when old George finally turned up grumbling, "There might be a lot of gold out there, James, but there's a lot of dirt in between."

They set up the still down by the creek away from prying eyes. George explained that the fire under the still had to be a slow fire because, if the fire got too hot, it burned the alcohol, and he warned James this could be fatal

James said, "What! The grog would be no good?"

"No, you idiot, if you drink it, you might die, it's poison."

So they went into the spirit business making whiskey out of Barley and Poteen out of the potatoes. George had worked in a hotel in Dublin before he had been transported and he knew all the technical details.

They erected a small shed down by the creek. The barley had to be spread out on the floor so they used a tarpaulin. It was the best they could do for the time being. Later on, they would invest in a bag of cement, and mix it with lime to form a mortar. The barley had to be turned and kept moist to make it sprout. George had explained this was to bring out the sugar. Finally, the mixture was brought to a slow boil and simmer. The alcohol would come off as a distilled liquid to make whisky. George said they only had to add burnt sugar to give it the right colour.

At first Catherine noticed James would work all day in the marble quarry and then would disappear down to the creek. It was a dead give-away with the smoke rising in the still air. One day she followed him as he was coming out of the shed with a cart full of bottles. He was whistling, *"It's a Long Way to Tipperary."*

Before long Catherine put two and two together and came up with their little scheme.

"You crazy Irishman! How long before someone dobs you into the Garda, James?" said she. James just shrugged it off and showed Catherine all the money he had accumulated in a biscuit tin he had stored in his shed. There must have been fifty pounds. Catherine grabbed the money, saying, "Thank you James that will come in handy. The girls need new clothes and shoes and I would not mind a new dress myself."

James promised Catherine that he would soon give it away as he was getting tired of all the travelling and his partner George had disappeared down to Sydney and left him with all the work to do. All the potatoes had gone. He would have liked to plant a bigger crop next year, however he swore on the bible in the kitchen a promise to his wife that this was the last batch.

He set out to deliver his last batch of Poteen. James had become quiet efficient in getting the amounts just right and was becoming an expert. He merrily pushed his cart down the Limekiln Road to a customer in Wattle Flat and was trudging up the incline past the Paling Creek turn off when he heard the muffled hoof beat of an approaching horse. He turned, but it was too late. He then thought he might jump behind the bushes, however, with a sheepish look on his face he was confronted by the local constable from Kelso, William O'Farrell. The constable pulled up his horse. He had been alerted by the tavern keeper that James was up to no good and had been selling black market liquor.

"Where would you be going, James lad, on this fine morning?"

"Well Sergeant, I am off to Wattle Flat on an errand."

"Would you now, James and what would you have under the hessian bag?" says O'Farrell. Reluctantly James lifted the bag and revealed the bottles underneath.

The constable, being of good Irish stock, gave James twenty-four hours to dispose of the goods. As James continued on his way he had a long face. "Nothing seems to go right," he muttered, then crows started to call, *"Caw, Caw, Caw."* He looked up into the tree beside the road.

"You can laugh, you bastards," he yelled.

He had agreed to show the constable where he was brewing the grog. He quickly delivered the bottles to his friend in Wattle Flat who was selling it out the back door to his mates. His mate was annoyed when James told him, "This was the last delivery, cobber."

"Why, James, what's the problem?" said his friend.

James explained that he had been found out. As James started to walk back, he contemplated selling the still to his friend, but then thought better of it. So next morning, O'Farrell turned up at James's house, with two black assistants. They walked down to the creek and the constable smashed the apparatus so it couldn't make another drop. The constable told Catherine he would call out next week to confiscate all the equipment.

With that Catherine started to cry. "Constable! I have really tried. Deep down, James is a good man but we seem always to be in trouble."

"Ah! Don't worry, me lass," said O'Farrell. "I'll put in a good word for James when his case comes up."

In 1852, when James' case was heard in the Bathurst Court of Petty Sessions, the Judge looked at James and finally gave him a warning saying, "Mr Fines, the state of New South Wales will not have its citizens flaunting the laws of the land. Distilling liquor for sale or for any illegal purpose will not be tolerated. I have taken into account your good record since being given your Ticket of Leave as well as your large family. I am in possession of three character references from some well respected citizens in the district, even from the publican of the local hotel who drew the constable's attention to the still. Mr Fines, for Goodness sake, pull yourself together and do the right thing. This court charges you two pounds plus court costs of fifteen shillings."

The Judge went on to say, "Mr Fines, if you are brought before this court again, I will have no hesitation in sending you to prison. This is a very serious offence."

Then the clerk of the court said, "All rise."

James had the last laugh as he travelled back to the Limekiln as after the fine he had pocketed, nearly sixty pounds, not taking into account the £50 Catherine had confiscated.

James now turned his spare time to drawing. Even Catherine was impressed.

"James, I like the way you draw the kangaroos and the koala" she said. "You have a good talent for drawing."

He had used up all the paper, so he put the drawings into a kero tin and placed them on top of the kitchen cupboard. Henry never returned, so he soon forgot all about the drawings.

Young Marsetta was born in 1850, however it took two years before the travelling priest had a chance to baptise her on Sunday, April 24th. James was on his way to the wine bar to celebrate the birth of his new daughter when he spotted the priest, Father James Keating arriving at the inn. It was Saturday afternoon and he was there to perform any necessary Catholic ceremonies including weddings and christenings. The Father had tried on previously and now again suggested to James that he and his good Catholic lady should be married.

James tried to avoid the good father, but could not escape.

"James, morning to you, would you like to have a drink with me?" asked the priest.

"Why thank you, Father," replied James.

Father Keating made small talk about the slow progress of the building of the new church and how some local marble around there would look good in the walls of the new church.

"Ah! You would have to talk to me boss about that, Father."

James knew the good father would get around to his favourite subject soon.

"James, why don't you and your good lady, Catherine, get married while I am here this trip?"

"Why, thank you Father," replied James. "But we'll get round to it one day."

It was late on Sunday morning, when Father Keating finally emerged from the inn. He had had a drop or two of the inn keeper's fine whisky and drove his sulky the short distance to the temporary church. Young Marsetta was baptised and her godmother was noted as Catherine Walsh. When the ceremony was concluded, they all went back to the house. Catherine had intended to get Father Keating to write in her bible and bring it up to date, but once again she had forgotten. They opened the door and on the floor was the biggest black snake they had seen. The ladies all screamed and went racing out the door. James and the Priest were bringing up the rear when young Mary came racing up to her father.

"Snake!" she screamed. "Father, it must be twelve foot long and it's in the kitchen under the table."

James and a slightly frightened priest tentatively entered the dwelling. James had picked up a shovel and when he was confronted with the reptile, he cut it in two. He picked it up and carried it out into the yard. The men quickly gathered round the black snake lying on the ground. Ants were already feasting on the flesh. James opened a bottle of his brew and toasted his new daughter.

Chapter 25

The old pub was nothing more than a wattle and daub hut and a new hotel of solid construction was finished in 1853. Both the stables and out buildings were of corrugated iron and it boasted solid wood flooring.

John Tobin was the son of James Tobin who was transported from Ireland for life in 1829 on the 'Larkin.' James had been a model convict and was granted Ticket of Leave 1838 Nos 310—557 on the condition he remain in the district. In the late 1840's John Tobin built the first Limekiln Inn. Its licence was granted by the government and it was called the Limekiln Hotel. The day of the opening was a big occasion, the entire town's people turned up from far and wide. John Tobin employed bar staff from Bathurst and the hotel was decorated with flags and bunting. He even had musicians from Kelso playing on the front veranda. The children were not left out either - games and races had been organised and everyone was presented with a prize and lemonade. The hotel even catered for guests who wished to stay overnight and break their journey before travelling on.

The Fines family were blessed with two more girls. Alice came along on 16th January 1854 and she was baptised without any trouble on 16th November 1854. Jane was born on 16th September 1855 and baptised on 2nd October 1856. The family now had seven girls and had lost two boys. This worried James and he could be heard mumbling to himself, "Will I ever have a son?"

Chapter 26

The Inn was always busy with travellers passing through to the goldfields from Bathurst, Sofala and Hill End.

The traffic from Bathurst and Lithgow also helped to keep the rooms full. If the weather was extra bad, then coaches would come to a halt. On those nights, the publican would place patrons in the stable and in harness room. The coach from Sunny corner would sometimes divert through Palmers Oakey and go direct into the Sofala and Hill End gold fields.

The hotel was always packed on Friday nights. Squatters, shepherds and gold diggers were there to tell their stories of triumphs and sorrows. James had promised Catherine that he would be home early that night as they were going to Bathurst in the morning. The girls wanted to visit a church market and the family had to be up early to make the sixteen-mile trip into town. They were staying with George Cott who had returned from Sydney. The girls referred to him as Uncle George. He was a confirmed bachelor and would joke that he was waiting for Catherine's sister.

The usual mob was holding up the bar and in full voice, singing, *"Bold Jack Donnan."* The authorities had banned the song and the publican was onto them to tone it down and sing another ditty.

A card game had developed. This was nothing unusual as there was always a game of cards on, but this night, James sensed something different. His boss, John Tobin had been on edge all that week. The word was out that he had got into a bit of trouble with gambling. He was known to back the racehorses in Sydney with the SP Bookie in Bathurst.

Samuel Taylor, who was related to John Tobin, had been drinking heavily since late in the afternoon, when James arrived at the hotel early in the evening. He recollected that he had promised Catherine he would be home early. One drink and he would be off.

But James, as usual, got involved with some old mates and by nine thirty was a little tipsy. It was after ten pm and the bar went quiet as the crowd gathered around the card players. The stake was getting serious. The other card players had dropped out as the stakes got to a ridiculous level. John had been dealt two black aces and two black eights. When he turned them over, he started to perspire as he had been told it was called the dead man's hand. He chucked it in and Samuel dealt the next hand. John Tobin had been dealt four kings and a seven of spades. He thought his luck had changed as he discarded the seven and one of the kings. There was a hush; not a sound. You could hear a pin drop as Samuel picked up his cards one at a time ever so slowly, whilst staring at his opponent,

"Are you out of your mind, Tobin, you mean to bet the hotel?" said Samuel.

"Yes, Yes, that's right, the pub," shouted John Tobin as he smiled and placed his hand on the table covering his three kings two Queens.

Samuel casually placed his cards on the table revealing an Ace, King, Queen, Jack and Ten of Hearts. John Tobin just sat there and realised what he had done, all the hard work, his life savings gone on a ridiculous game of cards. He just lowered his head, the place was silent, then Samuel said, "John, you can leave in the morning."

John jumped out of his chair and drew his revolver and shot two bullets into the floor causing a mad rush for the door.

Samuel was now the new owner of the hotel. The first thing he did was change the name of the hotel to *"The Rising Sun Inn."*

It was a well known saying in later years that Australians would bet on two flies walking up the wall.[3]

---

[3] Footnote 3: See page 377

The next morning, bright and early, the Fines family travelled to Bathurst. As they passed the hotel, James told Catherine the story of the card game that would later become a folk legend of Limekiln. They had arranged to leave Mary and Bridget with friends in Bathurst as they were now old enough to look for work. Samuel had offered Bridget a job at the hotel but her father said, "No," as he didn't want his daughter working in a hotel. Finally in 1858, while Catherine in her early forties and James in his fifties were visiting friends in Sofala, Catherine went into labour and a son James was born, but sadly he, like the other sons also died.

In 1859, the village of Limekiln had over forty-six children. The new publican, Mr Samuel Taylor offered a house to be operated as a non-vested school. It was open to all children regardless of what religion they were. James was talking to the new publican and he told Samuel about deeds to his plot. Samuel looked James in the eye and said, "Me lad, do you really want to go through filling out all those papers?"

"Ah! Sam, I see what you mean, I'll get back to you," said James.

He left the Rising Sun thinking, "What do I need the deeds for? Tobin tells me you have to pay the government something about rates. We're fine. We don't need a piece of paper to live on our patch."

James was now in his late 50's. A Hurling match was to be played between Bathurst and the Peel district. John as a lad had done some of this in his younger days back in Ireland. While down at the tavern in a fit of bravado, he offered to captain the Peel side. There were fifteen players on each side and you could hardly see the goal post at each end as they were six hundred yards apart, between the Vale Creek Bridge, Dennison Bridge and Gorman's Hill in Bathurst.

There were three umpires, Mr J. De Clovett for the Bathurst side, Mr Walter Cummings for the Peel side and Dr. Wilkinson as the overall senior referee. Three games were set down. The Peel side scored a goal in the first game. There was a carnival atmosphere at the park that day and three legged races, egg and spoon races and toffee apple eating contests were organised for the children. Mr Smith from the property Duramana, had also organised some donkeys for a ladies' donkey race. Bridget Fines entered along with other girls from the district. There was a betting ring and all the money was on young Molly Smith, whose father had stables in Duramana and owned the donkeys. The starter was Mr Walter Cummings. When he dropped the Union Jack Flag, the donkeys were off. Some refused to move and there were spills aplenty. Only two donkeys ridden by Molly and Bridget turned to enter the home straight, heading for the finishing line. It was declared a dead heat! There was wild cheering as the judges presented the winning ribbons.

The hurling teams had rested and were ready to resume the second match. Some staggered from the beer tent when the whistle blew to commence the game. It had only just begun when the ball exploded into a hundred pieces and that's when the riot started. One of the Bathurst players knocked young Archibald McKinnon to the ground with an illegal tackle, then it was an all-in brawl. One of the Bathurst players called James, "a no good, Catholic Mick."

About five pm, both teams made their way to the Shearers' Arms Hotel at Peel. There was to be a dance that night at the Peel Public School and the school parents had prepared the hall that afternoon. Sawdust was spread out on the floor, two lads would slide around on a bag to make the floor slippery, taking turns pulling the bag. The walls were decorated with bush branches and wattle flowers. The school hall was packed. They had erected a makeshift bar out the back, all the buggies were tied up to the hitching rail and some of the young lads had unharnessed the horses and placed them on the other side of the fence to confuse the adults when the function was over. They also turned the saddles around to confuse the patrons who were usually under the weather when they come out to mount up to return home.

By ten o'clock, the dancing was in full swing. The musicians were Joe Doolan on the fiddle, James Croft on the concertina and Roland Arrows on the drums and they were playing all the tunes of the day. At the first break in the dancing, a young fella jumped on the stage and started to play the gum leaf. He was pretty good. Some of the younger children were sound asleep under the seats. Finally, around midnight, the night came to a close finishing off with *"God Save the Queen,"* much to James' disgust as he still bore a grudge against all things British. Still, he had had a great night dancing the night away with his Catherine. James had been a good dancer in his youth and in a lighter moment he said to Catherine as he gazed into her eyes.

"Will you marry me, darling?"

Catherine replied, "James lad, you're drunk. We will talk about it in the morning when you're sober."

Then two young fellas got onto the stage, Len Cassidy on the fiddle and Jack Connelly on squeeze box and they played an Irish medley, *"The Wild, Wild Rover"* and *"The Irish Washer Women."* There was not a dry eye in the crowd. Even James had a tear in his eye. Young Catherine introduced her new man, the drummer to her parents and Roland asked James if he could marry his daughter. Then a young fella climbed onto the stage and started singing *"Danny Boy."* That brought the crowd to their feet and they all joined in. Finally, drunk as lords, the Limekiln players with their families finally dispersed, some on horseback and some in sulkies. They were all singing as they slowly made their way back to their homes in the early hours of the morning. James was in good voice as he hummed the tune of *"Danny Boy"* then, at the top of his voice, he broke out and started to sing. The sun was peeping over the horizon and the jackasses started calling as if they were singing along with him. Next morning all the girls could talk about was the wedding.

James and Catherine were still living in the wattle and daub house down by the creek, away from the main road. After the fire, James added to the dwelling, a back veranda which was enclosed for the girls to sleep in. As James sat down at the kitchen table, he quickly brought them down to earth saying, "It will be a long engagement Catherine. We haven't got any money for a fancy wedding."

The night before, James hadn't thought about going to work the next morning. His head and bones were aching. He tried all his tricks to stay in bed but Catherine moved him along, so he went off to work at the quarry.

By five in the afternoon James and John Tobin decided to have a drink. They had been slaving away all day getting a load of lime ready to burn. It was hard, dirty and thirsty work. So John said to James it was time to bury the hatchet and they would have a drink at the old Pub. John was going to shake Sam's hand and wish him all the luck. The bar was doing a roaring trade that night as it was full of gold prospectors all cashed up returning to Kelso to visit the bank. The new Licensee had introduced dancing girls on Friday nights to the delight of the crowd. The girls sang songs and the drinkers get merrier. Some of the prospectors would take the young ladies out the back to the stable and Sam, the licensee, would just look the other way. The constabulary knew it was going on, but turned a blind eye, as well.

John and James were discussing a new project to make money. They were always thinking of money making ideas - it was always on their minds. James suddenly said "Clothes Props."

"What you talking about James?"

"Well, you see John, I had a dream last night and it came to me we could sell clothes props in town. Everyone needs them."

John, being a bit slow said, "What are these clothes props?"

James went on by describing that he saw Catherine one day last week struggling with the washing and it was dragging in the dirt. He went on to say "Look, she was calling the dirt for all the names you could think of and a fine Catholic upbringing she had, so I cut a sapling with a fork and propped the clothes line up and she was happy. I was happy, and that night, I think she became pregnant again."

He was about to say something about selling them, when he was interrupted. The door flew open and two men crashed through the front door. A lull came over the crowd.

"Bushrangers," someone from the crowd called out.

The two men, both with their faces covered and with pistols, herded the crowd to the back of the hotel. One patron still with his drink in his hand was sculling it down when a shot rang out. One of the bandits had fired two shots into the bar wall.

"Get back there and throw all your money on the floor and be quick about it," he yelled.

While one of the gang held the mob with a gun, his mate quickly gathered up all the loot. Then a third member of the gang opened the front door and said "Hurry up there fellas, we ain't got all day."

Reluctant Heroes

The three members of the gang were last seen riding off in the direction of Palmers Oakey. There was speculation about which bushranger gang it was for months after the hotel at Limekiln was held up. There were all sorts of talk on the name of the gang. Some reckoned it was Gilbert's gang along with Ben Hall. But regardless of who held up The Rising Sun, no one was caught.

Catherine was hanging out the washing after she got the children off to school. Alice, who was too young to go to school, was in the yard playing with the pegs, when two men rode up at a great pace, dismounted and approached her.

"Morning Ma'am," the younger one said.

"What can I do for youse?" Catherine remarked as Alice hung to her mother's apron.

"Well, a cup of tea would do for a start," said the older one.

Catherine picked young Alice up and walked to the back door.

"Don't be afraid, Ma'am we won't hurt you or the young 'un," said one of the riders.

Catherine entered the house, got out two cups and boiled the billy. The two riders sat down.

Where are you from?" she said.

"Never you mind," the younger one said.

The older one said, "Where's your manners Ben? Sorry, Ma'am. Do you have any sugar?"

She nervously got the sugar jar and some of her biscuits down from the shelf and placed them on the table.

"My husband is working down at the marble quarry. Did you want to see him?" she said.

"No, Ma'am," replied the older one. "Thanks for the tea and biscuits. We have to be on our way. We're in a bit of a hurry."

With that they just rode off.

Just after lunch, two policemen from Kelso rode up to the back of the house.

"Afternoon Ma'am, have you seen two strangers riding through here today?"

Catherine had no love for the Garda and thought for awhile and said "Sorry Officer, no one has been here today."

"Well, keep your door locked tonight; there have been reports of two dangerous bushrangers in the area."

"I will officer. Thank you. Are they well known?"

As the troopers mounted, the older one replied, "Only Frank Gardner and Ben Hall."

Catherine grabbed Alice and went inside. The school was two miles away but as she drank her tea, she realised that those two men were wanted for numerous armed hold-ups, though she thought they would not harm the children. Still, she was on edge all afternoon looking out the window for her girls to walk up the track.

As the officers rode away, the senior officer remarked to his young assistant,

"Look Alex, horse tracks and I'd say from today. What do you think?"

"Ah! Sarge, the poor woman was frightened to death. Leave it there and let's follow what we have. See where they lead to."

Catherine was worried as she had not heard the dog bark at the intruders or the officers. So when the girls turned up from school she sent them off looking for Kanga. Young Marsetta found the dog lying dead down by the creek. Later when James came home from work, he found puncture marks on the dog and said to the girls

"It was probably a snake," he told them.

They buried Kanga down near the grave of James' son.

Chapter 27

The poster said "Sofala Cup - to be run this weekend, first prize 20 gold sovereigns." James looked and thought what might have been, maybe ten years ago he would have given them a run for their money.

John Tobin came up to read the notice.

"Gawd, James, we can go down and take the missies and our lot and make a picnic day of it," he said. "My nag Nelly is as fast as any horse around here and young Dylan can ride her."

James turned and said, "Not a bad idea. I've got a few bob saved and the grog down there's not bad."

John went on to say, "We can hitch up the dray, leave at the crack of dawn and be down there first thing Saturday."

So, all day Thursday, the families packed dampers, cakes and jars of goodies ready for the trip. James hitched the wagon with two of John's trusty bullocks. It was fifteen miles to Sofala and when they came down the hill into the village, the morning sun was just peeping over the eastern hills. There was a buzz in the air and a carnival atmosphere. Then they saw it, the circus tent that had been erected in a field next to the Turon River. Aston's circus had come to town.

The men made an excuse to cross the bridge and go over to the Royal Hotel, the excuse being to check out the field. After a few ales, they returned with a flag and a number seven. As the race was set down for nine am

Sunday morning, John was lucky as his horse, with Dylan riding was the last to be accepted. When John registered his horse in the race, he was allocated a plot over the river to pitch the family tent. They picked a good site next to the track so they would get a great view of the race.

Sofala was bursting at the seams as over 30,000 people now lived in the town and surrounding area. The area boasted thirty hotels. There was plenty of cash as nuggets were being found everywhere in the area. Only last week it was reported that a prospector had found a nugget weighing 120 ounces (3,400 grams), at Golden Point, Bells Creek. As they say: it was only a stone's throw from the hub of the town.

For every successful miner there were tales of woe. The people who were making all the money were the prostitutes and store keepers and spivs ready to take a drunk's money in a game of cards. The police were kept busy keeping the peace and the Mines' Commissioners were on the go, collecting the unpopular tax prospectors had to pay - thirty shillings a month.

That afternoon Catherine and James strolled down the many stalls, "Tell your fortune laddie" a woman called out as James passed by.

"Ah! Be off with you, you can't tell me fortune."

"Yes, I can," she yelled back to him.

"And I can tell you straight off you been selling illegal liquor."

James stopped in his tracks and he turned and whispered to Catherine, "How does she know that?"

"Come on in," she cried. "Tell your fortune for a shilling."

As Catherine and James seated themselves at the charlatan's table, she said, "Now let's see," as she looked into her glass bowl. She fumbled for a moment then said, "Is it six or seven girls and it looks like you've lost a couple of lads. That's sad." She paused to let the information sink in. "And you couple of scallywags, the Kirk is pestering you to tie the knot."

James was getting all hot and bothered.

Then she said, "I can see great things happening to you and your children's descendants, parliament. Yes, great things."

With that, James walked out of the tent grumbling, "That was a waste of a shilling."

Catherine was thinking and said, "What does she mean? One of our lot going into Parliament?"

James replied, "Ah! Don't worry about it, my love. Let me buy you some of this fairy floss they're all talking about. She was nothing more than a gypsy."

That night John had a fire going and boiled the billy and James took all the kids to see the circus. As he walked away, he yelled out to John, "don't drink all the grog."

James had stowed away a few of his home brew, so when he returned from the circus and had tucked all the kids into bed, he and John settled down for a few drinks. It had been a big day so they both went off for sleep to be ready for the big race in the morning.

The drinking houses were doing a roaring trade. The prize money for the main event was raised to twenty gold sovereigns. A ladies' race was soon organised and also events for the kids. This was to keep the crowd from drifting off as the main event, the Grand Turon Handicap Cup, was put back to run at one pm.

After a cup of tea and some breakfast, James and John went off to the marshalling yard where the race would start and they could meet the jockeys. John's son Dylan, was all primed up to ride Nelly. His mother had decked him out with a set of riding clothes that would have been at home at the race track in Sydney. They looked over the opposition.

"Gee, John, I think your nag will win," said James. "They seem to be a rough lot."

The steward and starter indicated that not all of the horses had arrived. A warning shot would be fired at eleven am. Most of the riders were local and John and James knew nearly all of them.

At five minutes to eleven, the last of the horses arrived, and John said, "James, look at that fine stallion. I think he is a ring in. He's going to be hard to beat."

The rider came over and introduced himself. The horse "Darkie," was ridden by a local called Jacob, but owned by a Mr Frank Pearson. At first, the name meant nothing to James but as he walked back to the girls he thought back to his convict days.

He was mumbling to himself, "Frank Pearson's face looks familiar. Ah! Well, whoever he is, I hope he doesn't win."

There were three bookmakers operating that day and James, never the punter, said "Why not?" so he laid out two pounds on John's colt, Nelly. The odds were five to one for a place, not bad. James thought. He would have to keep it quiet from Catherine as she would only nag him and want to know where it came from.

Captain Starlight and his gang, the Marston brothers along with an Aboriginal fellow called Warrigal, had been in all kind of trouble and had a price on their heads of £1000 - wanted dead or alive. They had robbed the local bank at Turon, and escaped with thousands of pounds worth of gold but every time the law closed in on them, they vanished into thin air. They had found a secret valley behind Nulla Mountain.

The gang drove a mob of cattle and horses (over 1,000 animals) overland to Adelaide and when they returned, they were captured. The Captain and Dick Marston were sent to Berrima to serve six years. The other member of the gang, Jim who was Dick's brother, escaped capture but with the help of Warrigal and some help from inside Berrima jail, Dick and the Captain escaped. They scaled the outer wall of the jail to freedom and returned to the Turon gold field on hearing rumours of prospectors finding nuggets the size of cricket balls. So not to be too conspicuous, they split up into two teams and worked separate claims. There were over 20,000 prospectors working the Turon River, so they soon melded into the scene.

Their claims were at the junction of Bells Creek and the Turon River. Dick and Jim Marston had been working a claim at Bells Creek where they had some moderate success with some small nuggets and some colour. What kept them going was a claim at Golden Point, one hundred yards down the gully where a nugget was pulled out weighing 120 ounces (approximately 3,400 grams). It had been hard work and they were going to give it to the end of the week, then they would go and rob a bank or hold up the stage coach, it was much easier work. The gold was shipped out each week and taken to

Bathurst. The bushrangers had been watching and recording the times and the day it left.

The Captain had figured out how they could rob the Turon bank. He paid a local lad to tell the constabulary he had overhead talk about a robbery to be held that night in the village of Peel, nearby on the Bathurst road. The senior officer had left a young lad, fresh on the job, to man the police station.

The gang had timed the raid on the bank for late in the day, right on closing time. Taking all the gold that would have been shipped out in the morning; they placed the bank manager in the back room and tied him up. The gold was quickly placed on a dog cart and Ben Marston, father of Jim and Dick, quietly left the town. The lads, who had tied up the young constable at the police station, even tied their horses in the stables out back of the police station. The gang casually left town on the Mudgee road. When they reached the crest of the hill, they were off as fast as they could go, back to their hideout behind Nulla Mountain. When they counted out the gold they had £7,000 worth of gold plus cash.

Some months had gone by when there was a notice in the *Turon Star* newspaper announcing the running of a horse race, the Grand Turon Handicap. The gang talked it over and decided Captain Starlight's horse, Rainbow would be entered under the name Darkie. They also talked to a local who had just been sacked from his job for drinking on duty at one of the local pubs and convinced him to ride Darkie in the cup. His purse would be ten percent of the winnings. The Turon Racing Club put up twenty gold sovereigns as first prize. The Captain guaranteed Jacob, the jockey, ten pounds for his time. Once again, the police led by Sir Ferdinand were sent on a wild goose chase on a tip-off about a gang that were going to hold up a stage on the other side of Bathurst near Blayney.

The night before the big race it was a typical Saturday night in a gold town. The law officers were kept busy with the usual load of drunks who were thrown into the small lockup, all crying out to be let out in the morning so they could see the big race. That night they were holding the Race Ball. It was being held in the reception lounge at the new Mechanic's Institute.

Reluctant Heroes

Dick and his brother Jim were standing out the front of the Royal Hotel when three gentlemen drove past in a trap.

"Gawd Dick, look at these three dressed up to the nines," said Jim.

"Yer, but see the gent in the back, that's our Captain. He's shaved off his beard. He looks like he's just arrived off the boats from London," Jim replied.

Captain Starlight rode into town and was going to gate crash the reception. Somehow, he had befriended two gentlemen from the old country. He had made a quick trip down to Sydney and returned in time for the Race Ball. They looked pretty smart, decked out with smart shirts, pants, coats and new boots.

As they pulled up to front of the newly opened hotel, called The Capital, Captain Starlight called out to the ostler, "My man, stable our horses please and there will be something for you when my horse wins the cup tomorrow."

There was a band playing and plenty of booze. Bold as brass, Frank (the Captain) asked Miss Bella Barnes, the bride to be, for a dance. They did a wild polka and he thanked her for the dance.

She looked into his eyes and said, "Sir, have we met before?"

He replied, "I don't think so, madam."

The Captain had promised Bella that he would dance at her wedding. Dick Marston had been quietly talking to his sister and had been observing the Captain. At first he didn't recognise him dressed to the nines, silk shirt and black coat, he looked a real dandy. Dick and Jim left the reception and rode back to their tent with Warrigal their trusty Aboriginal assistant. Captain Starlight, with shaved off beard looked a totally different person. His wanted posters were in all the towns west of the Great Dividing Range but it would have been difficult for anyone to recognise him.

Frank Pearson, alias Captain Starlight was the son of a wealthy noble family back in England. He had left the old country to try his luck at the gold rush in Victoria. Frank got into a spat in Melbourne and made a hasty exit to Sydney. The Captain had befriended the Marston family and he had his heart set on Ben's daughter Aileen. They had been drinking regularly at the hotel

Lucky Strike which was run by Bella's father, Vince Barnes at the village of Rylstone.

On the morning of the race the town was packed to well over twenty thousand people who crowded the fence around the track.

The Captain had Darkie in a tent some way from the track with Jacob the jockey watching over him. Jacob had been warned not to go anywhere near the drinking houses. The Captain had promised him a bottle of scotch after the race and Jacob had replied, "And don't forget the ten pounds."

The favourite for the race was a stallion up from Sydney, priced at even money. John had laid out ten pounds on Nelly and he was as nervous as all hell. A "tenna" was a small fortune. The odds were ten to one on Nelly. It was money he had stashed away, from his illegal grog selling and all he could think of was, if his horse won a tenna at ten to one, it was a hundred quid. All the horses in the race had weighed in except Darkie. Dick was getting nervous but finally he could see Jacob walking Darkie towards the weighing tent. The steward was going crook at Jacob, but he told the steward his timepiece said he had five minutes to go, so stop panicking. Jacob was starting to feel thirsty and was desperate for a drink. His mouth was as dry as stone.

Darkie (Rainbow) looked in magnificent shape. The price went crashing down from twenty to one down to eight to one and then back a bit to nine to one but the Captain and his new found friends had secured bets well over at ten to one. Most of the money was on the horses brought up from Sydney. There was tension in the air as the twelve riders in the race lined up at the start. The race was over two miles, twice around the track.

The starter's gun went off and they were racing. It was hard to make out who was in front until they passed the crowd for the first time. As they shot past in a cloud of dust, James called out to John that Nelly was in a bunch near the leading horses. Then, as they turned into the straight, Darkie shot to the lead with Nelly on his tail. They had left the rest of the field for dead. Some had even dropped off to a canter or to a walk. Nelly was neck and neck with Darkie but a hundred yards from the finish, Darkie shot through and raced over the finish line in first place. John's horse, Nelly, was second.

The crowd went wild as they had all had a skin full. As they gathered around the podium, the publican of the Royal Hotel handed out the prizes.

"Ladies and Gentlemen," he said. "It gives me great pleasure on behalf of the Turon Horse Racing Club to hand over to Mr Frank Pearson, the owner of winning horse 'Darkie,' the sum of twenty gold sovereigns. The second prize of eight gold sovereigns goes to Mr John Tobin from Limekiln."

At the edge of town, the winner stopped, looked back at the town and grinned.

"Well, Dick me lad, what a killing!" said Captain Starlight. "We made about £2,000 on the race."

Dick just grinned cheerfully and the two rode on.

As the winner quickly left the stage, the goldfields' commissioner started to think he had seen that Frank Pearson somewhere before.

Where were the damn police when you needed them? thought the Commissioner, Sir Ferdinand in irritation.

Just then, a young constable approached and informed him that his superiors had received a tip off about a robbery. In frustration, the Commissioner raced over to the tent where the horse Darkie was being held and he found the jockey flat on his back snoring his head off. By the time the police arrived, Captain Starlight and the gang had long gone and were back at their hideaway.

"Sir, I think this Frank Pearson is Captain Starlight," said the young constable.

"Are you raving mad, constable?" replied the Commissioner. "How could he have ridden right under our noses and got away with the prize money? Not only that, but the confounded man dined and drank our Champagne and slept at the new Capital Hotel."

It was soon established where the Bushrangers had been camping. A group of miners and police were formed and they rode to the Bells Creek camp site. There was no sign of the gang. They had flown the coop.

James and John and their mob had packed up their lot and on the morning, set off back up the hill to Limekiln. It was soon a buzz around the field and camp site that the winner of the race was a well known bushranger, Captain Starlight. John had a chuckle and remarked, "Good on him, gee, he had a nerve. It takes guts to do what he did in front of the law."

James was ecstatic as he had come away with over twenty pounds.

Nearly twelve months had gone by and not a word was heard about the bushranger Captain Starlight and his gang. They had disappeared. Then right under the nose of the police a notice appeared in the local newspaper the *Turon Star*. It read:

"Let it be known that Captain Starlight and Masters and Co. has ceased trading."

Sir Ferdinand was in a fit of rage and increased the reward for the apprehension of the wanted bushrangers.

Later that year, the police were tipped off that the Starlight gang was making a break for Queensland. The gang had passed through Cunnamulla and they could see the Warrego River up ahead. Jim's horse stumbled and as they stopped to help him, the troopers opened fire on them. The gang were trapped with the border of Queensland in sight. Jim Marston and Captain Starlight were shot dead. Dick Marston was captured and imprisoned to be hanged, but at the last moment was reprieved to spend fifteen years in gaol. Later, his sentence was reduced to twelve years because of good behaviour. [4]

---

[4] Was he Myth or Legend? See page 378

Chapter 28

By 1860, James' health had deteriorated and the travelling medico suggested he and the family move into Bathurst where James could get regular medical attention. The family packed their meagre belongings, closed the hut which had been their home for all those years. They had seen trials and tribulations, and the birth of all the girls and the loss of the three boys. As they walked down the track that led to the main Bathurst road pushing the cart with all their possessions, James held Catherine's hand and, with a tear in his eye, turned and took one last look. As he passed the Hotel, he was tempted to enter for one last ale, but Catherine steered him on. When they came to the bend in the road they all turned and took one last look at the village of Limekiln and made the sixteen mile trek into Bathurst.

They moved into a small house in Devonshire St, Bathurst. The older girls got domestic work, and the three younger girls were enrolled in the convent school. James seemed to pick himself up and actually gave up the drink. He started to run a few fowls and he soon had a sideline selling eggs to his neighbours. Every Friday he would go across the paddock to deliver his newly laid eggs.

"Good morning to you, Mrs Chifley."

"Good morning to you, Mr Fines. Are you feeling better?"

"I am thank you Ma'am, the bones are not what they used to be but I'm not one to complain."

"I will have one dozen, thank you. The last batch was all double yolkers. Mr Fines, we are taking up some land out at Limekiln, I hear you lived out there, did you like it?"

"Ah! Mrs Chifley, it was fine but it's hot in the summer and cold in the winter. Not much different from here, I suppose."

James had a small backyard, where he penned his fowls. He had Black Orpingtons and Rhode Island Reds. After school, young Marsetta help her father feed them and collect the eggs. James never got used to the cicadas that screeched in the daytime. The school children would bring home all the different types of cicadas, Yellow Monodies, Green Grocers, Black Princes and Flowery Bakers. He would sit on the veranda with Catherine late in the afternoon with a pot of tea. The doctor warned him off all alcohol and he would grumble about his only bit of pleasure being taken from him. He started to save the wings of the cicadas. Someone at the Black Bull had told him the dispensary would buy them. But, it was like a lot of things James had tried, all failed. All, that is, except his chooks.

Late in 1862, James' health suddenly took a turn for the worse and he was admitted to the Bathurst Hospital with dysentery. During the night he heard his mother's voice call from the past. He sprang up in bed and was sweating profusely.

The nurse rushed in. "What's up, Mr Fines? Are you all right?"

"Yes, yes, but can you get me the priest and get a message to my wife, please?"

The words kept coming up in his head. He could hear his mother saying, *"James you must be married. You know what the good book says. You and the girls won't go to heaven."*

So early in the next morning, with the priest, Catherine and the girls at his bedside, on 11th of February 1863, he formalised his marriage to Catherine. They had been together for over twenty years. Catherine had dressed in a pale pink ensemble as she stood beside James. His youngest daughter had picked a bunch of beautiful roses for her mother to hold.

"You know, James and Catherine," said the young priest, "before we perform the ceremony, we will bow our heads and give thanks to our Lord and hope that he will allow you to enter the kingdom of heaven, and let this be a lesson to us all."

The priest quickly formalised the union in a simple ceremony.

"You may now kiss the bride," he said at the end.

As James kissed his new wife and placed a gold band on Catherine's finger, he was steady as a rock. The wedding documents were signed with crosses as the wedded couple still could not sign their names. James the old devil was grinning and, as he kissed his daughters, he gave Marsetta a small box. Inside were two stones now wrapped in rag, that he had found when he first crossed the mountains back in 1825 when, with other convicts, he had mustered and drove the sheep down the mountain to Rooty Hill. He had kept them all those years.

"Marse," as he had always called her, "get Uncle George to look at them. I think its gold. They might be worth a fortune."

James had never bothered to get the stones identified or valued but he always thought there was gold in them. With the mention of gold, James suddenly remembered his stash of pound notes back at Limekiln. Since the time he and John had discovered the gold, he had only taken a few pounds from his stash from time to time and he reckoned there would still be about ten left. He held Marse's hand as he explained slowly where in the old barn they would find the tin. He started to talk like he was in the past.

"Marse, me darling daughter, look after me chooks. Don't let the Rhode Island Reds get all the feed, they are greedy buggers. Mrs McKenzie takes some of the eggs on Wednesday and then there is Mrs Chifley. Ah! She's a lovely lady. She will take all the eggs you can't sell." He paused as if in a dream and continued. "They're moving to Limekiln and she needs all her strength. She is having a young'in."

"They're OK, father, I know what to do. Don't you worry about them. Just get better," replied Marsetta.

"Jane, will you look after me drawings? If Mr Henry Howard ever turns up, he wants to buy them." With that James drifted off to sleep.

George Cott called in to see him. He looked down on his mate sleeping, and as he turned to leave him in peace, James opened his eyes.

"Where are you, Marion O'Connell?" said James.

"What are you talking about, James? Who is Marion O'Connell?" asked George.

James was wide awake now and looked at his mate,

"George, me old mate." He held out his hand and George sat down on the bed.

"Yes, what can I do for you, old fella?" said George.

James just lay there gasping for breath. "George, I'm dying. Will you look after Catherine and the girls for me?"

"Ah! you silly old fool, you can't die. What about you chooks? Who's going to look after you garden, all those lovely beans you got coming on?"

James had a tear in his eye as the matron came in.

"That will be enough excitement for one day Mr Cott," she said. "I thank you. Let me puff your pillow, Mr Fines and you try to get some sleep."

With that James closed his eyes and George left the ward.

James died one week later. The death certificate was signed by Dr George Busby.

There was not a big crowd at the cemetery. Catherine with all their daughters were there, Roland and Bridget, John, even Captain Raine and the residents from Busby Street and Mrs Chifley were there standing at the grave site. Then a sulky came to a halt and residents from the village of Limekiln, the Tobins and Sam Taylor joined the small crowd. At the last minute, another sulky pulled up and James' eldest daughter Mary, stepped down with a very smart gentleman. Mary quickly introduced him to her family as her fiancé, Dr Henry Swift.

James' two youngest daughters, Alice and Jane sang a lovely Irish ballad, *"Mountain of Morne."* The small crowd were brought to tears as the priest said a few words and they lowered the simple wooden coffin into the ground.

Although it was February there was a cool breeze stirring up dust as three crows called from overhead, "CAW, CAW, CAW." The crows finally settled in an old gum tree near the grave. The crowd of mourners looked up as if to say thank you. They also seemed to be saying goodbye to an old mate at the old Bathurst cemetery.

The family and friends made their way to the Black Bull hotel where the publican had put a great spread on and free beer all James old convict mates made the effort and turned up for the free grog Captain Raine kindly offered to pay for the occasion. There were a few speeches and there were some sore heads later that night.

Chapter 29

Henry Howard. Convict No. 642 sentenced to 7 years for forgery.

Henry Howard, a friend of James Fines from the convict ship the *Medina*, was a model prisoner and finally received his ticket of leave in 1827. He received a letter from his family with a notice to pick up a draft for £500 from the Bank of New South Wales with the proviso he was never to return to England.

So Henry presented himself to the Bank of New South Wales in George St, Sydney and wisely opened a bank account and promptly deposited the money he received from his father. He set about looking for a place to live, and while he was at it, purchased a brand new set of clothes.

He was wandering down a back lane near Circular Quay, called Reiby Place and he had only gone fifty yards, when there it was, a vacant shop, with an upstairs flat. The shop next door was a men's hair dresser and wig maker. Henry was peering through the window when a voice called out "Can I help you, mate?"

"Well I don't know, my good man" replied Henry. "I just might be interested in this shop and the sign says shop front and residence."

The wig maker had a key and let Henry in to have a look. Henry was pleased with the place and after negotiation with the shop owner, he became a shop keeper and had a place to live. He transferred his meagre belongings to the small flat upstairs, which had a pleasant view of the harbour. The room was airy and seemed to have most home comforts. The flat was certainly better than living rough in Bathurst, but nowhere near the standard he was used to back in good old Mother England.

Reluctant Heroes

He placed a sign in the window advertising his credentials. While talking to his neighbour, Albert, he learned where he could get anything for the right price. He set out looking for a small printing press, as he had in mind to print small business cards and the like. The rent was, he thought, a bargain, four guineas a month, which he paid in advance. In 1827, Sydney had now developed into a thriving town and before long, he was producing high quality cards.

One morning a well dressed lady entered the shop and asked Henry if he could do native birds and flowers. He said he would make some enquiries, and then Henry thought of his old shepherd mate, James, a great drawer of native birds and animals. He thought he should go out and see his old mate, so he planned to go out to Bathurst and track him down.

He had been busy working every hour of the day and his reputation was getting into the Sydney community. It didn't take long for the wrong element, who knew Henry's background to track him down. Late one afternoon when he was just about to close the door, two chaps walked in. Henry could pick them a mile off and he knew they were up to no good. One carried a large suit case.

"How can I help you gentlemen?" Henry wondered about their quality but he decided to hear what they had to say.

The younger of the two spoke. "We have got a job for you to do, if you're interested."

He undid the case. Henry straight away recognized the paper before he had a chance to touch it. He surmised that it had to be stolen, rice paper that was used for printing bank notes. He also recognized one of the chaps as James Dingle as they had travelled out on the *Medina* in 1823.

"Come now, Henry, you know what we have here," said Dingle.

Henry thought a moment and said, "How do you know me? And yes, I know what it is and it's a go to jail even by having it in your possession."

"Come now, Henry old mate. We were on the *Medina*. 'Ave you forgotten, already?"

Henry told them to sit down while he examined the paper.

"What do you want me to do?" he asked after a short period of study.

"Look, this is the deal," said Dingle. "We'll leave you with the paper and we'll be back tomorrow."

The two men turned up late the next afternoon.
"Well, Henry old son, what do you think?" said Dingle.
"I think you got rocks in your head," said Henry. "We will all be off to the Norfolk Island, and besides, it's not that easy to produce high quality bank drafts. It would need a small guillotine and special ink."
"Leave that to us, Henry old son," said Dingle.

A week went by and then they were back, armed with Henry's special requirements. The plan was to print five hundred five pound notes. Henry told them to call back at the end of the week. He would do some samples on ordinary paper to see if he still had the ability to do this type of printing. It had been a long time since he had done anything like this.

"I don't know if I still have the skills," he thought. In the back of his mind he was thinking he should refuse this and have nothing to do with printing forged money. He was also thinking that he was happy with his new life down in the new colony of New South Wales. He knew he had a chance to make a good and productive life. He may even settle down, find a wife and raise a family.

But no, as his soon-to-be partners in crime returned late the next day Henry knew he would give it a go. Dingle introduced his partner as William Blackstone who was impressed with Henry's handy work. So, Henry sat at his desk in his flat steadily forging five pound bank notes. His two partners in crime finally offered Henry £120 for his work which they paid in used notes. The lads were impressed until Henry told them there was one last process he had to perform. They watched him pour cold tea over the notes which gave them a brown colouring and made them looked like older soiled notes. His two partners in crime were a bit thick and did not realize that Henry had kept back two sheets of rice paper for his own purposes.

Henry's life went along as if nothing had happened. He was frugal with his spending as he didn't want to advertise his fortune. He journeyed out to Lime Kilns and spent the day chatting with his old mate James and had offered him some work supplying him with drawings of Australian flora and fauna.

About three months passed. It was late August, 1828 when Dingle arranged to meet with Henry in the new hotel at Circular Quay, Sydney.

"Look, mate, we are doing this bank job," Blackstone said. He went onto explain that they would be in possession of some valuable treasure soon. "We want you to help us dispose of what we get."

Look fellars," said Henry, "that's in me past. I'm trying to go straight."

Nothing more was said until about two weeks later. It was 14th September and late in the night when Henry answered the door and Dingle and two of his gang, William and George, pushed their way into the small shop.

"Be quiet," said Henry. "You'll wake up the neighbours."

"Come now, Henry," Dingle replied. "We won't be here long. We want you to mind the stash."

Henry opened the sack and found it full of coins and paper notes. "My god! There's a small fortune in here. Where did you get this from? "Look Henry, we just robbed the Australian Bank."

Henry, with his mouth open was in shock, then he said "But how?"

"Well there are five of us," said Dingle. "We left John Creighton and Valentine Rourke outside in the lane keeping guard."

It was all around town the next morning that the Australian Bank had been robbed of over £15,000 in promissory notes, Police Fund notes and coins.

It was reported in the Sydney Gazette, that a robbery was executed at around ten pm on Saturday night. It went on to say that the thieves burrowed into the bank through the sewer. The investigators advised the bank that the work would have taken up to three to four weeks as they had to pick their way through a seven foot wall.

The Bank staff worked all the next day reprinting new notes to replace all used notes presented to the bank.

Henry hid the goods in his upstairs flat and arranged to meet up with the lads in a couple of days at a watering hole in The Rocks. The traps (police) were watching Blackstone's every move and as they entered the Black Dog

Hotel in the Rocks, Henry told them he was finished, he wanted nothing to do with them anymore. The leader, William, quickly informed Henry that it was too late. "Now you are implicated just by being here. See that sailor in the corner? Well guess what? He's a copper."

Henry was getting nervous every time the door opened, as he thought it was the police come to search the place. It was time to make a move out of the country. He got talking to a fellow who said he could get him a passage on a whale boat if he ever wanted a change.

"Henry old son, I could take you to some sights in South America such as Rio," the man said. "The place is alive with women. On my last trip, I had two sisters for the price of one."

Henry thanked him for the offer and he returned to his humble flat but as he walked up Ruby Lane he started to think that he could do with some excitement. Since he came down from Bathurst, it had been all work and no play. As he got nearer the door to his little shop, a girl was waiting.

"Can I help you, love?" he said.

"I don't know, but I can give you a good time. Only cost you two dumps."

Henry was a bit tipsy and as he opened the door, the girl followed him in.

"What's your name, love?" said Henry.

"Pearl," she replied as he guided her up the stairs.

Henry was about to make his first mistake.

As they lay on the bed naked, Henry said, "Pearl, will you stay till the morning? It's been a long time since I have had any company."

Pearl agreed as Henry again mounted her. By three am, he was exhausted and was fast asleep. At six o'clock Perl dressed and was shaking Henry to wake him up. She wanted payment and to be off. When he didn't wake, she decided to help herself to the money in his pocket. As she emptied the money onto the table, she unfolded two crisp forged five pound notes.

Henry woke up and as he realized he had been robbed, started to panic. He thought it might be time he moved on, so he met up with his friend that morning and arranged to be on the whale boat that was heading for South America.

On the planned day he was to board the whaler, he couldn't sleep as he had arranged with George Farrell that he would take the bank loot down to the end of George St and meet him there to hand it over. He had taken some of the coins as his share. There was a brief meeting and George asked him to carry the bag down to the end of the road to the wharf. As they approached the wharf, Henry noticed a small boat tied to the pier.

"Over here George," came a voice from the dark. George didn't explain that he and his partners in crime were taking the loot to a place where they would bury it for safe keeping. Henry and George parted, never to meet again.

Henry made his way back along George St and on every corner he thought he saw a policeman. Rats were coming out of the drains for a nights scavenging in the area as it was not well lit. He finally made his way back to his flat and had his last meal there. After he gathered up his meagre belongings and packed his wad of money into his ship bag, he made his way to the wharfs to escape from this big brown land.

As the whale boat sailed out through the Sydney heads, Henry looked back on Sydney town. It had been an experience! He thought, "Never again will I be caught." He had put together a small sum of money that should set him up for the future, when the whale boat reached the Americas.[5]

In 1828, Australia experienced its first major bank robbery at the 'Australian Bank' in Sydney. Five convicts tunnelled into the bank through the sewer. They were led by William Blackstone who, with four others, all ex convicts, got away with over £14,000 in promissory notes and coins (equal to twenty million dollars today).

The crime was discovered the following day and suspicion immediately fell onto Blackstone, Farrell, Dingle, Creighton and Rourke. They escaped an indictment until Blackstone turned informer two years later and received a pardon. By then Creighton was dead and Rourke had left the country. Only

---

[5] Author's Note: This was the biggest bank robbery in Australia's history.

Dingle and Farrell faced the Supreme Court of New South Wales on 10th June 1831. Both were found guilty but escaped the gallows because of convict attained: that is, legal concerns as to whether Blackstone's evidence was admissible, because of a previous death sentence.

Chapter 30

William Henry Morris' family was in England. He had left a widowed mother, Eliza and he ventured to the colonies in search of gold. He migrated to New South Wales in 1868. He was quite a lad; he was what you would call a young virile country boy ready to conquer the world.

When he stepped off the boat in Sydney, he talked to a wharf labourer who assured him that there was plenty of gold left.

He said to William, "Sir, it's just lying on the ground waiting for someone to pick it up."

But before William made his way to the Gold fields, he promised his mother he would check out the property in Sydney town that his distant forbears owned. Edward Morris Esq. had arrived in Sydney around the turn of the century.

A letter had arrived at his grandmother's home some time before, boasting how Edward had purchased a hundred acres of prime land not far from the wharfs in Sydney town. William was keen to be on his way to the Bathurst goldfields, so he found cheap lodgings for the night. He entered the Brooklyn hotel down near the ferry wharfs and, after a few beers, soon had the directions on how to get to the claimed hundred acres of land. He caused a bit of a chuckle with the lads at the bar, one of whom, said "One hundred acres near Saint Mary's Cathedral? I don't think so, you must be joking."

William replied, "Not me, lad, I'm not joking. When I've seen the land, I'll be off to the lands department to confirm it." He caught a horse-drawn tram up Pitt St and was then given directions at Park St to head east. As he walked the short distance he arrived at what looked like a park. There were grass paddocks with cattle grazing so he continued on until he reached a road junction. Looking to his left he saw a Cathedral and he was starting to get excited. His relatives must be rich land owners! William walked up to the herd of dairy cattle and it felt just like home. As a lad he helped his uncle milk the family cow and later he got a job working for Mr Wilson at his dairy. He had fond memories of the farm and the early mornings walking down to the dairy and jumping into the cow pats to warm his frozen feet. It was there one day when Mr Wilson showed him the article in the local paper calling for lads to cross the world to New South Wales and take up positions in the emerging agriculture industries. William had also read about gold being discovered in the new south land and he decided this would be the reason he would leave good old England. His mother was now settled into her farm cottage and content with her weaving and her visits from her spinster sister. His mother had given William a letter explaining how a family member had purchased a parcel of land in Sydney town and she had suggested if he ever made the journey down to this new south land of New South Wales he should look into it.

The letter was safely in his pocket as he climbed under the fence and crossed the busy road. He asked a policeman how to get to the Lands Dept. and he was given directions to go down near the Circular Quay. He set off with a spring in his step. When he entered the building and started to ask questions relating to the hundred acres bound by Elizabeth and Liverpool St, there was a flurry and the clerk was in a quandary as to what to do. Finally, William was ushered into an office and a senior Lands clerk came in to attend to him.

"Mr Morris," said the clerk. "Glad to see you. I'm Gibbings, the senior land clerk directly under the Minister. Just out from the old country, are you Mr Morris?"

"Why yes, I am from County Warwickshire, to be precise."

"How can we help? I understand you're looking for a parcel of land?" said the senior clerk.

"No thank you, not now but maybe sometime in the future. You see, I am off to make my fortune on the gold fields"

"Yes, we are losing many of our staff that way. They all think they are going to make a fortune. Then how can we help, Mr Morris?" The clerk was getting agitated as it was close to his luncheon appointment with the Land commissioner and he did not want to be late. He also suffered from a urinary problem and he had to go to the toilet when he got agitated.

"Well, you see my distant relatives own a parcel of land here, and I was hoping to catch up with them."

"I see, and do you have any identification or do you know the name of the relative you say owns this rather large piece of land? We just can't have you walking in there."

William sat nervously on the edge of his chair, thinking to himself, *This public servant is supposed to be here to help me. You would think he owned the land.*

"Why no, I only have this letter which was sent to my Grandmother back in 1845."

Gibbings inspected the letter and started to perspire. He wanted to go to the lavatory, and placed the letter back on the table, along with the map of the said land, one hundred acres, Elizabeth Street bound by Liverpool Street and Park Street.

He said, "Look, Mr Morris, we really can't help you. The piece of land to which you refer was passed back to the Government some time ago because of unpaid rates. The land was not in the name of Morris, but Bowman and unfortunately he was assumed drowned. He fell off a ship near the Sydney heads which was leaving to sail back to England"

William just looked at him and said, "Did they ever retrieve the body? How can you be sure of your facts?"

"Mr Morris, the matter is closed," said Gibbings. "We can't have you marching in here making accusations as if there has been some sort of conspiracy going on."

As William stormed out of the office, he was not sure if he had been told the full facts. He stopped, turned and was going to return to Mr Gibbings and give him a piece of his mind.

How dare he talk to me like that? I am from the mother country and he is a servant of the people, thought William. Then, as he turned, he thought better of it and walked out the main door. It was a lovely warm day and as he walked back to the wharfs, he turned his mind to GOLD.

"I will show them," he muttered. "I will go and make my fortune and buy half of the city." As William stormed out of the office, the senior clerk Mr Gibbings, informed his junior lands officer to destroy all relevant information pertaining to the said piece of Park St land.

Next morning William caught a train to the Bathurst Gold fields. He had returned dejected from the Lands department to the Brooklyn Hotel and, after a few beers, let the issue of the land slip from his memory. Later that night whilst drinking with his new found friends, he teamed up with some lads who were on their way to the goldfields and he got talking about his time with the officials at the Lands department.

One of the lads said, "Look, William, I'm studying law at the University in Sydney. Give me the details and I will look into it when I return to Sydney in the New Year."

The subject soon got back to gold and after a few rounds of beer, agreed they were all going to be filthy rich.

"Hill End is the new Eldorado," said the young lawyer. "Yes, streets paved with gold."

They made it sound exciting.

They arrived at the railway station to find it with prospectors all heading west for the gold fields. It was late in the afternoon on a Saturday when the train finally arrived in Bathurst, so they set up camp in the railway yards. They were going to leave early the next morning and they had been given instructions on how to get to the fields. That night, after a few beers, they decided to go to the local dance, at the Catholic Church hall.

Chapter 31

Marsetta Fines, although shy, got on well with the local youths her own age and on her nineteenth birthday was at a dance at the local church hall, when she met a young chap named William Morris. He was fresh off the boat from England and had come to the Colony to make his fortune in the gold fields. William and Marsetta danced the night away and she let him walk her back to her house where he kissed her at the gate.

"When will I see you again, William?" she said.

"I am off to the goldfields at Hill End. I met up with some mates and we're off to make our fortune."

"I used to live not far from there at a place called Lime Kilns," she said.

"Gee! You are lovely. Come with me, Marsetta?"

"I will do no such thing, I have got a good steady job and what's more, I hardly know you. What sort of a girl, do you think I am?"

William was a bit of a lad and just laughed it off. Then he said, "When I make my fortune, I'll come back for you and sweep you off your feet and take you away from all this."

She entered the house but quickly came back outside and told him to be quiet.

"You will wake up the neighbours," she said.

William left that night and Marsetta forgot all about him.

William, with the mates he had befriended had stocked up with fresh supplies. They were on their way and they joined the steady stream of eager prospectors. Everyone was heading for places like Sofala, Palmers Oakey and Hill End. As they trudged down the hill into the village of Sofala, it looked like something out of a book. He had read about the Wild West in America and, as they crossed the dirt road, five riders on horses came racing at break neck speed and pulled up in front of them.

At the pub they were shouting, "Gold nuggets as big as oranges," as they mounted the steps and raced into the Royal saloon bar. William and his mates parked their barrows and followed them in. There was pandemonium. The talk was gold and plenty of it up at a place called Hargraves and another called Lewis Ponds Creek. It was all too much for William and his mates to take in.

That night, as they pitched their tents down by the stream running at the back of the town they discussed the outrageous price of goods in the town. In the morning, after a few drinks at the Royal, they heard about the miner's revolt back in '61 over outrageous mining lease fees. There had been gunfights and miners shot and it could happen again.

One of the lads who had been out here before tried to calm them and said, "Look, don't believe all you hear. There are seasoned spivs who will tell you anything to get you to part with your money."

They agreed to split up, as some of the lads wanted to go to a place called Palmers Oakey. William had no idea where he was going but he flipped a coin and heads had him off to Hill End. His mate Sparrow was with him. They pushed their barrows up past Monkey Hill and rested the night at Sally Flats. They unrolled their swags and after boiling the billy, slept like babies, too exhausted to move.

Next morning they made their way to Hill End. They followed the steady stream of prospectors all heading down the track to the Turon River. When they arrived at the river, William was shocked to see it was nothing more than a dry creek bed. There were dozens of other hopefuls, all going to try their luck along with other prospectors. There was quite a community, tent shops had been hastily erected where the cheats, card sharps and the girls had set up shop all eager to fleece the men out of their hard earned money.

William like a lot of other eager prospectors thought the gold was just lying on the ground. But he soon found it had to be dug out of the dry gullies and creek beds. It was hard work and no one told them about the flies, snakes, mosquitoes and the extreme changes of temperature. William could relate to the winter temperature, snow and freezing winds but the summer of over a hundred degrees in the shade!

William had been on the gold fields about eighteen months when he parted company with Sparrow who, one morning just announced he was off. William tried to go it alone and found some nice small pieces but he soon realised that to succeed, he needed to find a mother lode and quick.

One afternoon he was having a cool drink of sarsaparilla. He shied away from hard liquor but vowed he would crack open a bottle of bubbly when he found the big one. He only wanted to drink the good stuff at ten pounds a bottle. He got talking with two Germans, Bernard Holtermann and Louis Beyer, who also had little success. They had panned for gold along the Turon River bed but they had only found enough pay dirt to keep them in tobacco and food.

One night at the Royal Hotel, Hill End, they talked William into joining them in a partnership. The three worked well together so the two Germans wanted to form a syndicate called the "Star of Hope Mine." They begged William to invest some money but William decided to just work for them, as he had no money to invest in an unlikely scheme. William was also getting dejected with the whole thing as he was not making his fortune. Some prospectors had but as fast as they made it, they gambled or drank it away.

He went along with the Germans and, with hand tools and a lot of sweat, they dug a tunnel and reached about a hundred feet below with still no result. Bernard kept urging them on. Hill End was developing at a frantic pace, with twenty eight pubs and over 8,000 miners. In October 1872, Hill End was the largest country town in New South Wales. It boasted three banks and the main street was a mile long with shops of every description. The girls did a roaring trade as they preyed on miners who struck it rich and then they helped them spend it.

William was fed up and so he decided to leave the mad, gold fever Germans. He'd had enough so he wished Bernard and Louis well. He was heading back to Bathurst as one of his mates in the Royal pub at Hill End told him they were crying out for tradesmen in the building trade in the boom towns of Bathurst and Kelso. He packed up his meagre belongings, sold his wheelbarrow and gold panning equipment and, with his swag on his back, set out for Bathurst. He descended down the hill and crossed the Turon River to reach the main road.

He had been in the State of New South Wales for close on two years and, after the first shock of the weather and the snakes, he loved the bush. The different types of birds and lizards, the koalas and kangaroos he came across amazed him. He came to respect the bush and could see its beauty. As he entered the small village of Wattle Flat, he stopped at a shop that sold meat and asked the young lady the directions to Bathurst. "Just keep on this track. You can't miss the signs," she said.

"Why, thank you miss."

Just then, a fellow dressed in a butcher's apron, emerged from the back of the shop. "Get the gent some refreshments Bridget, please," he said.

"John Graham's the name. Purveyor of fine meat, at your service." Then in the next breath, he said, "Would you be interested in working in a butcher shop?"

William, after finishing his drink said, "Well thanks, but I will be looking for work in the building trade. In the old country, I was a bricklayer."

"Well, you won't have much trouble finding work here then," said John Graham.

William left the village of Wattle Flat with a spring in his step. He was unaware that he had just met his future sister and brother in-law. He finally made it into Bathurst town. As he walked down William St, there were signs everywhere, saying LABOURERS WANTED, so he started working as a Brickie's Labourer. He had only been back from Hill End a few weeks, but he did not have to be a genius to read on the front page of the local paper at smoko one day, and in big print (William had never had much schooling and could hardly read or write),

LARGE QUARTZ NUGGET OF GOLD WEIGHING 3,000 OUNCES
Two miners' strike it rich

Reluctant Heroes

The nugget was found by a Bernard Holtermann, the Manager of the Star of Hope Mine and his partner Louis Beyer at Hill End on the weekend. It was reported that the nugget would, after crushing, produce around 3,000 ounces of pure gold valued at £10,000.

William was happy for Bernard and was cursing that he did not stay on. The Star of Hope Mining Company that year payed twenty-five pounds dividend for every one pound share. It was never revealed that the day before Bernard struck the big nugget he had spoken to his stock broker and advised him to sell! sell! sell his shares in the Star of Hope Gold Mine. He was sick and tired of the heat and the flies and he wanted to try his luck in Sydney. It was on the last blast of the powder of the day that they uncovered the huge gold nugget. The partners had to keep it quiet all that night and Bernard stopped the sale of his shares in the morning before the local stock exchange opened at nine am. At ten am he proudly displayed his nugget. The share price that morning went through the roof.

William had been in town about a month when he bumped into a young chap in the pub. After much discussion, they finally realised that they had come up from Sydney on the same train.

"Barry Brighton, at your service, soon to be a member at the bar," said the young man.

William could not contain himself and said, "What pub?"

There was laughter all round when Barry finally told William that he would be serving at court. Then Barry said, "I remember now, you had a land claim in the heart of Sydney."

By this time they had all consumed a gut full of beer, then Barry's offsider, Gerald, stepped forward and called out

"Order in the court. All rise. The court is now in session and Judge Brighton will hear evidence. The case is the Lands Department versus Mr William Morris."

"Very good," Barry called out above the noise in the bar.

There was a lull then Barry turned to William and said, "Look, William I think we would have a solid case from what I remember. If you give me the papers you have, when I return to Sydney, I'll check it out."

William was completely stumped. No one had ever taken up a cause for him and he considered himself a born loser.

"Thanks all the same Barry but I will just get on with my life," he said. "Looks like I am destined to be a brickie's labourer."

The small mob then got down to some serious drinking.

Chapter 32

It was some weeks later when William, who had been residing at a hostel for single men, received a note to see a Mr Barry Brighton Esq. at the hotel known as the Miners Arms that Friday night.

Barry had a smile on his face as he entered the drinking establishment.

"William," he said. "I have some good and some bad news; but first let me buy you a beer."

William waited impatiently while Barry got two beers from the bar and sat down with him.

"Well, my good man," said Barry, "the good news is that when I approached the Lands Department re your said block of land, I was politely told that the matter was closed as the rates had not been paid and, as the legal time had lapsed."

"Well! What's the good news?" said William.

"My good man, if you could lay your hands on at least £1,000, we could take the Department to the Lands Court and we would win because of section 191 of the Lands Act set down in 1823."

"Ah! Forget it, Barry. Thanks all the same but its way out of my depth. I am destined to be a brickies labourer; but I appreciate your help. It's my shout."

Marsetta was born in Lime Kilns near Wattle flat and had been working in Bathurst as a servant. She had been raised by her mother Catherine, along with her sisters Mary, Catherine, Bridget, Margaret, Alice and Jane. She had three brothers, but the boys had all died at birth. The family had moved from Lime Kilns to Bathurst in 1860 so Marsetta's father James, could be closer to obtain medical treatment. Their father died in 1863 one week before he formalised the marriage with their mother to satisfy the church.

Marsetta was thinking back to when she was a child. She did not remember much about her father. He was always away droving, looking for gold or in trouble with the police and when he did turn up, Mum would be pregnant again. Her mother Catherine worked hard to raise the seven girls, scrubbing floors and serving behind the bar in grog houses all over the Bathurst Plains, Lime Kilns, Wattle Flat, Sofala and Hill End. The area was in the middle of a gold rush and the police were always raiding places as there were gangsters holding up banks and fights in the pubs. It was a lawless part of the Western Plains and Catherine did her best to raise her girls.

Catherine's sister, who arrived in the Colony's in the 1850's from Ireland, had run off with a con man who was going to make her rich. The last she heard from her was that she had was set up in a flat in Woolloomooloo, not the best part of Sydney. Her fancy man had left her for a younger woman.

As a youngster, Marsetta was told that her father was a French seaman who had served in the French navy. He had come out to the Colony and the Bathurst Plains ending up in Lime Kilns to strike it rich. Marsetta had grown up to be a nice girl which worried her Mother. She was a pretty thing, shapely, but not very bright, could not read and could hardly write her name.

After James had passed away, Catherine and the girls moved and found a nice semi-detached house in Bathurst. Marsetta found work as a general servant and her mother went back to work at the Black Bull Inn. Both Catherine and Bridget were married and off their mother's hands

On the third of July 1865, Catherine married George Cott. This came as a surprise to her daughters when George announced that he had married their mother after they came home from work. The girls were a bit annoyed but they were happy for their mother. George had been a long time friend of their mother and father.

Reluctant Heroes

The year was 1881 and the vivacious young Marsetta's life was about to change forever. Marsetta and her mother were shopping in William Street when, from across the street came this loud call, "Marsetta." She went red in the face as she turned to see who was calling out to her. On a building site, there he was, William Morris. Embarrassed, Marsetta and Catherine continued on their way. That night Marsetta and her mother were relaxing by the fire; she was knitting baby clothes for her daughter's baby, when there was a knock on the door. Her younger sister, Alice raced down the hall to see who it was. She opened the door and there was William, standing in the doorway, fresh faced and looking like the cat that got the canary.

"Good evening. Could I speak with Miss Marsetta Fines, please"

Alice looked him up and down and said, "Do you know my sister?"

"Who is it, Alice?" Marsetta cried out.

Catherine had been trying for the past ten years to marry her daughter off without much luck. All the boys that came around were either too tall or too short and they all seemed to lack something. This night, Catherine looked William over. He was handsome, well tanned from working in the sun and he had a twinkle in his eye.

"Come in, William, and sit down," Catherine said.

That was the start of Marsetta's love affair. William would laugh and have Alice and her Mother in stitches. He was a bit of a lad. He would meet George after work and have a drink at the local hotel, and when they both stagger home their dinner would be on the table most nights, burnt to a crisp. William was a few years older than Marsetta, mind you, her mother, Catherine may have worked in a grog house but she never let any hanky panky take place. You would think that Marsetta was only sixteen!

William who did not have a religious bone in his body, would have no part of getting married in the Catholic Church. He nearly caused a riot one night when he announced to Catherine and George that he and Marsetta would be married in the Church of England at Carcoar or not at all. This set Marsetta and her sisters in a crying fit. After a while, Catherine settled down and weighed up the situation knowing that this could be her last chance to get Marsetta off her hands. She talked to the local priest who strongly advised her to have nothing to do with the Proddie.

"It may be God's will that your daughter may never marry. Have you considered entering her into a Convent?" he said. "You realise that Marsetta will never be allowed to set foot in God's Church ever again, if she goes ahead with this union."

"Oh! Father that would be terrible," said Catherine. "We will think it over but Marsetta is set on marrying William."

She left the Church crying her eyes out. The wedding was planned for 24th of June 1882. William had picked up some work in Carcoar that would start in July and so he organised a small dwelling on the edge of town.

Marsetta and her bride's maid were to journey down to Carcoar a few days before the wedding and prepare the cottage.

Chapter 33

William was exhausted as he lounged in the guest smoking room of the boarding house. There was a knock on the door and as no one else was around, William answered it.

"Barry come in," he said in surprise. "Just downing some ale. Will you partake in one?"

"Sure William. It's been a hot day. Not like the old country, why in January, we would be sitting in front of a roaring fire."

"How can I help you, Barry" said William.

"Look William, it's been a few months since we last met and I have made some enquiries in Sydney with my father's law firm."

"Gee Barry, I thought I made it clear that we would let it rest as you mentioned a figure of £1000 and I haven't got that sort of money."

After a few minutes, Barry went on and explained that his father knew someone that knew someone who may be able to help William fight the Department at no cost to William if they don't get a verdict in his favour.

William thought about what Barry was getting to. Then he came out with it.

"Look, Barry, no one does anything for nothing these days. What's in it for them?"

Barry went onto explain how the system worked, that, yes they were in it for a piece of the land, if you won. "Of course, they would need to see all the documents you have in regards the piece of land. You do have them don't you William?"

William handed over the letters that he had brought from London and Barry was surprised to see that the documents were from a London Solicitor firm, Barker and Sons, Attorneys at Law. Barry was more hopeful when he left thinking that William had a good case. He bumped into William in the local Royal that Friday night and told William that he had sent the papers on to his father's firm of solicitors.

William went home and forgot all about the land. His attitude was he didn't care one way or another about it. If it came about, great. He was more worried about taking time off to go to Sydney if it came to trial.

Three weeks later, William received a message to meet Barry at the Royal after work that night. When he arrived Barry had lined up a round of drinks and was bubbling and jumping up and down like a cat on a hot tin roof.

"William, old son," he said. "Your case is to be heard 2nd May 1871, so we have two weeks to prepare you for the hearing."

"Look, Barry, I have told you everything. What else is there to say?"

"It's easy, William. You left Warwickshire with your heart set on being a dairy farmer on that land and you were devastated when your interview at the Lands Department was casually dismissed. William, we have a strong case."

So it was arranged that William and Barry would travel to Sydney to front the Lands Board on the Monday morning. That day, the train pulled into Sydney Central station and they caught the next tram down George Street. Barry knew the stop to get off and they walked across to the office of the NSW Lands Department. In the foyer Barry introduced William to his father who was in his wig and gown and to his understudy, Mr Martin Higginbotham. William was informed this was not a trial as such, but a hearing.

The small gathering was ushered into the court and the hearing commenced. The case was considered so important that the Lands Commissioner was presiding over the matter. The Lands Department was represented by a well known Sydney law firm, Garrick and Partners. As the case began, the Legal team representing the Lands Dept. was being assisted by Mr Gibbings, the Senior Lands Clerk.

William lent over to Barry and said, "Barry, that's him. That's the bastard who gave me short change, when I called here, last time."

Poor old Horatio Gibbings was still plagued by his incontinence. He was due for retirement and already he wanted to race to the washrooms. The small crowd stood as the Lands Commissioners walked into the room. The opening address was read out by the Solicitor for the Crown and was to be followed up by the well known Barrister, Percival Garrick. The case against William Morris was read out and the main argument was rather simple. The land in question was once leased by a Morris but the lease was never taken to a conclusion and, as no annual payments were paid, the lease was forfeited and considered correctly returned to the crown.

The court was adjourned for a short recess. Gibbings left the court and raced for the executive bathroom. It didn't take long for the Sydney press to get hold of the story and the three leading papers were at the court to pump anyone who could to tell them the outcome. It was too early, but Barry told one journalist that the Lands Department were riding roughshod over a land owner who was fighting for his parcel of land. The hearing adjourned at four pm to carry on next morning.

Gibbings was called into the Lands Commissioner's office. The Commissioner had a stern look on his face as he spoke to Gibbings.

"Look, have you seen the afternoon papers?" he said as he pointed to the *Sydney Gazette* on his table. The heading read, *"Lands Department takes land owner to the cleaners."*

"Tell me, how do we explain this to the minister?" continued the Commissioner. "My God! Gibbings. Can't you do anything right? We will be the laughing stock of Macquarie Street if this goes against us. Morris came out here, in what, 1867 and now is making claim to a piece of Sydney's top piece of real estate?"

Next morning, Barry and William, who had had a quiet night down at the Brookland Hotel, made their way to the Lands Department. The press gallery was packed to capacity.

"All rise. The case, The Crown versus W. Morris will continue."

The defence team were soon in action and put up a compelling case on behalf of William. They gave his background in Warwickshire, how he had been told by his family that the land in Sydney was there and it would make a great dairy farm to supply the locals.

Finally, in summing up for the Lands Department, the Commissioner who was at pains to point out that this was not a trial but a hearing, thanked his learned legal members of the bar for their tireless work for the Crown and Mr William Morris. In summing up, he proclaimed he had to deliver a verdict in favour of the Crown, mainly on the grounds that there had been no payments made to the Department for some time and the land known as the "Pasture," bound by Elizabeth and Liverpool Streets, would be left as is.

"This court is now adjourned. All rise."

William and some other friends who had gathered at the hearing, made their way down George Street to the Brookland Hotel, where they drowned their sorrows. William thanked Barry's father and his staff. The night was still young as the young lads made their way to the red light district of Kings Cross. Finally they made their way back to Barry's home and caught an early morning tram to the railway station for their journey back to Bathurst.

Later that week they were drinking at the Daniel O'Connell Inn in George St, Bathurst. The publican, Thomas McKell was celebrating the 25th year of the hotel with free beer at five pm and the bar was crowded. He had placed an advertisement in the *"Bathurst Free Press and Mining Journal."*

4th March 1882 "Daniel O'Connell Inn" (Actually the hotel was opened in 1857.)

"Thomas McKell begs to inform the good inhabitants of Bathurst and the surrounding districts, not forgetting his numerous friends of Carcoar and the Lachlan, that to celebrate twenty five years of service to the good people of Bathurst and surrounding district, Free snacks with grog, will be served all next week between the hours of five pm and six pm.

"I am thoroughly convinced that the first requisites of success for a licensed Victualler are civility, cleanliness, and good cheer," he begs to say and that those who favour him with a call will as always be served with a

good glass of grog, in a clean glass and that every necessary attention will be paid to their comfort.

"We have first class accommodation for weary travellers. Our staff are still under the supervision of Mrs McKell, who will see to the strictest cleanliness and order in that department and also to the culinary arrangements of the establishment.

"The stabling will be under immediate control of the Proprietor who will see that the horses left in his charge are well fed and properly attended to."

Chapter 34

24th June, 1882.

It was a crisp winter's day in Carcoar as the guests arrived at St Paul's Church for the marriage ceremony of William Henry Morris and Marsetta Fines. William was to start work on the new railway line at Carcoar.

The bride, her mother and her two sisters who were her bridesmaids had walked the short distance up the hill to the church. One of her new neighbours came out and gave her a huge bunch of lilacs. The bride looked lovely. She wore a serviceable travelling costume of heavy wool serge fabric trimmed with fox fur, and her matching navy blue bonnet completed the outfit. The girls were waiting in the small room at the front of the church for the Minister to start the wedding march and the boys to turn up. Marsetta was looking out the window and gazing up the hill to the Catholic Church and was miles away, dreaming of the past.

Her mother knew the licensee of the Royal hotel at Carcoar and the girls had a great few days doing all the things girls do before a wedding. They had William vacate the small garden flat on the Wednesday (he had located the place in Todd Street). Mrs O'Brien was a widow and in the few days he had been there, she wanted to know everything. She was a real nosey parker, forever sweeping the front pathway and one day invited William in for tea.

The girls decorated the two rooms with new curtains. George, her stepfather, knew all the travelling salesmen and he had acquired the latest range of pots and pans really cheaply. The best surprise was the latest in bedding, real eiderdown which came down courtesy of Cobb and Co. Cath, as she was known to her friends, had worked in the Black Bull Inn in Bathurst where the

Reluctant Heroes

Cobb and Co Coaches called in with the passengers from Sydney, and she had worked off and on in most of the best and worst taverns in Bathurst. If you wanted something, Cath knew where to get it or she knew someone who could get it for you, so by Friday the flat had all the latest kitchen appliances imaginable.

Chapter 35

The lads had decided to take William down to Lyndhurst, a short ride down from Carcoar. There were six of his mates and his best man John Pearman had organised a drinking session at the Golden Arms Hotel in Lyndhurst. The whole area was in the middle of a gold boom and as they rode down that Friday afternoon, they passed numerous gold prospectors on their way to the southern fields around Woodstock. One young Chinaman was probably off to Lambing Flat. His barrow was full of everything you could think of and his wife and three kids were trailing behind, all loaded to the hilt.

John Pearman had assured Cath that they would have the groom back in time for the wedding on Saturday but what John did not tell William, was that they had organised some entertainment for him. John knew someone who knew someone that told him down behind the pub you could get a shag for ten bob. William had been excited about the wedding and he thought this trip to Lyndhurst was a waste of time, but John was a good mate so he went along with it.

As they entered the Golden Arms, it was crowded as it was Friday afternoon and the place was full of gold miners all quenching their thirst. There was much talking about the nugget that was found at the gold field at the back creek that afternoon. It was June and supposed to be winter, but the weather was mild and the boys soon quenched their thirst. There was a mad rush by the drinkers to down the beer, as it was fast approaching closing time. Technically closing time was six o'clock, but standing at the end of the bar was the local Police Sergeant, so the Publican kept saying to the patrons, "Last drinks, gentleman."

Reluctant Heroes

As the boys with William were from out of town, the pub would allow them special privileges, so the boys booked in to the pub to stay the night as there was no way they could ride back to Carcoar. Most of the other patrons had left, but there they were, the six of them with the local Sergeant standing holding up the bar, singing away as the Sarge found out that William was getting married and was down there on his stag night. One of John's mates had collapsed. He was lying in the chair near the fire but someone took pity on him and threw a blanket over him. John explained to the Sergeant he had heard about a lass who could fix his mate up good and proper, "You know, wink, wink, nudge, nudge."

"Come with me lads," and, sober as a judge, the Sarge marched them out of the pub and around the back. As they stumbled along over fences, William kept saying, "Where in the hell are we going?"

Finally they arrived at a tin shed, where there was a light flickering., The Sarge knocked on the door called out "Mary, I have a couple of customers for you."

There was movement inside, then the tin door opened and, standing in the doorway was a woman. She was probable about fifty if she was a day, and big. She had huge breasts.

"What have we here, Gerald?" she said.

"Boys, meet Black Mary. Mary, we have tonight young William who is about to be married."

"Well, William, you better come in. Don't be shy," said Mary.

William all of a sudden became very shy and coy. He was not a stranger to love and lust as he had stopped off at some of the hottest ports in the Atlantic. He had even told the lads about a sordid night in Rio. But now he was having second thoughts.

"William, do I have to drag you in?" said Mary.

Then William started to laugh and they all started to sing the latest love song. William finally shuffled up to the door; all of a sudden he was sober. Mary took him by the arm and pulled him through the door. The room was pretty basic. The floor was dirt, but it had what looked like a Persian rug spread out, and there was a simple cupboard with a single bed.

"So, young William, you're getting married? What's the girl's name?"

William replied, "Marsetta."

Mary replied "What a lovely but unusual name, William. Well, young William, I think we better get on with it. Your mates are getting restless out there."

Mary was huge. She had some dark blood in her but when she slipped off her shift, her breasts were still uptilted and she was a light honey brown without the usual black's wide nose and skinny legs. She lay down on the bed. "Come on son, I won't bite you," she said.

Poor William was terrified, even though he had been with women all over the world and he had experienced sex every way possible. Even so, he dropped his pants, and mounted her, releasing his lot in quick time and it was all over in a flash. He went to pay her, as she got up off the bed, but she said, "No son, put your money away and I hope all goes well tomorrow."

As she opened the door, at the top of her voice, she said, 'Well, come on. Who's next?"

John, by this time was rearing to go and one by one they visited Big Black Mary. Finally, the Sarge went in, and as he went through the door he said, "Boys, I will catch up with you in the bar."

The moon was out and the air was crisp as they stumbled back to the pub. The door was still open and it was full, as a coach had just pulled in. The publican was doing a roaring trade as the Coachmen were changing the horses. A few minutes and the passengers would be off, so there was a mad panic to get a drink.

Gerald the Sergeant came in shouting, "Another drink, boys?"

The boys finally struggled up to their rooms to sleep it off as they needed to be up at seven am to ride back to Carcoar to give themselves plenty of time before the wedding. They assembled at eight in the dining room as none of them were eager to move. All were nursing sore heads. The young waitress sat them down and she fussed around, keeping them happy with toast, tea and coffee, then they all received a hearty breakfast. The cook was kept busy as they devoured huge helpings of toast, bacon, eggs and coffee and it was just on nine am when the group slowly rode off down the main road. Not much was said as they were still groggy from the night of lust and debauchery.

Suddenly, out of the bush rode four men. They all had scarves around their faces to hide their appearance.

One of the riders called out, "HAND OVER YOUR MONEY. THIS IS A STICK UP!"

John rode out in front and said, "Out of the way, you mugs. We're on our way to get young William here to his wedding."

There was a bit of manoeuvring and the leader finally said, "Give us your watches and any money and be quick about it. We're dangerous bushrangers and we're wanted by the law."

John's horse reared up and turned around towards William. John glanced at William and said, "We'll make a run for it," and with that, Charlie shouted, "Gee up, there," and they raced their horses through the bandits. The outlaws were taken by surprise and gave chase but the lads didn't stop till they reached the top of the hill near the Carcoar Hospital. The bandits gave up and slunk off into the mulga. John and William waited for the others to catch up and finally the six riders rode into town, crossed the bridge and pulled up behind the Royal Hotel.

It was eleven thirty am as the boys walked into the bar. William ordered drinks all round and they finally got him up to his room to change into his wedding attire.

They all looked pretty smart as they walked up the hill to St Paul's Church on the hill that overlooked the town. The Minister, the Reverend A.C. Hirst, had made a big thing of how the Catholic Church was higher up the hill. The forefathers of the town had given the higher site to the Catholics as the Priest back in 1840, switched the papers around, but it was too late. The Church of England was supposed to go there, so he would tell everyone, who wanted to hear the story.

The Groom and the Best Man assembled in the anti-room and waited for the Reverend to give the order to make their way into the church and await the bridal party. Marsetta and George were running late, which was accepted.

The Reverend brought out a bottle of fine Scotch whisky and said, "Ah! This should settle the nerves, lads."

William was still in a bit of a daze and he did not remember much but they got him there. John reckoned later on, after the wedding feast, he would see the local sergeant about the louts that tried to hold them up. "Bandits, I don't think so."

There were twenty of their closest friends in the congregation and as the boys were standing there, William had a slight sway but they had cleaned him up and he looked good in his new suit. The whisky had actually sobered him up, just a little.

"Good night last night!" John whispered to William.

William looked at him and said, "Where did we go? I don't remember."

As the organist started to play the wedding march, the bride with her step father joined William and the best man. Then the Reverend A.C. Hirst conducted the ceremony. (William said to John later that it was over in quick time as he thought the vicar liked the bottle and wanted to get on with it so he could get to the Wedding Breakfast.)

As they walked down the aisle, George nudged Marsetta who was in a dream. Uncle George, as the girls called him had been a father figure since their father died and had gladly accepted the honour to give her away.

After the couple had exchanged their wedding vows, the party filed into the Chapel and they signed the wedding certificates. William never said anything, but Marsetta signed with her mark. She was so nervous. William had been instructing her for weeks on how to write her name but in the end her hand would just not move, it was frozen, so she just made a cross.

They proceeded to the Church hall for some light refreshments. The Ladies' auxiliary had filled the hall with a great display of flowers and the perfume from the roses and lilac blooms filled it with a pleasant aroma.

George gave a speech, wishing the happy couple all the best then William's best man John, commenting on how lovely the girls looked in their wedding attire, got up and toasted the Bridesmaids.

The Cobb's coach left the Royal at three pm so at two thirty the small party walked back down the hill and waited for the Coach to pull in but there was always time for one last round. When it finally arrived right on three pm, the coach driver called out, "Attention to all passengers travelling south, please board the coach."

As the coach turned the corner and sped over the bridge, the lads returned to the bar for one last round.

The happy couple were off to spend a few days at Cowra. It was late in the night, when the coach finally arrived at the Cowra Hotel that William had booked into. Marsetta could not believe it but William deep down was a gentle person and he treated her like a lady. They enjoyed a couple of relaxed days before returning home to Carcoar.

Chapter 36

Mary, who was James's eldest daughter, married Dr. Henry Lascelles Swift and when they married, moved to Perth. There was some shadow of doubt whether James was the father of Mary but he always treated her the same as his other daughters. It had been twenty years since Mary had been in Bathurst and she was returning to visit her mother and the grave site of James. She was heartbroken when they told her the cemetery was no longer there. It had been turned over and sold and was now a police station. Mary had a chuckle to herself as Dad couldn't read or write but, to be buried under the law, he would be chuffed. That would keep him on the straight and narrow.

Her husband had moved to Sydney and set up a medical practice. Her son, Gerald, and his sister, met up with all their country cousins and were heart broken when they arrived at the old cemetery site. Not to be out done, Mary placed a bunch of flowers on the land in memory of her father. "But how did this happen?" she asked her younger sister Bridget who just said,

"It happened. There were hardly any monuments and they are over there at the fence. I can't for the life of me tell you where Da's grave was now. Mother knows but she just won't come out here anymore. She will say she is married to George now and that's that."

They had hired a sulky and when they returned to her sister's place in Busby St., her mother Catherine, was on the front porch, gazing into the flowers.

"Well, did you see him, Mary?" In the last twenty-three years Catherine had never been down to the old cemetery so she just lived in the past. She was happy now, married to George in a way, as he was most of the time in

Reluctant Heroes

Sydney looking after his frail brother. Mary's sister, Catherine Arrows, made them all a cup of tea and scones, then her husband, Roland, drove the sulky back to the station and saw them off, back to Sydney.

Chapter 37

15th October 1887.

The Morris family were always on the move as William worked for the railway. He had been shifted to Blayney, then onto Mandurama, Lyndhurst and finally back to Bathurst. William, who had the position as a works Foreman had been transferred to the railway sheds and was now working around the town. Marsetta was heavy in labour, William was not worried as Marsetta had delivered two healthy babies. Catherine had been born in 1883 and young William in 1885, so he went off to work. She was in good hands as Marsetta's sister, Bridget, had come around and had settled into the spare bedroom. She had the two young ones tucked up and in bed early when Marsetta cried out that the baby was coming. Bridget called out to the next door neighbour, who raced around to Mrs Bella Smith, the local Midwife. When William arrived home from work and walked down the hallway he could hear a baby crying so he rushed into their bedroom. Bridget met him at the door.

"Is she all right?" he said.

Bridget said, "She's fine, sleeping at the moment and you have a perfectly healthy daughter."

The doctor told William that his wife had experienced complications and should have no more children. Young Ellen was a robust child and was into everything, quickly gaining weight, and was walking before her first birthday.

13th Feb. 1888.

It was reported in the *Carcoar Chronicle* that the long awaited Rail link to connect Blayney and Cowra, was ready to be used by the public.

The train was due at two pm and the station had all the bunting draped from one end of the platform to the other. It was a big occasion, the local town band was there to play, and as the schools had declared a holiday, all the students were lined up on the platform in their Sunday best. The Mayor and the other town dignities including the local member were there to greet the train. As it crossed the rail bridge north of the town, it gave a loud blast of its horn and as it rounded the bend, the crowd let out wild cheering. As the great black beast pulled into the station, some of the children were afraid and started to cry as it gave a blast of steam.

The Station Master, Walter Levinge was there in his brand new railway uniform, fussing along the platform, herding children and keeping them well back from the edge.

William and Marsetta were there with their children as they had moved back to Carcoar. William had received a promotion with the rail gang and was now an Inspector of Works.

Young Sally who lived next door to the Layburn's had hold of John Joseph's hand as the train let off a blast of steam. The mayor introduced the local member who went on, telling the folks how the state was pushing ever forward in all directions. The rail was on the move and soon every part of the state would be connected by a railway line. After waffling on for what seemed an hour, he finally declared the new section of the line to Cowra open and there was a loud cheer from the big local crowd. The Railway Department had put on a spread of buns and drinks for the crowd. After the train had blown its whistle and moved off, the crowd dispersed back down the hill.

Sally, along with John Joseph, walked back down the hill past Stoke's pub. She went into Mr Bright's shop and bought two all day suckers and a packet of lollies. Then they sat on the old wagon behind the stables and chatted with Mr Lachie who told them stories about the old country and about John Joseph's father. Lachie's son, Angus was an apprentice working with the new railways dept. and he had worked on the stonework at the railway station. He had learnt the trade from his father whose father worked at the Rattle Bag quarry near the village of Gullane, seventeen miles from Edinburgh in Scotland. The stone from there had all the colours of the rainbow and had been used on some of the famous buildings and churches in Edinburgh.

Chapter 38

The Diamond Jubilee

All the states, except Tasmania, sent contingents to London to help celebrate the Jubilee. The Englishmen thrilled at the potential of the loyal Colonials, and the crowds were excited by the physique, stature and manliness of these keen but untried troops. The Colonials had met all the greater part of their expenses. (The New South Wales Government decided to establish a force of Mounted Rifles, about four hundred men stationed at locations around the State. They were to receive sixteen days training per year, and paid eight shillings per day. The Government supplied guns and uniforms, but the troops supplied their horses and equipment)

One of the reasons put forward for the military involvement, was that back in 1885, NSW sent 770 men to the Sudan campaign to assist the mother country in her hour of need, so if and when the occasion arose, it could come to the Colony's assistance.

Chapter 39

Although the family Doctor had advised William that Marsetta should not have any more children, Marsetta fell pregnant again in 1889. She confounded the doctor and had another healthy child, another girl they called Alice. The doctor again advised them not to have any more children, this would have to be the last, and he went to great lengths to explain to William why Marsetta should not have any more. However, they could not help themselves and as much as they tried to use birth control methods, Marsetta fell pregnant again. The doctor just shook his head and a boy was born in 1891. They called him Francis Joseph.

The family were like gypsies, always on the move and they moved again into a bigger house in Lambert Street, Bathurst. The children were attending the Catholic school. William had been abstaining from drink, but one night he had been drinking with his work mates and came home singing and shouting at the top of his voice. Marsetta met him at the door and quickly got him inside. William was a very lovable bloke and, as they hadn't made love for months, it was late, and the children had been put to bed, William led her by the hand and led her into their bedroom. They quickly undressed and climbed into bed. They were woken in the morning by young Ellen. They quickly covered their naked bodies but William rolled over and went back to sleep. Marsetta got up, dressed and got the children off to school.

In 1892 Marsetta was pregnant again and they visited the doctor at the Hospital. He was furious. He was pacing the floor and going red in the face.

"William and Marsetta," said with some anger. "This can't continue. This pregnancy will definitely have to be the last. I told you back in 1886 Marsetta that you should stop, my dear. You are now forty-two years of age."

Chapter 40

It had been some time since the family had moved into Bathurst from Limekiln and Marsetta had promised her mother that they would go out to the old house and retrieve some of the household things, especially the old wash tub they had left behind. William declared it would not be there, as someone would have lifted it after all these years

Catherine said she was too old to journey that far and had her hands full looking after the Grandchildren as they were scattered far and wide and also she had difficulty getting about as her bones ached with rheumatism. Bridget and Marsetta, with their husbands and children, decided to journey out to the old house and camp for old time's sake. So they packed food and sleeping blankets, tea, sugar, flour, billy cans and a tarpaulin just in case the roof had fallen in. William, had borrowed a horse and dray and on a fine spring morning, they set out past Kelso and up the Limekiln Road. As they pulled up at the old pub they found it was open and there were horses tied to the hitching rail. It was now called the Lime Kilns Inn, but it had seen some wild nights and you could still see the bullet holes in the floor after a card game that saw the hotel change hands. Both William and John went into the bar room to down a quick beer, but they got talking to two old timers who introduced themselves as Jacky Kidd and Arnold Feathers.

"There's gold in them there hills, sonny," said Arnold.

"We're not looking for gold, matey. We're with our families who used to live out here."

"Who were they?" replied Arnold.

"They're James Fines' daughters."

"Well, I never! Do you remember Jacky, the famous hurling clash back in 1860? I think we gave them fellows from Bathurst some curry."

"Ah, sonny, James was a hero."

The publican Thomas Tobin came out to the dray with a jug of lemonade for the girls and the children, and they were soon discussing old times about when they had grown up as children.

Finally after copious amounts of ale, the small party left and as the dray moved off, Thomas called out to them to be careful and be on the look-out, as a wanted bushranger had been seen roaming the hills.

They passed the remains of the old store which lay in ruins and the girls had trouble finding the track up to the hut. The briar bushes had over grown and the track was deeply rutted. Suddenly a kangaroo jumped up and bounded off. Finally, they made it to the old mud and daub hut which was in a sad state. White ants had eaten the timber rafters and they had fallen in. James had replaced one of the walls with stone so it was still standing. The small children started to cry but after a couple of hours and the billy boiling away, they settled down. A flock of black cockatoos flew overhead and settled in a gum tree close by. William picked up the billy, gave it a shake and hurled it around like a windmill.

"What are you doing, Uncle William?" cried out Margaret.

"I'm brewing the tea, it's called winging."

"Can I have a go, Uncle?" young Julia screamed out

"No, it's done now. Too much will spoil the flavour and you might scald yourself." They quickly made a damper in the hot coals in the camp oven. The children were looking forward to damper and cockies' joy (cane syrup).

"Marsetta, didn't dad say something about him burying a tin in the old barn?" said Bridget.

The children led the way up through the undergrowth that had taken over the track. They had only a shovel to push their way through and were going to give in but finally, they made it all the way through the briars and saplings to find that the barn had fallen in. Sheets of iron lay on the ground and the old horse stall had fallen down. Bridget yelled out "Watch out for snakes."

They were about to return to the camp site when one of the kids said, "Look, Aunt Bridget. Isn't that a kero tin sticking out of the ground?"

Sure enough, there it was. It had been hidden under a sheet of rusty iron. They lifted it out and were going to carry it back to the camp site. Bridget had to laugh.

"Look Marsetta, in the other corner under that iron there," she said.

Still standing and covered with cobwebs was the old spinning wheel, so after carefully uncovering it, they also carried it back with them. Marsetta was going to clean it up but their attention was soon distracted to the kero tin. The girls were excited as their uncle tried to open it. William finally prised the rusty lid off.

"Well, bugger me. It's empty," William shouted out.

"Well, someone had got to it or the old devil had taken all that was in it. Poor old Dar, he was losing it, in the end," replied Marsetta.

William told them how back in '72, he was working at the Star of Hope mine at Hill End. It was a stinking hot day when a flock of black cockies flew over and this black fella who was working with us said, "Hey, Boss, go'in to rain, big time." We all laughed.

"What a load of rubbish!" replied Bernard.

"Sure enough, down it came," continued William. "It rained for a week. The creek came up and you couldn't go anywhere. Our shaft was flooded and it took a week to pump it dry. After that, I used to take all things he said, seriously. Let's face it; they've been here for thousands of years."

The wives decided to sleep in the dray with the children. As they sat around the fire, William brought out a bottle of wine he'd brought along. They said goodnight and they were soon drifting off to sleep. William got up to relieve himself not far from the campsite over behind the old batted shed and in the distance through the trees he could see a flicker of light. He dismissed it as nothing more than a fire fly and returned to the camp site. They all demolished the damper and mugs of hot tea. Finally the children and the women turned in as it had been a long day.

Bridget said to Marsetta, "I don't think Da had any money buried here at all. I think he was away with the fairies."

Bright and early the next morning, the children had gone off to explore, calling out to their parents something about "a big hole." William came over to find the remains of the outhouse or, as it was now called, a Dunny. The sides had fallen in and as he lifted a sheet of tin, a snake slithered off into the undergrowth.

Marsetta then remembered the stones her father had left her. "I must get Uncle George to look at the rocks Da gave me," she said. "You never know, they just might be gold."

They didn't know it, but lurking not far away they were being spied upon by the bushranger called Slippery Jack.

His name was Jean La Fung, alias John La Rosa, and he roamed the rugged bushland around Sunny Corner in the Palmers Oakey region west of the Blue Mountains. He never staged a hold up or was involved in an armed robbery. He lived the life of a recluse, obtaining all his needed by stealing from miners' camps and lonely sheep stations, usually in the dead of night, then retreating into the bush never staying long in the same place. He had arrived in the area in the early 1880s and quickly obtained the name of "Slippery Jack." It was rumoured that he escaped from a prison in French Caledonia, which later in his trial in Bathurst, was proven to be true. Slippery Jack had originally hailed from Madrid in Spain and his trade was listed as plasterer.

As he looked down on the campers from his hideout at Mount Horrible, he had decided to leave them alone, as he had never in the time he had been in the area, hurt anyone.

The campers were woken in the morning by the sound of horses coming up the trail. Two policemen jumped off and approached them.

"Good morning, folks," said one. "I'm Police Sergeant Wright and this is Constable Bill McSpedden. Have you been here long?"

William came forward. "No, Sergeant. We arrived here last night. My father in-law with his family lived here thirty odd years ago."

He introduced Bridget and Marsetta.

"You wouldn't be James Fines' daughters, would you?" the Sergeant asked.

"Yes, we are," the girls replied.

The Sergeant went on to recall how he had been chasing two dangerous Bushrangers back in the early 1850s. "I was only a new recruit then. Look folks, I hate to frighten you but we have tracked down a dangerous bushranger called Slippery Jack and we know he is hiding out in these hills somewhere. Have you seen any one?"

"Sergeant, I don't know if this is relevant or not but last night before I turned in, I saw a light glow on that rise over there. It could have been the embers of a fire or a cigarette," said John.

"Thank you. We'll ride over there and take a look. Thanks a lot."

The two police mounted their horses, moved off and rode the two hundred yards up the slopes of Mount Horrible. The junior Constable slowly walked down a track that had been recently used.

"Look here, Sarge, he shouted. "Someone has been here recently. The ashes are still warm and there is some bedding and some old clothes."

The two police officers returned to the campers and advised them that they would return to Kelso for assistance and organise a search party. He advised them to leave the camp site and return to the safety of the Inn. As John had prepared a stew, they decided to stay and leave the next morning. All that night, the group sat around the camp fire. The sun had settled behind the distant hills and the birds had settled in for the night. A slight breeze came up and the aroma of the stew drifted over the valley.

Slippery Jack had returned, unaware of the police presence that afternoon. He had been scavenging all that day with no luck, so he was drawn to the campers and the food simmering on the camp oven. He was grumbling away in Spanish about how he was sick of this life and he was going to retire and move on down to the big smoke Sydney that he had heard so much about. In the twilight, he slowly moved down to the camp site till he could hear the men talking.

"William, what do you make of this character, Slippery?" asked John.

"Ah, John! I've heard some talk back in the hotel. He is harmless. Some think he's a bit of a loony, but when the police come back in the morning, they'll catch him. The Constable said they'd bring a couple of black trackers."

Slippery slowly backtracked to his hide out. "I'll give them loony," he mumbled in Spanish. He quickly gathered his belongings in preparation to shooting through.

True to his word, the Sergeant and his men returned the next morning.

"Folks, have you anything to report?" the sergeant asked

Then Fred King, the senior black tracker said, "He's getting careless Sarge. He's left tracks all over the place. We'll get him. Din't you worry, Boss."

It soon became obvious to all when Fred pointed out the broken branches. Soon the two black trackers were on his trail.

The girls soon decided to pack up and move closer to the Inn. As the dray moved back onto the road, they passed deserted shacks and the old school. Thomas let them stay at the back of the Inn. That night they were brought up to date on all that had happened in the small village since the gold had run out. The coach service no longer passed through and the old quarry had run out. Marsetta explained the story to William about the bullet holes in the floor and they sat around the bar, well into the night talking about old times. Next morning, as the children were getting restless, they packed up and went home to Bathurst.

Sergeant Wright, with his men tracked Slippery all that week across the Turon River, uphill and down dale, then the trackers lost his trail only to regain it further down the dry river bed. Constable McSpedden was first to see the camp site hidden below a rock ledge and they quickly established that someone had been there in the last twenty-four hours as the fire embers were still warm. There were fresh tracks leading away so they followed the trail for some miles over rugged hills and down a steep embankment and a dry creek bed.

Finally in May, the Sergeant was about to give up when the fugitive was spotted in thick scrub near Crown Mountain, near Capertee, but he was able to gave them the slip again. After searching for close on six months, early one morning the young constable moved a rock which started a rock slide. All of a sudden, out of a cave, a figure emerged.

The constable called out, "Stop, put your hands in the air," but the figure started to run. The young Constable lifted his rifle, fired and hit him in the leg. As the police moved up, he was quickly identified as the bushranger "Slippery Jack." As he was unable to walk, he was assisted to a nearby sheep station owned by a Mr Gallagher. He was taken to Wallerawang, where he was charged and placed under heavy police guard before being taken to Bathurst.

The Bathurst Free Press and Mining Journal published a list of stolen items retrieved from his hideouts, which filled two police cells at Sunny Corner. He was a real bower bird. There was everything from four bags of flower, tea, sugar, heaps of tobacco, clothing, miners' pants, toiletries, sowing kits and so on. It took two constables to collate the lists. The truth is that there were other camp sites, but he could not remember their locations. Homestead owners were asked to come forward to claim goods but few did, as they did not want to face embarrassment. The mountain of goods was auctioned off and the money donated to the Police Widow's Fund.

Slippery was finally sentenced on 27th July 1896 to five year's gaol. He was a difficult and hostile prisoner and had his sentence extended for assaulting a fellow prisoner. [6]

---

[6] The Story of Slippery Jack page 378

Chapter 41

Young James Fines Morris was born in 1893, and once again, Marsetta confounded her doctor and had a healthy normal birth.

Ellen on her fifth birthday, entered the convent school, along with her brother and sister, much to William's grumbling about the Catholics. Marsetta liked the nuns down at St Cecilia's, so Ellen happily went off to school.

The Catholic schools around the area had a sports day each year to celebrate St Patrick's Day. This year it was to be held at Blayney show ground and all the pupils were to attend. The ones that weren't playing in a team's event entered in running races. Ellen was in a three-legged race with her best friend Rebecca. There were teams from all the Catholic schools. The team from Carcoar convent was made up of two young lads, Jimmy Flood and his partner Frank Kelly. Sister Marie dropped the hanky and they were off. Ellen had obtained the nickname of Nelly and half way down the track she collided with the couple from Carcoar and bowled them over, (in later life, Jimmy reckoned Nelly did it on purpose) but the girls picked themselves up and went on to win the race. They were awarded a ribbon for their effort and were the toast of the little convent school

The Morris family was on the move again. William had been transferred back to Carcoar, still with the railway. The new railway station had been operating since 1888 and you could now catch the train to Cowra or down to Sydney. Old George Cott had gone to Sydney to be with his brother who had been unwell.

Reluctant Heroes

The Morris family moved into a cottage in Icely Street. Grandmother Catherine came with them. She was now getting on and at the ripe old age of 71, her bones ached, but every afternoon, she would walk to the Convent to pick up the children. It was a happy household, but one morning in 1895 William went in to give his mother in-law her morning cup of tea.

"Come on Cath. Wake up."

But she just lay there. William feared the worst, so he raced down to Doctor Hawthorne, who had been looking after the family. The Doctor advised William that she had had a mild stroke and to keep her warm and have no excitement. When William came home from work, he took a cuppa into Cath. She had, in her hand, a letter addressed to Marsetta. Her voice had been affected but, with a slow drawl, she said "William, give this to Marsetta, she should know the truth about her father."

William decided to put it away for the moment. He knew his wife couldn't read, so he waited till the children had been put to bed and then read it to her. In all the time William had known Catherine, he had never known her maiden name, so after she had drunk her tea, he asked her.

She replied, taking her time that she was born in county Sligo in good old Ireland. She went on to explain to William that her maiden name was Disney, her father was Daniel and her sweet mother's name was, "Oh, I don' remember, William, it was so long ago. William, I journeyed out on a big ship. I think it was the Neptune," and then she exclaimed out of the blue, "It was Mary Campbell, that was me mother's maiden name." She had a glazed look about her eyes. When her daughter came in, Catherine was rambling on about Ireland and the old people. Even Marsetta did not know it, she had never spoken of any relatives back home in Ireland, except for her sister, and they had lost contact with her years ago. They got her to her room and the Doctor said all she needed was plenty of rest. William waited to pick the right moment to open the letter that Catherine had given him that day. After the children had been put to bed and they were sitting by the fire he opened the letter.

Reluctant Heroes

Dearest Marsetta,

I never had the heart to tell you before about you father, James Fines. He never was a French Sea Captain, or even a seaman, but he was from the lovely Shamrock Island of Ireland, from County Kildare and was transported as a convict back in 1823 on the Medina. *He, with other convicts, were transferred to Bathurst, where he worked as a shepherd. He was a good man, your father. He worked hard, and before long, he got his Ticket of Leave. I hope you aren't disappointed. Try to get some schooling and learn to read and write.*

Signed Catherine Fines, now Mrs George Cott, with her mark.

Father Bernard O'Malley, their local priest, with George helped Catherine put her story into words.

There was a note on the bottom signed by George Cott saying he was a witness to the signing.

Marsetta just looked into space and said to William, "Well, it doesn't really matter. Who's going to know if he was a convict?"

William replied, "My folks are back in the old Country, I never really knew my father. My poor mother was a widow," and he left it at that.

Before long, Catherine regained some of her speech and some movement in her arms, but she would always have a limp and would need the aid of a walking stick. George, who had been away visiting his brother in Sydney at the time, had received a letter from William advising that Catherine had been ill and to return to Carcoar. George and Catherine returned to Bathurst and they moved in with her daughter, who was now Mrs Catherine Arrow, at Busby St. as it was decided that she could get better care in Bathurst.

Ellen's brother William was in the local football team and they would go to watch him play on Saturdays. He was in the junior football team and the family would stay on to see the first grade team play. There were teams from all over the Lachlan Valley and although Ellen was only seven years of age at the time, she had told her elder sister she was in love with John Layburn who played in the Carcoar first grade team.

Chapter 42

Matthew Grieves – 1886

Mathew Grieves tossed and turned all that night. The local ale had gone straight to his head. His pocket watch said six am as he opened the door to the balcony which overlooked the main street. There was a hive of industry going on. Shopkeepers were opening for business, the milkman was doing his rounds and there was a Chinaman plying his trade calling out, "Flesh vegies for sale. Cabbages, caulies and spinach. See me at the back of the Royal."

The sun was coming up over the beautiful green hills to the East of the town as the church bells started to chime. John Fagan told him at the funeral about his father's dislike for church bells. Then Matthew's head started to thump from over indulging the night before.

Sarah came out the door that led to the veranda and Matthew turned to greet her.

"Morning! Did you sleep well, Sarah?"

She looked radiant in her satin dressing gown, he thought.

Although Matthew's hair was ruffled somewhat, he looked handsome as he stood in the sunlight.

"How do you feel Matthew?" she remarked.

"I'll feel better with something to eat and some coffee."

They agreed to have breakfast together at eight o'clock. Sarah returned to her room, and changed into a green satin dress, a creation straight out of Piccadilly, London. As she ran her hands down the front of the dress and admired her still vibrant, young body, something tingled inside her. It had been sometime since she had felt the warmth of a male companion. She looked in the mirror and smiled to herself. She had just turned forty six but still had that something that made the men turn their heads.

Matthew descended the stairs and was going to catch up with Sarah in the dining room when he met John Fagan at the bottom of the stairs. John had a farm south of town so he had stayed at the Royal that night as he regularly did. As a past owner of the Inn, he regularly used the hotel on evenings that he couldn't return home.

"Morning! Matthew. Having breakfast?" inquired John.

"Yes! Thanks John. I'm waiting for Sarah. We agreed to meet at eight o'clock in the dining room."

As they had a few minutes to spare they went out the back door and walked to the creek. The stream was flowing gently over the stones and it was a peaceful scene.

"See that house over the other side of the creek. That's where your father lived," John remarked.

Matthew looked closely. What a beautiful but unusual setting was this Australian bush, he thought and then said "I will go around there and pay my respects to Mrs Layburn."

"She is your stepmother, you know," remarked John.

Matthew thought deeply for a moment and decided he would not say anything to her in regards to he being John Joseph's bastard son.

They made their way back through a maze of activity at the back of the hotel with a huge wagon unloading kegs of ale, a Chinaman selling vegetables and the laundry in full swing with a young lass carrying hotel linen to the clotheslines. They finally made it into the dining room where Sarah had seated herself and they had a real Australian breakfast.

"More lamb chops, Sir?" the young waitress said. Matthew had already had a large plateful of lamb chops, bacon, eggs, toast and coffee. The young lass was captivated by him and was flirting as much as she dared but she eventually moved off to serve the other diners. The new publican came in, sat down and asked them how long they would be staying. They both agreed they would be staying a couple of days to see the sights of the town, so they booked in for the next two nights. Sarah decided to give Matthew some time on his own to go round and see Jane Layburn.

Reluctant Heroes

Matthew crossed the bridge and passed The Stokes Inn, but just then, a coach came racing around the corner from the south. It must have been running late as it blew off Matthew's black bowler hat. A young girl picked it up and raced up to give it to him.

"Here t'is Mister," she said.

"Why thank you young lady, what's your name?"

"Sally Boxhall, Sir."

"Sally, I am looking for Mrs Layburn's home. Do you know it?"

"Just follow me, Sir. I live right next door." she said.

She skipped off down the track. It was not far and, before long, they stopped in front of the Layburn home.

As Matthew opened the garden gate he heard a loud cacophony of noise as a flock of coloured birds flew overhead. From the hill overlooking the dirt road he saw there were workmen on the rail track near the new Carcoar railway station. He walked the short distance to the front door and saw there were spring flowers in bloom. He had been told that his father loved his garden. The door was open and there were people milling around paying their last respects. He was greeted by a young lady, who said her name was Catherine.

Matthew greeted her and she said, "Would you like to see Mrs Layburn, Sir! Who will I say is calling?"

"Why thank you, Miss. My name is Matthew Grieves."

He was directed into what he thought was the drawing room and he introduced himself.

"Mrs Layburn, I am sorry to hear of your sad loss. He seemed to be well loved and known in the town"

Jane, through reddened eyes said, "Did you know my husband, Mr Grieves?"

Matthew thought for a moment, "My mother knew his family back in the old country."

Then she said, "In all the years we were together John never discussed where he came from."

Matthew decided to leave it at that for the moment and bid his farewell. As he opened the door to leave, there was a young boy pushing another boy in a wheel chair around from the side of the house. Out of the blue, the young lad said, "Did you know my father, Sir?"

"Why yes, young fella, what's your name?"

"My name is John Joseph, like my Dad's, and this is Freddie."

"The piece of paper blew away," Freddie muttered. "Yes Freddie," he said more loudly. "We know the piece of paper blew away."

"Did you know my father?" young John asked again.

"Well, not really, but my mother knew him back in England."

"I am going to go over there one day when I'm bigger," young John piped in.

Matthew left the boys and walked back down the lane to the corner where he met Sarah, who was sitting on a park bench admiring the scenery.

"Matthew, come and sit here for a while. It's so peaceful."

The stream was gently flowing over the stones under the bridge. It was so relaxing.

"Well, what did you find out?" she asked.

He told her how he met the family at the house and at the moment, he would let sleeping dogs lie. "One day I'll return and talk to Mrs Layburn," he said.

"Do you realise you may be able to gain from his estate?" she asked.

"I don't think so. John Fagan told me my father never knew I existed. He knew my mother was going to have a child but he was never certain. At the moment, I think I'll just return to the sea."

Matthew took Sarah by the arm and they walked over the bridge past The Stokes Inn and turned up the hill. There was a lot of activity going on, and the sign said the site was for the building of the new Carcoar Railway Station. The sun was high in the sky and Sarah was out of breath as she leant on Matthew's arm. When they reached the top, there was a gang of men working on the foundations for the station.

A young lad came over. "Can I help you?" he said. "We're not supposed to allow visitors on the site."

Matthew introduced Sarah and was about to introduce himself when the young lad said, "You were at my father's funeral yesterday; you were wearing that black hat."

"Are you John Layburn's son?"

"Yes!" he replied. "I'm Alfred." He looked at the Englishman then he said "Did you know my father?"

Matthew replied "I'm sorry but I have to say I never met him."

"Were you related to him?" Alfred asked.

Matthew chuckled to himself. "I don't know. John Fagan says your father knew my mother many years ago in the north of England."

"Are you staying long in Carcoar, Mister?" Alfred stumbled over the words.

Then Matthew said, "Call me Matthew and this is Sarah. We are both from England and the truth is, we both knew your father, but we were too late to see him."

"Look, I have work to do," said Alfred. "We are laying the rail lines south of here but I'd like to meet up with you after work and we could have a chat. At the Royal, if you like?"

Sarah held Matthew's hand as they walked back down the hill towards the town. As they crossed the bridge, a flock of parrots screeched overhead.

"The birds here are spectacular," he remarked. "We don't have anything to compare back home." As they walked up past the Court House, he said, "John Fagan told me my father worked fitting out the interior wood panelling in the Court house. "Sarah, what will you do now?" he asked, changing the subject.

"Oh, I don't know, I'll probably go back to Sydney on the train to my sister's place at Point Piper. I will be going back to London after Easter, back to a boring life of garden parties and attending to my charity work. My late husband Gerald owned a Cotton Mill in Manchester before he passed away. I was helping him with setting up a pension plan for the widows of his workers killed or injured at work. Will you go back to sea Matthew?"

Matthew explained that the sea was all he knew, but his friend on the last ship reckoned he had a way with words and maybe he could do something in that line, reporting or writing maybe? He had sent in short stories and had been successful in having them published on numerous occasions. He would explore a career in reporting for the papers. When he returned to London, he would be off to Fleet Street to see the *Chronicle*. At first the money he had earned from the short stories was small but he had been able to send money to his mother in Manchester on a regular basis. The publishers were now keen to get his writings about life on the high sea.

"Sarah, I'm 46 and I want to settle down and raise a family. I have been at sea for about twenty years."

He explained that his mother who was now in her sixties was frail and living with her sister in Manchester. He would write to her and give her the sad news that his father had passed away when he returned to Sydney.

They returned to the Royal and joined John Fagan in the Ladies' Lounge as women were excluded from the main bar. They continued to discuss Matthew's father and the more Matthew talked, John was certain that he was the son of John Joseph. Matthew and Sarah spent the rest of their time exploring the little town. Late that afternoon they hired a trap and made the short ride up past the Church to the cemetery. They arranged a small wreath on his father's grave and, although it was November and summer was about to start, a cool breeze drifted in over the deserted landscape. Matthew reluctantly walked away and turned at the gate to view his father's grave and wondered if, in time, it would have the luxury of a proper headstone.

The coach pulled out on time at nine am and made its way up the hill. As they passed the Catholic Church, Matthew noticed a woman coming out and he recognised her as Jane Layburn. The coach continued on to Blayney where there had been good spring rain and the paddocks were lush, and green. The coach pulled into the Blayney railway station and, as Matthew helped Sarah down from the coach, she slipped and fell into his arms. She lingered and Matthew found her perfume to be something special. He loved her womanly fragrance.

The train was on time and would leave at one pm. It must have been a sale day as there were cattlemen all around the sale yards next to the railway station with dust and the sound of cattle lowing. It was a good earthy country sound and smell. Matthew thought he liked it and he would return one day to the western plains of New South Wales.

Chapter 43

The train passed through Bathurst and stopped at Lithgow. Matthew and Sarah had thirty minutes to wait as the train took on coal and water, so they strolled down the platform. Matthew started to read about the engineering feat of the Zig Zag railway line.

The concept of a railway line down into Lithgow was first planned in 1856, but most surveyors decided that the gradient was too great in some places, as much as one in eighty. It was suggested that a line be built to the base of the mountain and passengers walk or be taken by coach to the top to reconnect with the line. Early travellers would take a whole day to travel the few miles. When work started, surveyors had to lower their assistants by rope down cliffs. Tunnels were first considered but it was estimated they would need over ten million bricks to complete two miles of tunnel, so the engineers decided to build a Zig Zag at Lapstone Hill and a viaduct at Knapsack Gully. The Zig Zag principle was a line built so the train backs and fills to ascend or descend the grade. The line was to be built across the face of the incline roughly in a Z shape with the upper and lower arms of the Z extending beyond the oblique central arm. A train approaches along the lower arm and continues until the last of the train is beyond the intersection, then the engine pushes the train backwards up the angled section until the engine is clear of the top arm and so continues on its way. This is a lift of 613 feet from Lithgow to the top of Lapstone Hill. It crosses a Viaduct 126 feet above ground on seven stone arches.

As Matthew walked back to board the train he looked at the mountain in the distance and shook his head in amazement at the work and the engineering feat

They continued their journey up to Mt Victoria. As the train manoeuvred through the Zig Zag, Matthew was out on the viewing platform. It certainly was marvellous engineering. They were now in the Blue Mountains and as he looked back over the Western Plains, he was dazzled by the setting sun in the western sky. He moved back inside as a mist descended and then it started to rain and the wind howled. Sarah cuddled into Matthew and went to sleep. The guard came through the carriages announcing that there had been an earth slip covering the line further down at Blaxland so the train would be stopping at the old Weatherboard Inn. It was now closed, but the railway had an arrangement for situations like this to use it while the rail gang cleared the track. Any passengers that would like to depart the train could do so, as it would be morning before the train could continue its journey.

Four passengers disembarked including Matthew and Sarah but as they crossed the lawn to the gate which led to the old guest house, the rain came down in buckets and, although it was summer, there was a chill in the air. An older couple now in their twilight years, were the caretakers. They met them at the door and soon the two couples quickly gathered around a roaring fire. The hosts offered them steaming hot tea and he offered Matthew something stronger, which Matthew gladly accepted. Sarah took off her coat and relaxed in the leather lounge and soon closed her eyes and drifted off to sleep. Matthew was looking through the old visitors' book and was surprised to see so many names from the old country.

The host came over and said "Mr Matthew Grieves isn't it? I'm Patrick."

"Just call me Matthew."

Patrick went on to say, "We only get bush walkers now as we closed the Inn for travellers when the railway was put through. My wife Millicent was getting too old to run the place but we now organise bush walks and soon there will be organised tours of the newly opened Jenolan Caves."

Matthew picked up a newspaper from the table. It was a copy of the "Sydney Gazette" dated 1836. The headline read;

Famous English explorer visits Sydney.

It went on to say that Charles Darwin, on his World voyage, visited Sydney in his ship the Beagle.

Patrick interrupted Matthew and went on to say, "Well, it was before our time but Charles Darwin visited here in 1836. He was, according to the article, enthralled by the beauty of the view of the Valley which is now called Jamison Valley after one of our early explorers. Charles Darwin marvelled at the spectacular cliff formations and the sound of the water cascading over the falls into the valley below. He also trekked out to the waterfall called Govett's Leap out from Blackheath then he went on to visit Bathurst also. The Inn goes back to the early part of the century when it was used by the military as a sentry station checking travellers moving west. The first Licence was issued back in 1832 and it was called the *Bathurst Traveller*. The name changed to *The Weatherboard Inn* in 1847.

"Patrick, I must come back if I stay in Sydney," Matthew said. "When did you open for business?"

"Way back in 1865, my wife and I have managed the Inn about the same time as the train reached this point and met by the coach to take passengers further on to Bathurst."

And then Matthew could not believe his eyes as he read in the paper, "8th August 1867, Elizabeth and John Joseph Layburn, Just Married."

Patrick said, "Did you know John and Elizabeth?"

Matthew hesitated for a moment. "Well, he was my father," he said. "My friend and I were going out to Carcoar to see him but we were too late. We arrived on the day of his funeral."

He went on to explain how he had been searching for him all over the world and had finally tracked him to NSW.

Patrick called out to his wife, Millicent. "Do you remember John and Elizabeth Layburn, Millicent?"

"Yes" she replied "How could we forget dear Elizabeth's happy smiling face. Why Pat, what has happened?"

"Why my dear, Mr Grieves was his son and he has been out to Carcoar and sadly arrived just in time for his funeral." Millicent's hand went to her face with shock. "We had heard that Elizabeth had passed away some years ago, but now John. How sad."

Sarah was still sleeping peacefully as the day dawned, light filtered through the window and the raindrops sparkled in the emerging sunlight. Sarah had slept most of the night and Millicent had placed a rug over her in the early hours of the morning. Matthew and Patrick chatted well into the night while the other couple were snoring away.

The train guard came over and announced to the passengers that the line had been cleared and they would be ready to proceed as soon as the engine had steam up, however there was still time for breakfast. As the two couples walked outside in the morning sunlight, the parrots were screeching and there seemed to be dozens of them hanging upside down in the lovely trees with yellow flowers. Sarah quickly pointed out to Matthew that they were Wattle trees. They waved to the hosts and said they would return and stay awhile if they had the chance.

Patrick remarked, "If you write to us care of the Inn, we can tell you about the caves. They have built new accommodation so you don't have to rough it in tents."

Sarah and Matthew moved to the train, turned and waved to the caretakers. They were helped aboard and the train blew its whistle as it moved away around the bend.

Chapter 44

The village of Weatherboard had grown from a couple of bark huts in the 1860s catering for travelling stockmen which moved up and down the mountain, there was now a general store, a stock feed and produce store and cabins springing up.

Sarah moved closer to Matthew and looked into his eyes and said, "Don't leave me just yet. Stay in Sydney and we can see the sights. I will take you to Manly to the beach. They say in the brochure that it's seven miles from Sydney and a thousand miles from care."

As the train made its way down the Blue Mountains in the early morning, the sunlight glistened on the lush green paddocks down on the Nepean River. Soon they passed over a stone bridge across a gully called the Knapsack Gully. It was named after early pioneers who used to stop over for a break before continuing their journey over the mountains.

After they pulled into the station at Parramatta, they decided to leave the train and spend the rest of the day seeing the sights around town. They walked down to the park and fed the swans on the lake, dined in a restaurant near the wharf and strolled arm in arm down to the river. It was alive with small ships coming and going and there was a ferry which went to Circular Quay. They were tempted to catch it, but their luggage was back at the station and their train was due to leave at three pm.

"Well Matthew, what are you going to do?" Sarah remarked as she turned to him and stroked his arm.

"Well, I was going to sign on to the next available ship but you make the sights around Sydney so inviting, that if I was not being too forward, I would love to escort you to some of these places and a trip to Manly down on the beach sounds nice. I would love to stay."

Before boarding the train, they turned to glimpse the distant mountains and Sarah commented on the blue haze. Although they had only just got to know each other there was something that was warm and vibrant developing between them.

When the train pulled into Sydney's Central Station, Matthew hired a cab and they were off to Sarah's sister's home in the exclusive suburb of Point Piper. The cab pulled up the hill that went through the locality called King's Cross which was starting to gain a name for gambling, night clubs and the red light area of Sydney. The driver also told him that the notorious razor gangs roamed The Cross after dark.

Chapter 45

The cab descended through Rushcutters Bay, then entered a leafy street which meandered along the harbour. The houses were all two storey mansions and it appeared to be the wealthy part of town. Sarah gave the driver the address and it only took a few minutes before the cab pulled up outside a magnificent house. Sarah knocked on the door and a servant greeted them.

"Good afternoon Ma'am!" the girl said with a pleased smile. "Come in. The mistress is still in the country."

"Thank you Millie," replied Sarah. Just then a young lady came bounding down the stairs.

"Aunt Sarah!" she cried. "Mother has gone to Parkes to the property. Who is this?"

Sarah frowned and just shook her head and muttered to herself, "the younger generation!" Then she spoke louder. "Emily, this is Mr Matthew Grieves. We have been out to see a friend of ours at Carcoar but alas, we were too late. He had just passed away."

Not long after, Josh came in from work. Amy and Stephen had two children, a son Josh, who was working part time at the famous Cobb and Co head office in Sydney The next year he was going to go to Sydney University to study law.

Matthew was given one of the guest rooms next to Sarah. Emily arranged everything just a little bit coincidental, as there were four guest rooms but the other two rooms were being re-decorated. Matthew and Sarah came down the stairs for the evening meal served by Millie. Emily was talking away about her new clothes her Aunt had brought from England and how she was the envy of her class mates at the school she was attending, Ladies College at Dover Heights.

Matthew and Josh talked well into the night about world events and England's involvement in China and the Boers in South Africa. Matthew believed it was only a matter of time before there would be trouble between the blacks and the whites in Southern Africa.

Matthew explained that he had been at sea for over twenty years and, when he returned to London, he had an interview with the Chronicle newspaper for a reporting job. He went on to explain to Josh how he had had a few short stories printed and how he was getting too old to be travelling around the world.

"But what about all the places you have been to? They must have be exciting," said Josh. He explained to Matthew that he had a friend who worked at the Bulletin newspaper here in Sydney and that he may be able to get him an interview.

As Matthew climbed the stairs that night, he had a warm glow from the whisky. He normally did not drink but with the events of the last week, he had dropped his guard and explained to young Josh how he had been searching for some time to see his father only to get there too late. Matthew thought to himself that he should have tried harder when he was here in 1873, as he would have met his father. Little did he know that he had met him in the hotel in Sydney.

He opened the door to his room. It was the beginning of summer and it was extremely warm so he undressed and washed his face. He lay down on the bed and was going to get into his pyjamas, but he drifted off to sleep, Sarah, who was in the adjoining room, slowly opened the door and entered his room. There was a full moon that night and it filtered through the window and cast a shadow across the room catching her sheer night gown.

Once again she was falling in love. His body was so athletic. His chest rose and fell as she approached the bed and she slowly got down on her knees. She started to kiss his naval and worked up to his nipples and he groaned and woke up. His hands reached down and caressed her back slowly as she moved up onto his body. Their lips met and they kissed passionately. His eyes opened and they embraced, then his hands moved over her ample breasts and she moaned and lay on her back. Matthew was now very aroused and he started to kiss her mound. She opened her legs and when he entered her, she wanted to scream but held it back. Matthew was an experienced lover as he had made love in every major port around the world, but it had been some months since he had experienced love like this. Finally he could not hold back any longer and he exploded in her. She let out a muffled scream and lay back exhausted. Sarah pulled up the sheet and went to sleep in his arms.

She woke up at six am and slowly got out of bed and returned to her adjoining room. Matthew stirred and went to the bathroom. He looked into the mirror. He looked awful but after a wash and shave, he dressed and slowly made his way down to the dining room. Breakfast was set out and he helped himself to bacon, eggs and coffee. He was soon joined by Sarah who greeted him, and he took her in his arms and kissed her.

"Good morning, Matthew!" she said with a small smile. "Did you sleep well?"

"As a matter of fact I did," he replied, returning the private smile. "It was the best night's sleep I have had for some time."

Emily came into the dining room and said, "Aunt, why don't you and Mr Grieves go out to the property at Parkes and see the real outback. You can saddle up some horses and ride the hills. They seem to go on forever. We have over seven thousand acres and Mother said to ask you if you returned before she got back."

"Thank you Emily!" replied Sarah. "We will think about it, but today we are going to visit Manly."

The maid Millie had packed them a picnic lunch.

"Aunt Sarah, would you like me to arrange a cab for you?" Millie said.

"No! Thank you Millie. It's such a lovely morning, I think we will walk."

Arm in arm, they set out for the main road and caught a tram to Circular Quay. They arrived just in time to catch the *Queenscliff*, one of the many ferries plying the sea route to all the wharves around the harbour. They found a seat outside as the sturdy craft moved away from the wharf. The vessel was packed as it was a Saturday, and there was a carnival atmosphere about the trip as the ferry rounded Bennelong Point and moved down the harbour past Pinch Gut, now called Fort Dennison. It was built earlier on to repel an expected Russian invasion.

Sydney harbour was alive with craft going each and every way. One of the ferries was heading to the new zoo at Mosman. As they approached the Sydney Heads, the ferry started to roll. There was a swell coming through the heads, and seagulls were landing on the deck. One of the passengers told Matthew that, on a good day, the swell would spray passengers on the outer deck and they would have to go inside.

Chapter 46

Sarah had thought about packing a port but in the end decided against it. As the ferry started to roll, Matthew, being an experienced sailor, was used to it so Sarah moved close to him to keep dry but the rolling was soon over. As they passed the north head, the sea went calm again and the brightly painted craft continued on its way to the Manly wharf. Along with all the other weekend passengers, they walked down the Corso which was full of shops and hotels, and onto the beach.

Matthew had been told about the pine trees planted at Manly. The young pines were now growing into fine specimens. He had been told the seeds had been brought from Norfolk Island and were planted some twenty years ago. Matthew helped Sarah down onto the sand and they walked hand in hand along the water's edge. Matthew asked a young chap where there was a nice place to have a picnic lunch.

The young man told him about Fairy Bower, just around from the main beach. There was a promenade for walking, so they set out for the Bower as the locals called it. They had lunch on the sand and Matthew kicked his shoes off. They held hands and walked down to the water's edge and Sarah kicked water onto Matthew. As they laughed and looked into each other's eyes, they embraced and slowly walked back to their picnic. Matthew lay back and started to doze off. He was woken when Sarah planted a kiss on his cheek.

"Matthew!" He rolled over and their eyes met.

"Yes! Sarah?"

"Make love to me!"

Matthew was embarrassed. "Here now, look, let's find lodgings for the night," he said, so they packed their things and walked back down the path which led to the main beach to sounds of thunder in the near distance. It was a Sydney thunderstorm or, as the locals called it, a southerly buster. The sky became black and lightning started to strike in the distance. The birds seemed to meld in the foliage to escape the oncoming storm. The rain started. At first it was gentle but before long, it was coming down in torrents. Holding hands they started to run, but they soon become drenched. In the mist around the bend through the trees they came across the Bower Private Hotel. They entered the foyer and rang the bell.

"Yes!" came a voice from the back room. Matthew called out in a loud voice as the storm was deafening, "We would like a room please." Sarah started to laugh. She was drenched and Matthew was no better but at least his hat had kept his head dry.

The owner of the lodge came from behind a curtain. "The room will be seventeen shillings and six pence. Towels, bath robes and soap an extra shilling. Will that be one or two rooms?"

Sarah replied, "One, please."

He gave them the key to room number four and said, "Second on the left at the top of the stairs."

Matthew's shoes started to squelch as he climbed the stairs. He opened the door. The room was plain but tidy. There was knock on the door.

"Yes!" Matthew said.

"Sorry to trouble you," said the owner, peeping his head in. "The bathrooms are along the corridor, ladies on the left and gents to the right. I hope your stay in my humble hotel will be an enjoyable one."

Sarah opened the French windows and walked out onto the veranda. The storm had passed as quickly as it had started. The sun was out and the giant black clouds had drifted out to sea. Matthew had gone down to the bathroom and when he returned, he had organised with the owner for a meal to be brought up to the room at six thirty with tea. With the passing of the storm, the sea birds came back and settled on the pathway in front of the lodge and the swifts and swallows were diving in great flocks. Matthew thought they were diving for the insects brought out by the rising heat from the storm. As the sun set in the west, they sat on the veranda silently eating fish and chips.

Sarah wondered how this had happened. She was falling in love with a man she hardly knew but somehow she felt that she had known Matthew a lifetime.

As the sky settled and darkness took over, they joined hands, entered the bedroom and climbed naked into bed. They lay in each other's arms and made passionate love. Exhausted, they finally drifted off into a deep sleep.

The owner, for a small fee had arranged to have their clothes dried and pressed for the morning. He could not do enough for them. Breakfast arrived with their clothes neatly folded and Matthew's shoes had even been dried and polished.

They waved to the Lodge owner as they set off down the pathway to the main beach. It was a lovely summer's day and everything looked green and fresh after the storm. Hand in hand they walked back to the wharf along the Corso. As it was Sunday, the people were streaming off the ferry, all bound for the beach. The bay was filled with small sailing craft darting this way and that, and they looked like they were having a good time. They entered the amusement park and Matthew thought it looked like Blackpool with the Ferris wheel and a steam-run Ghost Train. When they went into the Haunted House, Sarah was scared out of her wits and was hanging on tight to Matthew. They stopped at the window and looked out into the bay and kissed.

Sarah said "Matthew, make love to me tonight like you made love to me last night. I will never forget that as long as I live."

Matthew just held her and was about to say something when a young couple came up from behind them.

"Can we pass please?" the young lad said and with a pleasant smile, Matthew and Sarah moved over. The young couple left the park and entered the wharf.

There was a half hour wait for the next ferry so they wandered over to the milk bar. It had a sign new to Manly, *"Super Juana Sling."* Matthew ordered two doubles with strawberry toppings, and the young female assistant served them at the table.

Matthew asked the young lady, "How long have you been open?"

The place looked brand new.

"We have just opened, Sir," the girl replied. "Welcome to Bert's Milk Bar."

Sarah struggled to get through her Juana Sling, then over a loudhailer came the call for all passengers to board the ferry for Circular Quay. They rushed to join the other sunburnt merry makers and climbed the gangplank. Safely onboard, they stood at the rail and watched the stevedores throwing the ropes as the ferry cast off from the wharf. The SS Manly made its way back to Circular Quay and the City. It was beautiful summer's day, and as the ferry passed North Head, Sarah said, "Look Matthew."

There on the wall, the sign read, 'Seven miles from Sydney and a thousand miles from care.'

The ferry docked at Circular Quay and arm in arm they walked over and caught a Hansom cab. They passed the Mitchell Library and the naval dockyards, and then wound their way up through Kings Cross and home to her sister's place.

Dinner was served as the children, both young adults now, chatted away.

Josh said, "Matthew, I spoke to my friend today and if you can see him at the Bulletin office tomorrow, he could see if he can arrange an interview with the chief editor. You may only get a job as a Junior Reporter, but it would be a start if you are seriously thinking about entering the world of newspaper reporting."

"Why, thank you Josh. I have to make up my mind if I'm staying in Sydney, but I'll certainly go and see what he has to offer."

That night when the house was quiet, Sarah made her way into Matthew's room and climbed into his bed. Matthew stirred and placed his arm around her shoulders as she snuggled into him. They lay there for a while, when finally Sarah said "What are you going to do Matthew?"

They were naked and the sheets were pulled back as the heat was oppressive. He turned and looked at her and said, "Sarah, I know we have only just met, but I would like to stay in Sydney for a while yet. If this offer is what I am looking for, then I could stay. I like it here. We could perhaps find a place together?"

Sarah jumped up. "You mean - live together?"

Sarah had lived her married life as a good wife knowing what society expected of her. She had never strayed once. She thought for a moment. *What harm could it be? Except for my sister, no one knows me here.*

The following morning, she wrote to her sister in Parkes and told her the news. She expected her to return a letter full of scorn as she, Amy, was a good church goer. When the letter came, her sister stated that she thought she was crazy but also said she thought it would do no hurt to see if they were suited to each other. Was he good looking? was all she really was interested in. I can only vaguely remember him she wrote.

Chapter 47

Carcoar – 1874

Back in Carcoar, young John came running into the house and informed his mother that there was an important letter at the post office and the postmaster says she had to come around and pick it up and sign for it. But Jane was in no hurry to visit the post office until she did her weekly shopping.

On Friday, as she went into the butcher's, Mrs Fogerty was quick to tell her that there was a letter waiting for her. Jane chuckled to herself as she crossed the road. Everyone she bumped into knew about the letter. As she opened the post office door she bumped into Mrs Stammers who also put her two penn'th in. She signed for the letter and placed it into her shopping bag and walked home. When she had made a cup of tea, she carefully opened the letter. It was addressed to Mr J. J. Layburn Esq., care of Carcoar, NSW. It was from the court house of York England. It looked like it had been around the world as it bore post marks from Canada, St Helena, and other places through which it had passed. Some had even rubbed off over the years. She carefully cut the string that was holding it together. Finally, Jane had digested the contents of the letter which stated that John was under arrest for failing to appear in an English court in 1864. She quickly glanced through the pages of legal jargon and found there was one entry for 19 November 1868 against a Martha Layburn of Otley for fourteen shillings and sixpence, failure to pay for goods received, given as "coal."

She reread the letter and could not believe that her John could be involved, but she said to herself that he was a bit of a lad, sometimes. She thought that she should show it to Mr Fagan but wondered what good would it do now? As her John was now deceased, she placed the letter in the fireplace. Poor Jane, her world had been turned upside down, but nothing was going to upset her world of the church and bringing up her family. *No, best to let sleeping dogs lie*, she thought, as she drank her cup of tea and watched the fire consume the pages.

Chapter 48

Johnny Layburn had been working in the Stokes Hotel as the Cellarman, moving beer barrels. He also looked after the horses in the stables and he was as strong as an ox. He lived in Stokes Lane with his mother and his step brothers and sisters as his father had died back in '87. His father had been the talk of the town, as his wishes were that he was not to be buried with a church service, especially not a Catholic service, and he had instructed his friend that he wished the funeral service to take place in the Royal Hotel. It was unheard of and it shocked certain sections of the community.

Johnny was only a boy when his father died, but he remembered the day as if it was yesterday. All the people from far and wide had gathered at the Royal and the service spilled out into the main street. His mother would not go to the funeral service and Jane, who was a strict Catholic, vowed she would never place flowers on his grave site in the unconsecrated ground. She had been shocked at her late husband's wishes. He gave strict instructions it was not to be conducted in the Church, but to be carried out in the hotel. But John Joseph and his mother joined the procession as it passed the Catholic Church and climbed up the hill. Mr Cobb gave them a lift in his carriage. He had come down especially for the service.

Johnny was in the local football side and they were playing Woodstock. Both were sponsored by the Royal Hotels chain. The publican at the Royal in Carcoar paid for their jumpers and travel expenses. As now the trains were running, they could play in Cowra on a Saturday and be back at the Royal for drinks by six pm. The Carcoar side were leading the local premiership as they had not been beaten. The players came out onto the field; it was a cool afternoon, and the crowd numbered about a hundred. There was a carnival atmosphere and the local brass band was there to play at the interval.

The nurses from the Hospital and the girls from the convent came down to cheer on the local side. One of John's biggest fans was Sally Boxhall, who had been working with John at Stokes Hotel for some time. She had a hidden desire that one day they would get married, but John, being shy, would avoid the situation and tell her they were just good friends. They had known each other since going to school.

At half time, as the players left the soggy field as it had started to rain, the visitors were leading ten points to six. The Coach of the Carcoar side said the Woodstock side had a ring-in from Sydney The new kid was working on one of the outlying stations and was strong, playing in the centre.

The Carcoar coach said, "Look, boys don't let that Number Six get away. He's fast, but don't forget, tackle hard around the legs and he'll fall."

The players went back onto the field after half time, and as a light snow started to fall, it got bitterly cold. The game had only a few minutes to go; Number Six scored again, but the Carcoar side had kicked two penalty goals and were only trailing by four points. It had been a hard match except for the last runaway try scored by the Number Six player for Woodstock, but there was nothing in it.

The Carcoar coach was looking worried as the Woodstock side kicked the ball from their half and the visitors were chasing the ball towards Carcoar's try line. Young Johnny Layburn, playing fullback, caught the ball under the goal posts and started to run. He quickly gathered speed and shot past half the Woodstock side before they knew it. He crossed the half way line before the visitors realised what was going on as he swerved and side stepped. The locals were cheering, and he scored the try in the corner with Number Six tackling him as he crossed the try line. The captain of the local side gave Johnny the ball to kick the conversion goal and save the match, as the visitors were in front by a point fifteen to fourteen .The crowd went quiet as John lined up the ball. It was a difficult kick from that position and to make matters worse, the ball was heavy and wet as it started to rain and the fog came down over the field. However, John was not fazed as he was a good kicker but he knew this was not going to be easy. He lined the ball up, moved in and put his boot into it. The ball sailed through the air and it seemed to take forever to reach the cross bar but finally it went over the black dot and was awarded a goal. The locals had won and the crowd went wild.

The visitors shook hands. There were two tents rigged up for the players to change in, then they all moved off down to the Royal Hotel. The mail train was due in at six fifteen, so there was a mad drinking session at the pub. The visitors with their supporters, left the Hotel as the train blew its whistle, about five miles back down the track, giving them time to get to the Carcoar station.

Johnny was a hero that week and written up on the front page of the *Chronical* with the headline saying:

LOCAL BOY SAVES FOOTBALL MATCH

Johnny's mother, at the kitchen table the morning the paper came out, said, "Don't go getting a swelled head now Johnny. It's only a game, you know."

All the girls at the Convent were talking about Johnny. Young Ellen, who was only seven thought he was cute, but could not understand what all the fuss was about. Every afternoon walking home from school she would pass the Stokes hotel.

Ellen was visiting her friend up near the showground and on some days, she would see John cleaning out the stables. One day, nearly six months after the football match, some of her school mates crossed the road and ventured down by the creek; it was a short-cut, as Brown's Creek meandered through the village. They would jump across and climb up the other side and continue up the hill. On this occasion her friend Patricia, slipped and fell. She was screaming, and the girls thought she had broken her arm. She was lying in the water so Ellen ran up the bank, crossed the road to the Stokes hotel and called out, "Help! Help!"

Sally Boxall, who was now working as a maid, ran to the front door and around the back to get help. She quickly summoned the stable hand to come, telling him there had been an accident.

Reluctant Heroes

Johnny came running out of the stables and she quickly told him what had happened. Ellen led Johnny across the road and down to the stream. He gently picked Patricia up, carried her across the road to the hotel, and placed her in the office while one of the kitchen staff ran to the hospital for help. She was taken to the hospital and her arm, which was broken, was put into plaster.

The village had been quiet for years, after the bushrangers had terrorised the town. But on the morning of the 25th September 1893, the inhabitants woke to learn that there had been a murder at the City of Sydney Bank. The local paper, the *Chronicle*, worked through the early morning hours, to get the first edition on the streets.

24th September 1893 "Bank Manager Murdered

> *The Manager, Mr John William Phillips, and a family friend, Miss Cavanaugh were hacked to death at the residence of the City Of Sydney Bank in the early hours of 23rd Sept. The alleged culprit escaped on a horse, stolen from the Anglican rectory. Later that day a Herbert Glasson was apprehended in Cowra and was to be returned to the Carcoar Lockup.*
>
> *A local girl Miss Mary Friend, was witness to the grim finding when she called into the Bank's residence early in the morning and found the murder scene.*
>
> *"The two bodies had been hacked to death," she said.*
>
> *When Mary had regained her composure and had been given a stiff drink to settle her nerves, she told police how she found Mrs Phillips and her three-year-old daughter hiding upstairs in a cupboard.*
>
> *"Mrs Phillips had blood on her face, and was holding her daughter's hand which had two fingers chopped off. She was terrified and screamed when I opened the cupboard door," Mary said.*

Mary had been employed as a domestic servant at the Royal Hotel, which was next to the Bank, and, as she was traumatised by the event, was given the rest of the day off. Her fiancée, Alfred Layburn, who was working down on the Whitney property in Woodstock, got on his horse and rode up to be with Mary as soon as he found out what happened. The young couple were to be married the following year.

As the story unfolded, it was reported that Herbert (Bertie) Glasson, the son of a wealthy land holder, had forged cheques for £1200, which was hushed up. The Bank was about to foreclose on his Butcher shop, so to get even, he entered the Bank through the back window and committed the murders.

TRIAL FOR CARCOAR BANK MURDERER.
As reported in the Carcoar *Chronical*

Herbert Glasson was taken to Bathurst where he was charged and placed on trial before Mr Justice Innes, the circuit Judge. He was convicted and sentenced to death. He is to be hanged at Bathurst Goal at 9 am, Wednesday, 29th November 1893. The murder weapon at the time of the trial had not been found.

Chapter 49

Carcoar - 1898

The town of Carcoar, was hosting members of the Federation committee who were travelling around the state getting support for the states to become a Federation. The local hall was packed. It had been built back in the 1860s but there had been moves to have a more permanent building erected. The main speakers were Mr Henry Parkes, the local Mayor, and a member of the New South Wales Government, Mr Waddell. The Mayor introduced Mr Parkes and a hush came over the crowd. He was the last speaker.

"What I want to talk about tonight, is Federation," said Mr Parkes, "bringing all the states in line throughout this great country of ours, which will mean no more duty to be levied on goods crossing state borders and a whole range of minor changes. Do you realise the drama in taking a body across from one state to another? There is excise on the casket if the timber was locally grown, and I could bore you with a list as of details as long as your arm. But, on a serious note it is important to remind you about the Ideals of the British Commonwealth of Nations.

"The Empire, is to-day our serious link, binding Britain and our states and the other countries of the Commonwealth. This has been established by the gradual spreading throughout the world of British political ideals by which citizens in every colony have been encouraged, stage-by-stage, to attain the same status as British citizens in the Mother Country.

"Freedom of conscience, freedom of the press, freedom of speech! In the campaign for these, Britain was always the leader, and they were won by the citizens of Britain. For these, and for our rights of self-government in a family of nations, we, as New South Welshmen, (hopefully soon to become part of the nation of Australia)."

There was a roar from the crowded hall.

"Ladies and Gentleman." Mr Parkes raised his arms and the crowded hall became quiet.

"Thank you," he continued. "We will always remain grateful. It is the ideal of government by the people that has distinguished our Empire from other great Empires of the past. This great ideal has been best described in the words of a distinguished American, Abraham Lincoln. During the American Civil War, when the Northern States fought the Southern States, to free the land from Negro slavery in the cotton fields, Lincoln delivered this speech at the opening of the National burial ground at Gettysburg."

"Four score and seven years ago, our fathers brought forth on this continent, a new nation, conceived in Liberty, and dedication to the proposition that all men are created equal. Now we are engaged in a great civil testing, whether that nation or any nation so conceived and so dedicated, can long endure. We are met on a great battlefield of that war. We have come to dedicate a portion of that field as a final resting place of these who gave their lives that a nation might live, but in a larger sense we cannot dedicate, we cannot consecrate, we cannot hallow this ground. The brave men, living and dead, who struggled here, have consecrated it far above our poor power to add or detract. It is rather for us to be here dedicating to the great task remaining before us, that from these honoured dead, we take increased devotion to the cause for which they gave the last full measure of devotion; that we here highly resolve that these dead shall not have died in vain; that this nation, under god, shall have a new birth of freedom, and that government of the people, by the people, for the people, shall not perish from the earth."

"This is, not alone, an ideal of the American Nation, but it also represents the ideal of government of the British Commonwealth of nations. It is an ideal which has taken more than a thousand years of British History to evolve, and it is this ideal which we honour to day. The hope that,

Government of the people, by the people, for the people, shall not perish from the earth."

There was loud acclamation and everybody stood and sang "God Save The Queen."

A well known Sydney journalist, Mr Matthew Grieves, was travelling with Mr Parkes and reported for the Bulletin newspaper. They were staying at the Royal that night and, after the meeting, the official party adjourned to the bar. It had been sometime since Matthew and Sarah had been in Carcoar. The hotel was packed with local dignitaries, the Postmaster, the Bank Managers, the new Station Master and half the town was spilling out onto the pavement. All wanted to talk to Mr Parkes about the advantages of Federation and the disadvantages. He excused himself as they had to catch an early train in the morning.

Matthew and Sarah reacquainted themselves with Mr John Fagan. They had a few drinks and the three climbed up the stairs as it was too far for John to travel back to his property at Sunny Ridge. The train was due at nine am, so the press, who were also travelling with the main party, trudged up the hill to the waiting train.

Chapter 50

African war possible – 1899

In June 1899, the Carcoar *Chronical* published an article stating New South Wales had emerged as clearly possessing the most efficient military organization in Australia, including all arms of the service. Recently a force of 500 men had been raised to form the NSW Light Horse.

A Sydney paper printed that a Canadian offer of 2000 picked men for service had been made in the event of war.

The Bathurst paper reported that they had twenty five trained horse men ready to volunteer from the Mounted Rifles.

Although the Queensland Government were the first Colonial Government to offer troops to the Imperial cause in South Africa the sending of the troops was hotly debated by the Parliament and finally passed in late October 1899.

The London cables revealed the gravity of the Transvaal situation.

One headline in the Sydney Bulletin read,

POSSIBILITY OF WAR
Correspondent Matthew Grieves.

> The British Government is concerned, that the Afrikaan Nationalism could pose a threat to British supremacy in South Africa. There could be no compromise on such fundamental issues.

The British Government had asked the New South Wales Government, to consider training troops in case of trouble in the African continent, believing that her Majesty's Government would come to the Colony's rescue if and when the need arose. There was always the threat of trouble from the French, Russians and the Germans who were now stationed in the Pacific.

There had been at the time a large number of Australians working in the Transvaal mines; the dispatch of an Australian force would relieve them of the white tyranny exercised over them.

Headline, 18th September in the Sydney Bulletin:

BOERS FOR WAR

War Considered Inevitable.

Article written by Matthew Grieves

Not all South Africans were for the war against the might of Great Britain. One such military general, Koos De La Rey, was totally against the war, but he went on to say that he would do his duty if called upon.

29th Sept.

A meeting of all the Colonies was held in Melbourne. The Premier of Queensland, James Robert Dickson, happily regarded it as a Federal incident of no small importance in the history of Australia. The states of Victoria, South Australia and Western Australia favoured a Federal force, but New South Wales and Queensland opposed the move in the strongest manner. Their argument against a Federal force on the grounds that it would take too long to sanction - they favoured sending state troops.

3rd October

The Colonial Office in London, cabled the States saying they would accept the Colonial offers of troops and laid down the composition of the Australian forces. They also stipulated that troops were to embark no later than 31st October. Why the Home Office would have wished to have the Colonial irregulars in South Africa so quickly is a matter for some conjecture.

3rd October

The Victorian Government committed troops to the war in South Africa.

5th October

Western Australia and South Australia introduced legislation to send contingents.

6th October

The New Zealand Government to send troops to South Africa.

Matthew Grieves interviewed the poet, Henry Lawson (writer for the Bulletin, the *'Bushman's Bible'*), who gave one of his rare interviews on the South African problem.

He said, "What does it all amount to? Only this; that, because of the craving for the sensational, born of the world's present social system – the mad longing for change, intensified in Australia by the hopeless flat monotony of the country and its history, some of us are willing – wilfully, blindly eager, mad! - to cross the sea and shoot men whom we never saw and whose quarrel we do not and cannot understand. Our cry is "For England!" or "Blood is thicker than water!" and so we seek to blind and deceive ourselves as fools who are unanimous in our eagerness to sacrifice right, justice, truth - everything to satisfy our selfish craving for what we consider a picnic-to have "some fun' -to have a spree." - Henry Lawson.

The Australian press were particularly hard on the enemy and some of the local press set out to label them as a cruel and fanatical race.

10th October
The Tasmanian Lower House approved the dispatch of a contingent.

17th October
The NSW Legislative Assembly began debating the dispatch of troops to the War effort in South Africa.

Chapter 51

Back in Carcoar, Johnny Layburn went bush as much as possible with a few of his mates; Iggie Smith, John Fox and Ernest Howarth, who were all excellent horsemen. They would ride down to his late father's friend, John Fagan's property called Sunny Ridge, near Lyndhurst. They had left early in October of 1899 to do a bit of fishing in a stream at the base of Mount Macquarie, build a fire, have a good time, a few drinks and set up camp for a few days. Sometimes John Fagan would come down and spin a few yarns about the old days and inevitably, one of the boys would ask him about the time he was driving the mail coach carrying a consignment of gold when he was shot in the hat by the bushrangers. They had heard it many times, but he told a good story about the hat, which was still in the bar at the Royal Hotel in Carcoar.

John Fagan had been given power to act on the late John Joseph's estate. He had attended to everything except where young Johnny was concerned. His father had stipulated he was not to be brought up in the Catholic religion but Jane, young Johnny's mother, was strong willed and he was not going to fight her. As far as she was concerned, she had God on her side so like a good tyke (Catholic), young Johnny attended Mass every Sunday morning with his Mother and family. Catherine, John Joseph's elder half sister had moved to Sydney and she was boarding with her uncle who had arranged for her to work for the railways as a typist and office clerk. He had become a successful solicitor.

The lads returned late in the afternoon of the twelfth and as they crossed the bridge over the Belubula River, or as the locals called it Browns Creek, there were wild scenes. The town was out parading in the main street and the Union Jack was flying.

"What's happened?" said Igge.

A young lad, twirling a flag on a stick said "WAR! They have declared WAR on the BOERS."

It was 12th October. The boys hitched the horses behind the pub, and walked back around to the bar. The publican called out, "Free beer to the lads who will sign up."

The four lads had been involved in the NSW Light Horse training at Molong and they were top of their group, so it was only a matter of course for them to enlist.

Igge was the first to speak. "Gee! Free beer! Count me in."

Jack and John looked at Ernest and said, "Well, why not? We're in."

The Royal ran out of beer that night, so the four lads, rolling drunk turned up at Stroke's hotel, but Johnny's boss sent them home and said, "Don't be late for work in the morning."

Johnny struggled down the lane to his house and at the top of his voice shouted, "Rule Britannia, Britannia rules the waves."

Freddie, his disabled brother, sitting in his wheelchair met him at the gate, and Jane came racing out the door.

"What's all this commotion, John?" she said.

"I am going to war, Mother."

"You are doing no such thing," Jane replied.

"But Mother, I have given a pledge and the four of us drank to it, HIC!"

"Come inside and have your tea."

"But, Mother, I gave a promise to me mates."

Jane replied, "Well, we will see about that!"

Next morning Johnny was up bright and early, ate his breakfast and, as he was leaving the house his mother put her arms around him.

"Johnny, I am real proud of you and I know you will do a good job, but you will come back, won't you?" With that, she started to cry.

They were taking possible recruits in Bathurst, so the four lads went up on the train so they could report for duty.

The Sergeant on duty yelled at the top of his voice, "Form a line here, you lot. If you're not between twenty and forty and single, you may as well leave now and you must be at least five foot, three inches."

The four boys remained in line, but two of the other boys from the district dropped out. As they passed, John said to young Archibald Stacy, "When are you twenty, Archie?"

"Are next year," he replied.

Johnny whispered in his ear, "Just put your age up."

18th October

Finally the QLD Government sanctioned the enrolment of Volunteers to form the Queensland Mounted Infantry.

It was then reported that all the States will be represented in the War in South Africa.

Chapter 52

Matthew Grieves, a reporter for the Bulletin since 1888.

Mathew and Sarah had settled into a flat in Liverpool Sreet in the City and went to all the shows around town. Sarah had been out to visit her sister in far-away Parkes. She loved the country life and she and Matthew would spend weeks out there when possible, calling on their way at the Weatherboard Inn now in the town of Wentworth Falls in the beautiful Blue Mountains. They had even ventured out to Jenolan Caves, camping out under the stars. Matthew obtained a position as junior reporter at the Bulletin (although he was 48). He loved the life and the challenge of the job reporting on events all over Sydney.

He had been travelling around the state with Mr Henry Parkes and reporting back to Sydney on the State becoming part of a Federation.

He had been asked to report to the Chief Editor in the head office in Sydney. Matthew was waiting nervously in the outer office, looking through the latest real estate magazines. He and Sarah had been keen to buy into a new subdivision on the Manly Peninsular, just near the beach at North Steyne. The blocks were being auctioned this Saturday on site and they wanted to be there. They had arranged to stay at the Bower Private Hotel where they first stayed back in 1886.

The door opened and Matthew's boss came out.

"Good morning Grieves," he said. "Come in."

"Thank you Sir," replied Matthew.

As the door closed, Matthew sat in the only chair available.

"I have asked Miss Jones to bring in some coffee and cake," said the Chief Editor. "I remembered your liking for coffee instead of tea."

He took a breath as if about to impart serious news.

"Look Matthew, things are getting pretty serious in the Transvaal," he continued. "I would like you to consider going over there with Patterson. He has shown a lot of promise lately though I thought you would be a steadying influence on him and to see he does not get into trouble. You know the drill and I think you have earned some leave. Keep up the good work. That was some speech you reported that Parkes made in, where was it, Carcoar?"

"When do you think we will have to leave?" Matthew asked.

"The first consignment should leave early next month," the Editor replied.

"Do you think a few days off to get things in order, would be ok?"

"Sure Matthew. Keep in touch and I will let you know the procedure. You will have to come in to the office for a final briefing"

"Thank you, Sir."

"Do you realise the *Bulletin* is not in favour of this war?" said the Editor. "It's Britain's war. We really should not be involved but they will be our soldiers from the Colonies, so the paper should be there."

Matthew and Sarah caught the Manly Ferry on Friday from the Quay.

The musicians were playing and collecting money as they serenaded the passengers. Sarah reached out and held Matthews hand. Since they had been together, there had been love and magic between them. She loved him and they were so happy together.

Sarah was unaware that Matthew had been talking to her sister, when they arrived at the Bower Private Hotel that a wedding had been planned. Sarah's niece, Emily, had arranged everything even down to having someone from the Manly Court House take care of the marriage ceremony. Amy, Stephen and family, with close friends, had made excuses and went over to Manly late in the week.

As the ferry pulled into the Wharf, Matthew took Sarah in his arms and in front of the other passengers said, "Sarah, will you marry me?"

"Matthew, what did you say?" she replied.

"Will you marry me?"

"Yes, Yes," she replied.

They walked arm in arm up the gangplank. Sarah had stars in her eyes and then she started to cry.

The Bower Private Hotel provided a carriage service from the wharf. It made its way up steep Daley Road and turned into Bower Ave into the quiet leafy grove down to their piece of paradise. For them the hotel was private heaven. They had been here each summer since they had been in Sydney. The driver unloaded their baggage into the foyer and they were met by the owner, Mr James.

"Welcome back, Mr Grieves. Same room, Number Four?"

"Yes please," Matthew replied.

Just then from behind the curtain, Sarah's sister emerged.

"Surprise, Surprise," they shouted.

There was a mad rush with everyone hugging and kissing then a waiter emerged with bottles of champagne and accompanied by a young lass with savouries.

Sarah said to Matthew, "What's going on?"

"Well, we are getting married."

With that she burst into tears. She threw her arms around Matthew and his old black bowler hat went flying.

"There is going to be a wedding," Matthew replied, trying to drink his champagne.

"But how can you arrange it so fast?" she said.

Stephen stepped forward. "Sis, everything has been arranged."

With that, Sarah's sister Amy, took her by the hand and whisked her up to her room.

Amy and Matthew had arranged through the week to have Sarah out of the flat so Amy could get her some clothes to wear. Stephen and Matthew adjourned to the bar. A quick drink and Matthew went upstairs to change; he had come prepared with the latest dinner suit and he looked the part of the groom. Stephen came in with the bride. The Proprietor of the hotel Mr James, had got to know Matthew and Sarah as they came over on the ferry in the summer and spend time lazing on the beach at the Fairy Bower or walking down the Corso on the bright summer nights.

Mr James was recently widowed. His wife had died giving birth to their first child, a boy. They both died and it was a very sad occasion.

One night having a quite drink with Matthew, he told him the story of how he had corresponded with his wife back in England and she finally migrated out to Sydney to join him.

They had arranged for someone to play the piano for the wedding and on cue, he started to play the wedding march. The only guests at the hotel that night were the wedding party. After signing the wedding register they all adjourned to the dining room for their wedding feast. After consuming more than enough champagne, Stephen rose and proposed a toast to the Bride and Groom.

Finally the wedding party climbed the stairs. Matthew and Sarah parted from the rest and, as Matthew opened the door, confetti rained down on them. They undressed, got into their new night attire, and slowly climbed into bed. They were exhausted as it had been a long day. They lay in each other's arms and Sarah was the first to stir as her arm had gone to sleep. It was three am. Matthew got up and went to the bathroom and when he returned, Sarah was lying on the bed with the sheets pulled back. He gently lay down beside her and kissed her, slowly moving down to her exposed breasts.

Sarah whispered into his ear, "Matthew, I have loved you since the first time we met on the train going to Carcoar."

Although they were in their fifties, they had experienced a good and healthy love life as they were both fit and strong. They made slow, passionate love and lay there as the sun came through the window. It was seven am, so they dressed and met the others downstairs for breakfast.

The Auction Sale of the land was at eleven am so they had plenty of time to make the short journey to North Steyne. The Proprietor of the Bower Private Hotel, Harold James, had organised a sulky and driver to take them to the auction, as the road was now macadamised all the way from the Corso to the area known as Queenscliff.

The real estate firm handling the auction, Weight and Co., had a tent gaily decorated with bunting and flags flying. They were stationed at the corner of Pine and Whistler Sts and it was a carnival atmosphere for everyone to enjoy. There were about fifty people all enjoying the refreshments on offer. One young chap was heard to say, "Can't see too many people living this far from the City. Why, there are natives living down at the Lagoon."

The auctioneer started out by giving the terms and conditions of the sale. The two streets Matthew was interested in were Whistler and Pacific Sts but they started out with the lots further away which went for ten pounds a block.

Matthew and Sarah were more interested in blocks at the southern end of Whistler Street. The bidding got higher as they got closer to Pine St and the auctioneer started the bidding on lot Number fifteen, the block they were interested in. There was a bid from the back at fifteen pounds and Matthew came in at twenty pounds. As there were more blocks than people, the bidding slowed down.

The auctioneer said "Sold to the man in the black hat for twenty pounds."

Matthew was more than happy with his purchase.

In the background a tram passed. It ventured down Pittwater Road going clang, clang, clang. The crowd dispersed and people laughed and shouted. Everybody seemed to be happy with their purchases.

The group strolled down to the Pacific Ocean near the North Steyne Surf hut. The ocean front was growing with holiday shacks and dwellings and a new shop had sprung up on the corner. Sarah and Amy raced down to the sand, took off their shoes and paddled in the surf.

It was still against the law to swim in the ocean during daylight hours but some of the bathers were getting gamer and were venturing out into the water.

Stephen and Matthew crossed the road and entered a tavern where there were tables and chairs out on the pavement. It reminded Matthew of some of the ports on the continent. The girls said they would be over in a moment, and as they crossed the road, Matthew thought he recognised Henry Lawson. He called out to him but he just walked on with his head down. They decided to wait till the girls came over from the beach before they ordered tea and fresh scones and cream.

The pine trees had started to get some height and looked impressive.

Matthew said "Stephen, where are those trees from?"

"They're native to Norfolk Island," Stephen replied

Stephen went on to explain that the First Fleet were told to investigate the possibilities of their uses (they had been sighted by Captain Cook as he ventured past Norfolk Island between the mainland and New Zealand and he thought they would make good ship masts, but alas, they were not strong enough for the job). They made beautiful street trees, which have been planted all over Sydney and the seeds have even found their way to Kew Gardens in London. Also the palm trees, native to Lord Howe Island, you will see them in the bigger hotels. They have been sent all over the world.

"Matthew, what are you going to do now that you are a married man?" asked Stephen.

"Well Stephen, I have been offered the chance to go to South Africa with the paper. I haven't told Sarah yet, but I thought it would be good opportunity for a honeymoon. Then we could go on to London. My mother is now eighty and in her last letter she said she is not doing well. She has been staying with her younger sister and they are thinking of putting her into a nursing home. The War can't last that long."

Sarah and her sister joined them and they enjoyed Devonshire tea. On their way back to the Bower Private Hotel, they called into the Ivanhoe Park native flower show. They were greeted by the Mayor, Mr Hayes, who proudly stated that the native flower show had been going since 1881. Matthew had not seen flowers like them and bought a bunch of Waratahs to take back to the Bower Private Hotel. They fascinated him. They were called the native rose.

One of the country newspapers, *The Eureka* made headlines around the country when it suggested that the Australian volunteers were going to war for the sake of four shillings a day and not out of loyalty. The Catholic Daily wrote disparagingly of the "valiant volunteers of the colonies."

Cardinal Moran stated that true Australian patriotism was to stay at home to defend one's own country.

Chapter 53

The Scramble for Africa by the great nations of the world.

England, France and Belgium and to a lesser extent Portugal and Germany, by the middle of the 19th Century, were the main controlling powers of the Dark Continent. Early in the 19th Century the main powers of Europe were busy at home fighting wars, and it was not until 1857 that the heroic explorer and naturalist Livingstone first appeared on the African scene. Then others followed.

In 1884-85, at what became known as the Berlin Congress, the countries came together to lay down the rules to slice up the Continent of Africa.

At a glance of the map of Africa, and at the beginning of the conflict, Great Britain's interest extended from the Cape to Tanganyika, a distance of 1800 miles and if you included the Sudan, Egypt and the minor colonies of the Gold Coast and the Niger territories, it had an area of about 2,300,000 square miles. Between 1879 and 1883, Stanley Livingstone founded what eventually became the Congo Free State.

The territory claimed by France in the Dark Continent was a few square miles more, 3,300,000 square miles, and England very magnanimously ceded to her European rival the Sahara desert. Lord Salisbury rather wittingly termed it "very light soil," but it did not dawn on the French the implications of this until the agreement had been drawn up. Although France may have been the biggest land owner in all Africa, she had purchased the biggest White Elephant.

At the time it was reported in the *London Times*, that "the British Empire dreams of a "Cape to Cairo" rail link," entirely under British control. The rail contractors had reached Bulawayo in the south, and in the north, Lord Kitchener had pushed the rail link about the same distance.

The stumbling block was the Boer-held territories called the Orange Free State and the Transvaal.

The prominent British capitalist, Mr Cecil Rhodes, after whom the country, Rhodesia was named, played an important part in the politics of the South African region. He became Premier of the Cape Colony in July 1890 and a member of the Privy Council in 1895 leading up to the conflict between the British and the Boers. He was heavily involved with diamonds and gold mines in the Kimberley and Witwatersrand, and the railway.

The Boer Republic was led by Oom Paul Kruger, elected 9th May 1883. He was a man of strong will and simple habits, and a firm believer of the Bible. He was a person of regular habits and he could be found any day of the week, sitting on his front veranda.

It all started with the Boers leaving the Cape back in 1833-37 because of their dissatisfaction with the ruling British liberal policies with the natives. History will record it as the "Great Trek," but they eventually settled in the Transvaal with the capital at Pretoria. There were a number of British subjects called "outlanders" (by the Boers), who were being persecuted and heavily taxed. The two taxes that brought everything to a head were first, the Dynamite Concession tax, levelled at the mining industry, $22.00 per case that gave the Boer Govt over $2,500,000 per year, and was far higher than what the local Boers paid, $4.00 a case, and second, the tax levelled at freight on the railway. One incident involved a traveller who arrived at the border near the Vaal River, and the train was held up for over eleven hours whilst it was thoroughly searched for diamonds and gold.

On 29th December 1895, four hundred volunteers set out from Mafeking, where they had assembled four days after Christmas. Dr Jamison had received from the outlanders of Johannesburg, an appeal for help to overthrow the governing body. They were to join forces with the Cape Mounted Rifles and the Natal Mounted Police, but it was a complete disaster as they met a strong force of Boer fighters and the volunteers soon raised the white flag. This became known as the Battle of Doonkop.

Reluctant Heroes

On 9th October 1899, the British Government was given an ultimatum by the Boer Government, to withdraw all of its British troops from their Transvaal border, plus the mass of troops camped in South Africa. An answer was demanded by five pm on 11th October. The British Government did not meet the Boer request, so war was declared and the Boer Republic called on all Afrikaners to rise up against the British.

The British were soon taken aback by the strength of the Boer troops and the first British causality was an armed train under the command of Captain Nesbitt, carrying guns and ammunition to Mafeking. It was destroyed by the Boers at Kraal-pan.

Chapter 54

On the day that the troops of the first contingent were to leave Sydney, they marched down from Victoria Barracks to the wharfs. The streets were lined with people and it was estimated there were between 250,000 and 300,000 people pushing and shoving to get a better view of their lads. Local authorities did not anticipate the crowd, it appeared that everyone in Sydney was there. Chaos was imminent when a north bound tram tried to get through the crowd. As the Sons of the Empire proudly moved down through George Street on their horses, the crowd surged forward, women waving hankies and throwing them to the boys.

Then it happened. A lad fell and was trampled by one of the horses. The soldier had to keep moving and he kept looking around but it was too late. There was nothing he could do. When the parade had passed an ambulance cart was summoned to carry the lad to the hospital. He had suffered internal injuries and he lay in hospital for weeks, being left with a limp for the rest of his life.

The crowd started to sing *"Rule Britannia," "Sons of the Sea,"* and *"Soldiers of the Queen."* The first to leave Sydney Harbour was the steamer *Kent*. Matthew and Sarah were on board the ship, and it was brimming with dignitaries, all trying to get in on the act. It was 28th October 1899. It started to rain. Matthew had been writing and giving the copy boy last minute stories to take up to the paper. Matthew and Sarah had a first class berth on board the vessel for its eight-week trip to the Cape. They would be stopping and picking up troops on the way in Melbourne, Adelaide and Albany.

Reluctant Heroes

The *Kent* moved away from the wharf. The crowd standing in the rain went wild and as the ship sailed away, the crowd started to sing, *"The Girl I left behind"* and *"Auld Lang Syne."* The harbour was awash with all types of craft, large and small, all blowing horns and escorting the ship out the harbour.

Chapter 55

The War In South Africa

Sarah was complaining bitterly, as she wanted to go with Matthew, but he would not allow her. When they landed at the Cape, he booked her into a hotel under protest, but Matthew was adamant, that she could not go near the fighting.

The British forces had suffered their worst week in the short conflict; it was reported as the "Black Week." The Boers inflicted huge defeats on the British on three fronts and had the British forces under siege in three towns, Mafeking, Kimberley and Ladysmith. The battle of Magersfontein on 11th December, where the Boer forces attacked with about 2,000 commandoes, inflicted heavy fatalities, on their British attackers.

One of the British foot soldiers had divulged to Matthew that the enemy were too damn quick. They were there one minute, then they would melt into the bush and just disappear.

He said, "They fight like men possessed and they were in possession of new German Mauser rifles. They also had got hold of the new American Maxims Gatling gun that could fire rounds of bullets at a fast rate. We have old carbines and they are useless when they get hot, they just jam up,"

The *London Press* headlines that afternoon stated:

AWFUL BRITISH DISASTER.

It was yelled by the newsboys as shoppers in Piccadilly rushed to get the latest on the war. The crowd soon advanced to the War Office to see if their love ones were on the dreaded list.

In 1899, a squadron of a hundred colonials under the command of Captain C. Cox proceeded to England to take part in the annual military tournament at Islington, and for extra training at Aldershot, but when war broke out, they proceeded to Cape Town instead. On arriving they were received with enthusiasm by the locals.

The squadron was formed in 1883 first, as The Light Horse, but in 1885, after they had returned from the Sudan, was renamed the Lancers as a complement to the 5th Royal Irish Lancers. The New South Wales Lancers were the first troops from the Australian continent to go to the war front. It was attached to General French's command and were employed on patrol duty in the Colesberg District. They were involved in some minor skirmishes, but on 6th December, joined forces under Major Lee and were present on 8th December at the capture of the town of Arundel.

The century was drawing to a close when the New South Wales Lancers went into action at a small village called Sunnyside near the town of Belmont. The battle continued on and was still raging on the first day of the new century. Colonel T.D. Pilcher, an Imperial Officer, led an attack on a Laager. The Lancers were joined by a force consisting of two hundred Mounted Infantrymen from Queensland, a hundred Canadian infantrymen and forty British regulars, mounted infantry and artillery support.

The first casualties of the conflict in South Africa came when five Queenslanders on scout duties were ambushed when they rode into a Boer camp. At Sunnyside, two riders from Queensland mounted infantry, Lieutenant Alfred Adie Number 450 of A Company and Private Victor Jones Number 219 of B Company, were badly wounded. They were taken back to camp.

Matthew, who happened to be attached to the contingent, had the sad duty to report back to his office in Cape Town and the news was relayed back to Sydney that Private Jones had become the first member of an Australian contingent to be killed on duty in South Africa.

Colonel Pilcher repeated raid after raid, attacking the Boer positions, sending the Canadians and Queenslanders straight into the Laager surprising the enemy. Another young Queenslander, Private David McLeod Number

91, was killed before the artillery was brought into the battle bringing the fight to an end. Forty one Boers were captured and taken prisoner.

There was jubilation and sorrow as the troops arrived back at the barracks. The *London Press* described the victory as strategic and the colonial troops were magnificent.

The cartoonists back in Australia had a field day when it was made obvious that the Australian troop's superior fitness was evident when the British uniforms would not fit the colonials.

Lord Roberts arrived in mid January and immediately took control and went about correcting the mistakes of General Buller and Lt. General Methuen. The second contingents from Australia and New Zealand arrived in February, so he decided to convert the infantry Battalions into Mounted infantry.

New Zealand shows her patriotism

His Excellency the Governor, the Earl of Ranfurly, GCMG, informed the Prime Minister, Richard Sneddon that he has received a telegram from the Secretary of State for the Colonies to the effect that her Majesty the Queen, desires to thank the people of New Zealand for the striking manifestation of loyalty and patriotism in their voluntary offer to send troops to co-operate with Her Majesty's Imperial forces in maintaining her position and the rights of British subjects in South Africa. She wishes the troops God-speed and a safe return.

Intense enthusiasm in Wellington.

A 'Red-letter day' in the annals of Wellington will be Saturday, 21st October, 1899.

The native-born had no event in his memory which compared with the enthusiasm displayed by the citizens towards the sons of the colony who volunteered to risk life and fortune in South Africa in the interest of the Empire. Townsfolk and visitors assembled in thousands along the whole front of Jervois-Quay. Upon the southern portion of the street a platform had been erected for the accommodation of His Excellency the Governor and party, and the speakers who were to take part in the official ceremony. The whole length of footpath and roadway along Lambton-Quay was crowded by 2:30 pm.

The youngest of the colonies had the honour of being the first able to telegraph to the Motherland, that our contingent has this day sailed for the Cape! New Zealanders realised the sentiment expressed by the late Vincent Pyke, in his well-know song, *"The Old Flag"* composed in Dunedin in 1885---

>Three crosses in the Union,
>Three crosses in the Jack---
>And we'll add to it now the cross of the South,
>And stand by it back to back,
>Though other skies above shine,
>When danger's tempest lowers,
>We'll show the world that Britain's cause
>And Britain's foes are ours!

On October 21st 1899, the first contingent of two hundred and fourteen troopers from the New Zealand Mounted Rifles departed Wellington on SS Wairewa for South Africa.

On 21st of December, 1899, Private George Bradford was the first New Zealand soldier to lose his life.

January 1901, William James Hardham from Wellington, won the Victorian Cross at a place called Naawpoort when he rode to the rescue of a fellow Mounted rifleman whose horse had been shot from under him and had been injured as he fell to the ground. While a group of Boer marksman were trying to cut him down, Hardham lifted the injured trooper onto his saddle and ran to the safety of a rock outcrop, pulling his horse behind him.

At dawn on 16th January, Lancers from the Australian Light Horse, commanded by Lieutenant W Dowling, set out to reconnoitre the Boer positions at Slingersfontein. They rode into a trap and, with between sixty and a hundred Boers in pursuit, it was every man for himself. However they were trapped by a wire fence. Six troopers escaped, one was killed and fourteen captured and taken prisoner. When the news got back to camp, the Australian troops wanted to go and rescue their mates but they waited till first light to mount an ambush. When they arrived on the scene, the vultures were feasting on the two dead horses, and the dead body of Sergeant Major Griffith of the Australian Light Horse lay close by. Corporal Kilpatrick of the New South Wales Lancers, a teacher from Leichhardt Superior School in Sydney, whose wounds had been roughly bandaged by the Boers, died and they buried him where he lay.

Matthew reported back to his paper in Sydney, *"The Australian Solders were the finest solders in the Empire."*

He went on to say:

> *"The campaign did not need soldiers in fine red tunics but boys who can ride and shoot and blend into the African bush. The South African campaign needed cavalry. The Boers were fighting a different battle of hit and run and the British soldiers on foot were getting slaughtered. The days of a gentlemen's war were over. With their modern rifles, the enemy could hide unnoticed in the kopjes then, before the British troops had time to spot them, they would be off. There was a great need for more Colonial troops with riding experience."*

The London papers slashed some of the references he had made regarding the scandalous ineptitude of the British Generals and the cavalry equipment that did not suit the horses sent. The list went on. Matthew, who was writing for the *Bulletin* in Sydney, submitted articles to the London press but his features on the war soon made it into other capitals throughout the Empire. This immediately caused other members of the Empire to raise troops. Canada pledged 1,000 experienced rough riders, men who lived life in the Canadian back country.

The day it was published in Sydney, the NSW Government established a committee tasked to raise money from public donations. It quickly raised

£30,000, thanks to donations from S. McCaughey, W.R. Hall, and S. Hordern and it also received a generous donation of five hundred horses.

The State Government of New South Wales decided to form a Contingent of Bushman who were experienced riders and good shots, men from the bush, rough riders and drovers who could handle a gun.

Chapter 56

The Carcoar Railway station 1ˢᵗ February,1900

John and his mates dressed in their khaki jackets and Bedford cord pants, slouch hats with red puggaree hat bands and Cossack boots marched from the Carcoar Town Court House. There were four boys going off to war that day. What a glorious scene! The town Brass Band marched with them and the school children lined up across the bridge, along with the town's people, waving Union Jack flags and banners. They were meeting the morning train to take them to Sydney. It became the Lachlan Valley troop train that started in Cowra, picking up the troops on the way. Some of the boys were in their finery but the rest were in mufti. They were to be issued their uniforms when they arrived at Victoria Barracks.

The band was playing *"When Johnny Comes Marching Home Again"* as they crossed the bridge near Stokes's hotel.

Young Ellen was there with her brothers and sisters, waving and cheering along with the rest of her school friends as the boys marched past the crowd that followed them up the hill to the station. The train pulled into the platform with a loud bang and whistle, blowing steam with smoke billowing out of the engine. It was already half full of families and friends, all going to Sydney to see their boys off.

Mr Waddell, the local member was there to wish them well and a safe return home to their loved ones, and to "do your best for Queen and Country."

John's mother and his half brothers and sisters were there to say goodbye and Jane Layburn broke down and started to weep as she thrust a brown package into John's arms and said, "Son, something to eat on the way to Sydney. We will be praying for your safe return."

John held her in his arms and said, "Don't cry Mum. I will be all right. We will stick together and look after each other."

Igg's, Henry Fox's and Ernest's parents were there also saying good bye. As the train pulled out of the station, the band played *"Rule Britannia"* and the crowd drifted back down the hill. Ellen had walked to the end of the platform and was crying her eyes out, saying, "Come back, Johnny. Come back."

Jane Layburn waited for Freddie in his wheel chair to catch up. Young Ellen caught up with them and said, "I will help you, Mrs Layburn."

"Why, thank you Ellen," said Mrs Layburn.

Then in a fit of emotion, Ellen said, "Mrs Layburn. I waved and waved but he did not see me."

Then she started to cry again. Ellen had been coming around to Stokes Lane to the Layburns' place for some time now ever since Johnny had saved the day and won the football match. Jane was not worried as she knew the crush Ellen had on her son Johnny would pass as the young girl met other good, young Catholic boys. Ellen kept crying but as she was only thirteen, Mrs Layburn took her in her arms, consoled her and said, "Come around and have a cup of tea with me, Ellen. A strong cup of tea will make things better."

So they pushed Freddie back down the hill and turned into Stokes Lane for home. As it was Saturday there was no school. Jane and young Ellen, sobbing her eyes out, sat at the kitchen table. When Ellen recovered, she told Jane what she was going to do after she finished school.

She said, "I want to be a nurse Mrs Layburn and help our troops in South Africa."

Jane replied, "That's very commendable Ellen, but how long do you think this conflict will last?"

"I don't know, Mrs Layburn. The Matron at the hospital has said I can start training as a nurse as soon as I leave school."

The troop train was packed, picking up recruits along the way and by the time the train came down the mountain and pulled into the siding at Saint Mary's, there were troops everywhere. Finally, it pulled into Central Railway Station in the "big smoke," and as they lined up outside, there was silence then a few moans as they were told that they had to march to Victoria Barracks, to have uniforms issued to those who did not have them. Then they were back on the road again for the march to Randwick race track.

When they arrived it was a sea of tents. They were marched in single file to a shed where they were all issued identification numbers.

John Layburn, No. 147 Lance Corporal/Sergeant, C squadron;

Ernest Howarth, No. 373 Trooper, D Squadron'

Ignatius Loyola Smith, No. 520 Trooper (You can understand why they called him Iggie), D Squadron; and

John Fox No. 504 Private C, Squadron.

Iggie Smith asked to be placed in the same Squadron as Johnny Layburn but he was quickly told by those who were in command exactly who was running the show.

The men were to have their photos taken in one of the pavilions. They were given twenty-four hours leave and told in no uncertain terms to stay away from Kings Cross. The four lads from Carcoar teamed up with boys from the Blayney and Bathurst area and as it had been a long day, someone suggested they go out on the town but there were no takers. They were literally exhausted. Some had been up since four am and after the train trip, then the march from the railway station, most of the boys flopped on to stretchers and were soon fast asleep.

Next morning there was a bugle call at six am, so the men made their way to the mess tent where they all assembled and were given orders from Lt. Colonel Airey. He gave the men the *departure date, 28th February on the transport ships, "The Atlantian" and the* "Maplemore." The troops were finally given their horses and they moved off.

It was reported in the Bulletin

Reluctant Heroes

"NEW SOUTH WALES CITIZENS' BUSHMEN"

The New South Wales Contingent of Citizen's Bushmen was raised in the first instance by public subscription, hence the name. The object was to enrol a regiment of countrymen acquainted with the vicissitudes of bush life, good shots, good riders, and of sound physique. Such a class of men, as would be fitted to cope with the enemy, according to the matters of the latter. Preference therefore, was given to men who had previously served in South Africa, and especially to those who had experience in Country work, management with horses and bush travelling.

The Quarter Master then read out a long list of who was in the Citizens Bushman from the Lieutenant Col right down to the number of horses and what they were taking.

"God," Iggie whispered to John. "It's a wonder they don't tell us how many pairs of socks and longjohns were taking."

The four lads from Carcoar were talking about the payment and Ernie said "Gee, fellas, five bob a day, that's not going to go far."

Then Iggie piped in, "Don't forget we are now on full board, with clothes supplied and we are off to see the world."

John Joseph, being the wisest of the lot, said, "Before you get carried away with this great adventure that we are about to embark on, some of us may not return and as far as food is concerned, one of the travellers staying at Stokes Hotel said that in the Sudan campaign it was not all steak and fancy food." He went on to say, "We'll be lucky if we get bully beef and hard tack."

There was silence for a minute, then Johnny Fox chimed in with his jovial manner.

"Well, I don't care. I'm looking forward to going to South Africa. We might bump into some lions," he said.

They all laughed and went off to have a shower, set out their uniforms, polish their boots and turned in for the night. Tomorrow was going to be a big day. They settled into the pub close to the racetrack on their last night in Sydney before they set off the next day to fight the Boers. It was packed to the rafters but they found a spot out the back and started to talk about families. They had known each other since school days although Iggie was a 'Proddie' and went to the local school. The other boys were Catholics and went to the Catholic School.

"Foxie how long have you lived in Carcoar?" asked John Layburn.

"Me folks lived in Sydney before we moved to Carcoar," said Johnny. "Dad got a job on a sheep station near Orange but we decided to stay in Carcoar."

John Layburn continued. "What about you, Ernest?"

Ernie pondered for moment then said, "My family have lived here forever. Charles, me dad and his dad Thomas came out as a convict, they called him Long Tom. He came out on the Waterloo in '29, sent out for life for stealing his own cow. Can you believe that? Never met the old fella but dad said he was a gentleman."

John chimed in. "How could you be sent out as a convict for stealing your own property."

"Well if you didn't have legal representation back then, you just copped it sweet, replied Ernie." [7]

Ernie said, "What about you, John? My mum said your old man was a bit of all right, a real dapper especially with his hat."

John sat there for a moment and said, "God, me mum is still finding out things about me dad and he has been gone for twelve years now. We still get letters from the old country. I can't see what all the fuss is about. He is dead you can't send a dead man to prison."

They all laughed and drank another round.

The next day, the New South Wales Bushmen marched down to the Sydney wharfs. The streets were packed just like when the last contingent left, back in the closing days of the last century. Down George Street, the flags were flying and the crowds were cheering. Every vantage point was taken up and there was even cheering from the tops of shop roofs and

---

[7] Thomas Howarth: See page 379

balconies. As the parade passed down Pitt St. there were magnificent banners across from the New York building in big letters which read, *"America salutes the Brave Bushmen of Australia."* Another banner read *"Good Luck."*

The boys from the bush looked magnificent in their khaki uniforms with the feathers in their hats flying high. The Sydney police bands was playing and it was a sight to see. It was chaotic. Trams were held up and an estimated crowd of 300,000 people was there to cheer the boys off. (Later in the afternoon papers, it was reported the crowd number of nearly 300,000 was pretty accurate, as every man, women and child from far and wide, had flocked to Sydney to see the boys off.)

There was a lot to do, getting the horses on board and settled, as well as all the equipment. However, the two ships sailed on time on 28th February. Down the harbour, small sailing ships were there to cheer them on their way. It was a beautiful summer's morning and the harbour shimmered with a gleam and a sparkle. Every vantage point was taken up on the headlands with people cheering and waving flags.

The ships called into Albany, on the Western Australian coast, to pick up more troops. It was an easy passage to the Cape. Crossing the Indian Ocean, the sea was calmer than usual, and at one stage they would have been stationary, except for the auxiliary coal burners to fire up the huge Lister motors. They arrived in South Africa on 2nd April, for a brief stop at Durban and then sailed north to the port of Beira, in Portuguese East Africa.

Chapter 57

When they disembarked, they found they had arrived in the middle of a hot and sticky season. It was the wet tropics. Their heavy uniforms stuck to them and perspiration poured out of them. (The Colonial army top brass however had advised the British that the men needed light uniforms to cope with the harsh humidity.)

Then there were the insects. Igge remarked to John, "Bloody Mozzies! You would think we were back home."

Their orders were to proceed to Bulawayo via Marandellas and then onto Rhodesia. The troops made their way through malaria-infested country. John had teamed up with a fellow from Lagoon near Bathurst, Freddy McSpedden who was in D Squadron.

"Wild animals, John,: said Freddy. "Do you think we will see any?"

John replied, "I don't know Freddy. I think with all the noise we're making, they would be miles away."

Although next morning John saw some strange foot prints on the ground, he let it pass.

The boys were excited and keen to impress. Their aim was to join up with Sir Fredric Carrington and protect Rhodesia from the possibility of a Boer and native attack.

They were offered wagons but the men decided to walk. After six weeks at sea, the idea of fresh air was just what they needed. They were to pull out in the morning. The men quickly formed into their Squadrons and got some shelter as it started to pour. The rain came down in buckets but the cooks had a fire going. Bully beef, biscuits and weak tea were on offer.

As they passed through Portuguese Africa, some of the horses dropped and it was soon realised that they had died from the Tsetse Fly. The terrain soon changed to open plains and the weather became milder. After they had gone a few days, they noticed the countryside was similar to their home in country New South Wales.

Then John saw the man in the black bowler hat and strode over to him.

"Mr Grieves, what are you doing here?" John asked.

Matthew turned around and with a smile on his face said, "Well! I never! John Layburn. I read where the boys from Carcoar had enlisted. I'd like to write a story on you blokes, about when you beat the Boers. You are off to Rhodesia, I hear."

So much for intelligence! The press usually knew before the troops. Although John's mates were in three different Squadrons, it was not that hard to keep in touch. At first it was easy going, only 289 miles to Bulawayo and the bravado of the boys from the bush reckoned they could march it. It was finally decided by their Commanding Officer, that his men would walk with their horses. Most of the troops walked. John walked 250 miles but rode the last thirty nine miles. At first the going was tough, through hot and steamy jungles. There were few roads and at times they had to hack their way as they travelled through some primitive country, finally reaching their goal at Bulawayo.

Matthew was on his way to Mafeking. It had been under siege for seven and a half months. It was important that the British hold the town as it was a strategic rail link to the northern town of Bulawayo, near the border of Bechuanaland. It was an important win when the siege ended as it had tied up 8,000 Boer fighters for the duration. Heroic tales were told of the citizens and their struggle.

Lady Sarah Wilson had been held hostage by the enemy, but in the dead of night when the moon was at its lowest, she escaped from an outlying homestead into the town. The messages she had tried to get to Colonel Baden-Powell when all other avenues had been exhausted finally were sent by carrier pigeons. Lady Sarah was the 11th child of John Winston Spencer Churchill. She was the first war correspondence to cover the siege of Mafeking for the Daily Mail in the UK Colonel Baden- Powell pleaded with her to leave the siege city for her safety She set out with her maid to cross hostile enemy territory they were finally captured by the enemy and were returned to Mafeking and exchanged for a horse thief.

Relief came from Col. Mahon's 1,000 strong troops who had marched 250 miles in less than a fortnight, to meet up with Col. Herbert Plumber and his troops. He reported that the breaking of the siege of Mafeking had been an important faze of the war. When the news reached the Capitals of the Empire, the headlines called:

MAFEKING RELIEVED

People went wild in the streets and public holidays were declared.

After the dust had cleared around Mafeking there was much to do as the Boer army that had held the town had ripped up the rail line on both sides. The British engineers re-laid the track that allowed the trains to run again and bring up much needed supplies to the people of Mafeking.

The summer that year in South Africa was hot and very dry. An outbreak of Typhoid Fever, also called Enteric Fever, was endemic and British soldiers were dropping like flies. There was also chaos as General Sir John French's troops lost 460 horses. Fifty died, fourteen strayed and the remainder were unfit to proceed. On the 27th February, Piet Cronje had raised the white flag to Lt Roberts at the battle of Pieter's Hill.

The Bushmen had at first been given subordinate roles, as the British Generals did not believe the Colonials would be able to take up positions at the front. This approach changed as time and time again, as the Colonials constantly challenged their superiors' orders. The Queenslanders were given the task of supporting the Fusiliers but as the British troops moved forward, the Colonials were up there with them. The Australian troops soon got the reputation of being fierce fighting outfits.

The three New South Wales Bushmen Squadrons set out for Rhodesia and John's squadron were the first to get there. They were given new orders to move onto Mafeking. The town had been held under siege for some months but had finally been relieved. John met up with Igge. Both their horses were lame and they had to arrange remounts. There were major troubles with the horses that had been overlooked by the Army officials. The dreaded Tsetse Fly had caused horses to drop in their hundreds.

The Bushmen arrived after the Boers had been captured but most had just melted into the bush. There had been some sniper attacks as they rode into town and Jack Fox had copped a bullet in the leg. He was going back to the Army Hospital at Johannesburg by train with other wounded. He protested, but his superior officer said it was for the best, so the boys got him drunk and escorted him to the platform on crutches and with a very sore head. The trains were running down to the Cape now that the siege was over. Jack boarded along with other wounded and, although his leg was hurting, his head was his main trouble after the heavy night's drinking. He drifted into sleep, but when he woke, he was shaking and in a cold sweat. The infection around his wounded leg was inflamed but the orderly in his carriage could do nothing to relieve the pain and Jack, at this stage, was drifting in and out of consciousness. When the train pulled into the station at Johannesburg, the wounded disembarked and Jack was carried off on a stretcher. He was taken to the Number Six General Hospital. When he finally came out of his delirious state and opened his eyes, he thought he was in heaven or back home in Carcoar.

"Nurse! Don't I know you?" he said.

She replied, "Look soldier, just lie still and get better and we will have you back on your feet and with your mates in no time."

"What is your name, Nurse?" He was now certain he knew her.

As she reached the tent opening, she turned and said, "Nursing Sister Emily Hoadley, soldier and yes, I knew your brother, the rat who went off to marry that girl in Bathurst."

It all came back to him. She had been engaged to his older brother when he left town to be with that girl Betty from Bathurst.

After that, Jack's injuries improved and he was sent to the Army barracks in Cape Town to await passage to Sydney.

The town of Mafeking went berserk as the train brought fresh supplies from the South. The grog shops had reopened and the boys got drunk. They had twenty four hours leave, but couldn't go anywhere so they drank the bars dry.

Chapter 58

Back home in the state of New South Wales, the citizens had voted to form the new Federation of Australia along with the other States. The Bushmen were trying to get used to being called Australians as most of them had come from inland country towns in NSW and thought they would not live anywhere else. They believed they would be New South Welshmen forever.

John was starting to get homesick. When one of the lads started to sing one of the new songs, *"Waltzing Matilda"*, it started to bring tears to his eyes. As the boys moved away from the centre of town and down a back lane in the seedier side, they entered a grog shop. It was the sort of place his mother and his priest back home, Father Kelly had warned him about.

The sermon was ringing in his ears.

"Me boys, soon to venture to fight for our country in South Africa, the good Church believes we should have nothing to do with this war but if you must go, be careful of the hidden traps, not only Johnny Boer, but there are many other traps, the dreaded drink and most of all, loose women, who will want to do terrible things to you."

John had stopped and was in a trance when Igge shouted, "Hurry up John, you look like you are in a dream."

As bold as brass they walked up to the bar and then some black girls started to talk to them about having a good time. After a couple of beers, the boys high-tailed it out of there and returned to the barracks with their virginity still intact.

Early next morning they were on their way again to places with unusual names like Rustenberg, Koster's River and Zee-rust. The troops started to complain they were ready for action, but some of the men were ill from bad water and monotonous food, mostly bully beef and biscuits.

The weather was hard to fathom. The days were stinking hot but the nights were bitterly cold and they had been issued with only one blanket each. It looked like it could snow and they had gone from searing oppressive heat to freezing cold. None of the lads had seen any real sign of Johnny Boer yet, except for the skirmish on their way into town when the enemy shot and ran. All you would see was the flash from their guns. The Captain told them to be on the lookout because the enemy was known to be in the area. They reached Zee-rust and the most of the squadrons slept out under tarps, but D squadron was lucky as they were garrisoned in town

On 7th July, A squadron under General Baden Powell were involved in the relief of Rustenberg.

John started relating the experience to a crowd of his friends.

"We raced through the town and then it happened. The Boers attacked and charged us. There were hundreds of them, all firing at us, they were stationed on a slight rise with the sun at their backs and we could hardly see them. Our men were firing back at them, but as the sun disappeared below the horizon, all went quiet as they withdrew their fire. As we lit camp fires, it started to rain and a wind came up. It was bitterly cold, and reminded me of back home. We dug trenches and bunked down for the night, waiting for the Boers to attack again.

"As the sun rose in the east, we had the advantage of having the sun at our back. There was a fierce battle, and they were shelling us. I saw one of our blokes cop it in the shoulder. It did not look good, so the orderly called out, "Stretcher bearers!"

(Taken from the book *"History of the war in South Africa"*
James H Birch, Jnr.)

A Boer, who was only a lad, described to one of the war correspondent, the magnificent courage displayed by the Australians when they attempted to rescue the Worcester's Regiment which had fallen into a Boer trap. The fight took place near Colesberg during the struggle round the town.

"What do you think of Australians as fighters?" said the correspondent.

Carrying one arm in a sling, with a bandage around his neck to hide a bullet wound, the Boer said simply, "The Australians can fight. They wounded me and they killed my father."

"Tell me, comrade, of the Australians who fell. They were my countrymen."

"It was a cruel fight," said the young Boer. "We had ambushed a lot of the British troops. They could neither advance nor retreat. We had them penned in like sheep and our Field Cornet, Van Leyden, was beseeching them to throw down their rifles to save being slaughtered, for they had no chance. Just then we saw about a hundred Australians come bounding over the rocks in the gully behind us. They were making such a racket that at first, we thought there were about 1,000 troops coming at us. There were two great men in front urging them on. We turned and gave them a volley, but it did not stop them. They rushed us everywhere, firing as they came, not wildly, but as men who know how to use rifles, with a quick sharp, upward jerk of the shoulder, the rapid sight, and then the shot.

"They knocked over a lot of our men, but we had a splendid position. They had to expose themselves to get at us and we shot them as they came rushing to the rescue of the English. It was splendid, but madness. On they came, but we had cover, as we lay behind boulders, and our rifles snapped and snapped again, at pistol range. Amazingly, we did not stop those wild men until they charged right into the little basin which was fringed around all the edges by rocks covered with bushes. Our men lay there thick as locusts and the Australians were fairly trapped. They were far worse off than the English who were up higher in the ravine.

"Our Field Cornet gave the orders to cease firing, and called on them to throw down their rifles or die. Then one of the big officers, a great, rough looking man, with a voice like a bull, roared out, "Forward Australians! No surrender." Those were the last words he ever uttered, for a man on my right put a bullet clean between his eyes, and he fell forward dead. We found later, that his name was Major Eddy, of the Victorian Rifles.

"He was as brave as a lion, but a Mauser bullet will stop the bravest. His men dashed at the rocks like wolves. It was awful to see them. They smashed at our heads with clubbed rifles or thrust their rifles up against us through the rocks and fired. One after another, their leaders fell. The second big man went down early but he was not killed. He was shot through the groin but not dangerously. His name was Captain Mc'Inerney. There was another one, a little man named Lieutenant Roberts, he was shot through the heart. Some of the others, I forget. The men would not throw down their rifles, they fought like furies. One man I saw, climbed right onto the rocky ledge where big Jan Aldrich was stationed, but just as he got there, a bullet took him, and he staggered and dropped his rifle. Big Jan jumped forward to catch him before he toppled off the ledge, but the Australian struck Jan in the mouth with a clenched fist and fell over into the ravine and died.

"We killed and wounded an awful lot of them, but some got away; they were tough and fought their way out. I saw a long row of their dead and wounded laid out on the slope of the farm house that evening. They were all young men, fine big fellows. I could have cried to look at them lying so cold and still."

He continued, "We lost some fine men also."

Chapter 59

Although John Layburn was a shy non talker, when he had a couple of beers in him, he could talk the legs of an iron kettle. One evening, he was telling his mates in the canteen about one episode.

"Lieutenant Colonel Airey, our Commander, gave us our orders and we were on our way again to Koster's River. The Bushmen had been given permission to try out a new form of warfare (they would run the enemy down and take them off their horses). On the 22nd July, B, C and D squadrons took part in several small skirmishes. On one occasion, we had the enemy pinned down behind a kopje. They were masters at camouflage, one minute they were there, then they were gone. Suddenly, for no apparent reason they stopped firing at us. Our Lieutenant thought they had run out of ammo, so the order was given to rush them. We yelled out and shouted, sounding like a yard of wild animals but when we got there, they had vanished into thin air.

"We moved on and took Rustenburg on 23rd of July. There were twenty three of us at a place called Elephant's Neck. Who in God's name would call a place Elephants Neck? However, we were there. We were under Lieutenant Jell.

"Sadly we lost another good man, Joseph Russell Number 149 and then finally we were on our way again to a place called Eland River. We did not know it then, but that name would go down in history."

Chapter 60

The Siege of Eland River

John's squadron was keen to be on its way, as since they had arrived in South Africa, they had not had any real opportunity to test their skills. They were given orders to relieve the guard at the Eland River supply dump. It was late in the month of July 1900, the weather was cold and the sky was crystal clear with not a murmur of wind. John said to his riding companion, "There looks like being a frost in the morning, I reckon."

As the column of soldiers rode along, there was something in the air and they knew the Boers were close as they had quickly come to recognise the signs. The birds and wildlife had gone quiet. John's squadron came to an opening. As they silently moved along through a valley, he did not like the situation as it rose up with bushes on both sides. It was late in the afternoon and in the distance, they could see the tents through the trees.

"I don't like it, John," Freddy McSpedden said in a quiet voice.

Suddenly the Boers appeared out of nowhere, firing at will. Most of our squad were dreaming of home 5,000 miles away, amongst gum trees, blue skies, inland rivers and sandy billabongs. They reached the safety of the supply dump which was in a natural amphitheatre. The 505 Bushmen and others, Commonwealth irregulars, had been sent by Lt. General Sir Frederic Carrington to defend the vital supply dump.

Quickly, the Commander gave the order, "Squadrons from NSW to the right. Queenslanders to the left."

There were bugle calls, so they quickly dismounted or they would have been shot off. They were given orders to dig in. It was hard going as the ground was mostly slaty chips. They were lying there protected by a mound of earth and shells were landing all around them as the enemy was now firing cannons. Thankfully, they were dropping short. They were firing twelve pounders and Pom-Poms which were quick firing guns and very effective against the old carbines of the Australians.

Sandy Watson, who was a big bloke, said out of the blue, "Gee, fellows, I hope we don't run into any lions."

Anderson, who was in charge of the horses, came up to take their mounts and said as he led the horses away, said, "They wouldn't eat us Aussies. We're too tough. They only eat Limeys."

Just then a shell dropped in front of their bunker spraying dirt in their faces.

"That was bloody close," remarked Sandy.

Then more shells landed, no more than twenty feet away. They were surrounded by the Boers who had dropped back to a safe distance. Then, as quickly as it started, it went quiet. As they lay in our protected trench they were able to get some tin bully beef and biscuits and some hot tea. As the moon rose in the distance, they could hear some big cats roar. John looked at Sandy, then just smiled and said, "Don't worry, mate, they're miles away."

The full force of the Boer assault came at daybreak on 4th August, when they were attacked by the Commandant De-La-Rey's forces.

It was hard to tell how many there were in the Boer force, but they estimated a figure totalling around 6,000 highly motivated and trained in hit and run combat. They were under the command of Commander General Piet Cronje who was in charge of the Western Transvaal. The command was to patrol the border between Bechuanaland and Kimberley near Mafeking, which was about 200 miles to the north of Kimberley. They would send out raiding parties to disrupt the Railway.

General Koos De La Rey, on 12th October 1899 had already been responsible for other raids on the Commonwealth forces. He had captured an armoured troop carrier at a place called Kraaipan. He now found himself in charge at Eland River.

Koos De La Rey was initially against going to war with the British Forces. He was born in 1847 at a place called Weinberg and he had five brothers and sisters. His first taste of war was in 1865 against the Basuto and again in the first Boer War in 1880, so he was a seasoned campaigner. His scouts had established that the enemy forces were Bushmen from the new country of Australia, mainly from New South Wales and Queensland and a force from Rhodesia, so he told his men not to take the enemy lightly.

The Boers had tricked the British forces time and time again, but these Colonials were a different matter and they were quickly gaining a reputation for being tough fighters. The Bushmen had dug in and were ready to fight. The Boers were relentless in the bombardment of shells. John could not believe his eyes as one of the A Company troopers, Tommy Harris, crawled out towards the enemy line towards a fellow trooper who had been shot. His horse was dead and its entrails were hanging out of its side. The soldier, who was injured was lying beside it under cover. As Tommy crawled closer, the boys opened fire to give him cover as the Boers were now concentrating their fire on the injured soldier. Tommy reached him picked him up and ran back to our lines. A great cheer went up as he reached safety, but he collapsed and there was blood on his uniform. At first we thought it was from his mate, but we later found it was from a Boer bullet. Tommy was recommended for a Victoria Cross.

John and his platoon had started to build half moon stone walls on two sides of the main camp. They put empty biscuit boxes to good use, stacking them in rows to form a wall, filling them with stones and earth. At sunset, when the firing had ceased, some of the men set about packing dirt onto the outside of the wall. It was positioned on a Kopje and commanded by Capt. Butters with eighty men. The hospital was inside the camp and we had three ambulances. The horses, oxen and mules were on an exposed slope and suffered heavy losses as we had no way of protecting them and hundreds were killed. We were outnumbered eight to one and the Boer then started firing night and day. Word had come through that 1,000 Bushmen were on their way to help fight off the Boers and we could see them in the distance. They were under the command of Sir Frederick Canning but the Boer superior fire power stopped them in their tracks and they had to retreat to safety. They suffered seventeen casualties but no fatalities.

On 8th August there was a lull in the firing and from the enemy position came a runner with a white flag and a message from the Boer.

General De La Rey summoned the Commander Colonel Hore and demanded he surrender. The general wanted them to raise the white flag. His terms were very reasonable; Officers would be allowed to retain the firearms and to march the men to the nearest British post. The men, especially the Bushmen said, "No!" They wanted to fight on and they shouted that they would not raise the Coward's Flag. The surrender terms were refused. The Australian Imperial Commander in Charge, Colonel Hore sent his reply and it read:

"To General De La Ray. Even if I wish to surrender and I don't, I am commanding Australian troops, who would cut my throat if I accepted your terms."

There were three cheers from the Bushmen and when someone yelled out, "Forward! Bushmen never surrender," there was more cheering.

One of the Boer solders wrote home to say that, "for the first time in this war we are fighting men who have copied our tactics against us. They are volunteer troops from Australia and though small in number, we could not take their positions. At night they scout our outposts and kill our sentries. They are far more dangerous than their British brothers."

The intensity of the Boer guns kept up until 9th August and then they retreated out of range and a strange lull and an eerie quiet came over the battlefield. The Bushmen were running out of ammo. John had only about a hundred rounds left.

They learnt that one of the boys from Orange, a town not far from Bathurst had been hit by shell fragments and was in a bad way. John was passing the hospital tent when he overheard the Surgeon, Captain Duke, tell trooper W. Hunt that he did not give James Duff, Number Thirty Four, much hope of surviving.

The guns were becoming a problem and he had repeatedly explained to his superior officer that the seven pound muzzle-loaded, screw guns mounted on a nine pounder gun carriage, kept jamming. Things were getting desperate and John thought, *How could we last the week out?* They were running out of food and other supplies. Then we heard cheering from the other side of the

Kopje. Lord Kitchener was seen approaching on 15th August with 10,000 men and he marched into the camp on 16th August.

General De La Ray's men were routed, so they dispersed and melted into the bush. Kitchener could not believe that we had held them off for so long. Some of the Bushmen had collected bomb fragments and were going to take them home and sell them for souvenirs.

Lord Kitchener had the troops assembled and said, "Gallant members of the Colonial troops from Australia and Rhodesia, in years to come, the last few days will be looked at as being a moment in history. I am proud of you, and I will be relaying a message back to your Prime minister, well done!"

There was a loud cheer and hats were thrown into the air, then Colonel Hore stepped forward and spoke of how proud he was of his men, but in a sombre voice, he went on to say, "We lost some good men at Eland's River, including Private James Duff Number 34, Sergeant Major James Mitchell Number 504 and Private James Walker No. 75.

He continued, "Let us pause for a moment with a minute's silence to reflect on our fallen comrades."

"Permission to speak, Sir?" said John.

"Yes, what is it, Trooper Layburn?"

"Well Sir, I have noticed how the English trenches are laid out in straight lines."

"Yes! Yes! So! What's the problem?"

"Well Sir, if they were laid out in a Zig-Zag pattern, any men in the trenches would be protected from artillery fire as they would be protected by the bends in the trench."

"Yes! Well, thank you my lad. I will take that suggestion and give it some thought."

The action at Eland's River won wide praise for the defenders. An assessment of the action by the Boer General J.C. Smuts is most significant and it was reported in the press in the Orange Free State.

Never, in the course of this war, did a besieged force endure worse suffering, but they stood their ground with magnificent courage. All honours to these heroes who in the hour of trial rose nobly to the occasion, and amid retreats.

When De La Rey was questioned later for the Johannesburg Paper he said, "Let me fight the British any day." But he admitted that there would be more encounters with the Colonials.

When they arrived back at Zee-rust they were greeted with cheers and members of the press. John noticed Matthew first by his black bowler hat. Matthew got John and his mates a drink and they gave him the story of the Siege of Eland's River. Matthew wrote it all down, how these boys from the bush, outnumbered eight to one, performed magnificently. That weekend, the Sydney papers had on their front pages that it was reported in the *London Times* that the battle of the Eland's River possibly changed the course of South African history. Forces from Rhodesia (198) and Australia comprising troops from Qld, Victoria and NSW (307) under the command of Lt. Col. H.D. Hore, kept the Boers at bay until reinforcements arrived. The papers promised to reveal more details the following week when a Sydney reporter, Mr Matthew Grieves, arrived in London.

The town of Carcoar was abuzz when the Sydney paper arrived in the town the next day proclaiming the story of the Siege of Eland's River.

Matthew had the opportunity to talk to one of the Boer prisoners who had been captured at the River.

The Boer, carrying his arm in a sling, described the Colonials as magnificent, courageous fighting men. He said, "Those buggers can fight you, no doubt about it. We had them surrounded. They could not get away, neither advance or retire. Our Commander gave them the chance to surrender when, out of the bush came this mad man shouting, "Forward Australia. No surrender." They were the last words he ever uttered as he was charging and firing, one of our fighters shot him in the head and he fell. He was mad, but brave."

Matthew thanked him for his recollection of the battle.

Chapter 61

Matthew returned to Cape Town, from where he was heading off to London. His mother, in her last letter stated that her health was failing and she did not think she would last much longer, so this was his last news bulletin he would be reporting on the war. His editor back in Sydney wanted him to continue from London. The boys from the Australian contingent got talking and drinking at the hotel near the railway station. Matthew was catching the late train back to the Cape. He took John aside and told him everything he knew.

"Mate, we are brothers. I wanted to tell you before, well we're half brothers," said Matthew.

Matthew realised that he might not get back to see Sydney again, so he explained to John that he had purchased land in Manly on the harbour. He was building a holiday house and he would leave the block of land to him. John was dumb struck and couldn't say anything but just sat there. Matthew went on to tell him about his father and how he could check the details with old John Fagan back home. Young Johnny just shrugged it off and said to Matthew that he never really knew his father.

John's Mother Jane was still bitter towards his father for denigrating the Catholic Church. He was buried in the unmarked Proddie section, of the Carcoar cemetery. His grave was falling into disrepair as no one was looking after it. His mother would not spend any money to do up the grave site, although she would visit the cemetery each Sunday to place flowers on her

Reluctant Heroes

beloved Michael's grave. John decided when he got home that he would get the stonemasons to make up a headstone for his father.

Next morning Squadrons B, C, and D rode south out of town as they were going to patrol the rail line to Kimberly. After setting up camp at Kimberly, the squad had a few days furlough and then they were off patrolling the main rail line. They found the Boer fighters were as elusive as usual. The Australians just never saw any sign of the enemy.

They came around a small hill and before them was a Boer homestead with smoke coming out of the chimney. John and three other Bushmen knocked on the door while the others kept guard front and back. The door opened and a young girl came outside. John could not believe what he was hearing as she spoke in perfect English, "Mother said, would you like to come in and have a cup of tea and cake?"

The four troopers entered through the front door which was fashioned out of reeds. The windows had no glass just hessian curtains and the floor was packed dirt. After a few minutes they had tea and cake and left.

The Sergeant drilled them for any information about the incident, but John said, "Nothing to report, Sarge."

"What were you doing in there?" cried out Sergeant Payne. The four just started to laugh and the Sergeant, weeks after the incident, still reckoned that they had been up to no good. The lads did not have the heart to tell him it was all innocent as there was no way he would believe they only had tea and cake. They all rode back to camp.

After that things got a bit slack but they never knew when Johnny Boer would strike next. John and Igge were standing around the camp fire and were about to relieve the sentries on guard duty about one mile from the main camp, when out of the night came seven Boer riders. The two Squadrons quickly formed into two lines of defence and they fired on the enemy but the Boer escaped into the night.

After that, the sentries were doubled and the rail gangs, mainly black labourers, would walk down the line checking for damage and to see if it had been tampered with. The afternoon train was running late. It was late in November, and the boys were heading back to Kimberly in a few days where they would take a few days rest. Johnny and Igge were on lookout duty on a Kopje where they had a good view of the rail line south and north. The sun was high in the sky, when Igge said, "John, did you see that?"

They both crouched low and cocked their rifles. Anderson, who was steadying their horses, moved out of view, then John said, "Look over there, Igge." On the other side of the low line of hills there were about thirty men on horseback, riding towards the Squadrons' Camps, which were about one mile north up the line. John quickly got onto the wire, and sent a message to base.

Igge said to Anderson, "They're coming closer."

The Captain told them to lay low and let them pass, as they were to try and hold a rear guard position. The Boer riders passed and the Bushmen could not believe that they had not been seen. Anderson had muffled the horses, to keep them quiet.

The main camp was ready for them and they heard the gunfire, but it was all over in minutes. They mounted up and were about to ride back to camp, when a Boer rider came riding through fast as a bullet. They commanded him to stop, but he kept going past. Igge fired a warning shot but the Boer rider kept right on going but threw his arms in the air as he had been hit.

They jumped on their horses and chased him, but he finally he stopped and fell to the ground. He was only a lad of about fifteen. He started to cry as he was in agony. Igge had got him in the leg, so they bandaged him as best they could and led him back to the main camp. The Squadron had captured all the opposition with no other casualties on their own side. The Boers had a few broken bones but no one died.

The Australians were slowly making their way down to Kimberly. The three Squadrons had split up and were patrolling different sections of the railway line.

They finally made it into Kimberly for Christmas and were granted one week's leave. Their Commanding Officer informed them that Jack Fox, had made it back to Sydney. He had written and was having a great time in the Army Hospital at Victoria Barracks. He finished off his letter saying he missed his mates and wished them a speedy and safe journey home.

The three Carcoar boys went on a drinking binge as the bars in the Diamond town were something they had only dreamed about. Every second place was a bar. The boys were in civvies because they could not drink in uniform. Finally, they went into the Diamond Nugget which was a bar on the wrong side of town. Igge wanted to go but John was a bit worried when they got past the front door as there were naked black women on the stage. They bumped into a few blokes from the Fifth Victorian Mounted Rifles and after a couple of beers, were on first name terms. One was a Veterinary Captain who was telling the boys the trouble they were having controlling the equine problems with the horses. The Victorian boys left and there was a loud noise from the entrance as a bunch of British soldiers turned up. John wanted to leave as they had been in this hole for what seemed like hours but he recognised one of the blokes from the Bengal Lancers, so it was back to the bar for a few more rounds. Then a few more boys from the Fusiliers arrived. The place was packed and they could hardly hear themself talk above the noise and the singing.

A Scotsman in a kilt got talking. He was Jock McTaggart from Aberdeen and was attached to the Second Fusiliers. He was telling the group how he, single handed, held off the enemy in a raid. He covered his fellow mates who had made a run for cover behind some rocks but when he started to run, he accidentally dropped his sporran. The rest of the group were firing volleys of shots as he made a quick retreat to the cover of the waddy when he suddenly remembered that he had a gold sovereign hidden in lining of his sporran. It was lying there on the ground and the Boers were firing at it.

"What happened next, Jock?" asked Igge.

"Well, my blood started tae boil. My fellow mates tried to hold me back but I just hightailed the thirty odd yards to my sporran. There was bullets flying through the air left and right, but I reached me sporran, so I picked it up and ran like hell."

One of the boys then said, "Did you make it back safely, Jock?"

"Dina be daft. I was riddled with bullets and died."

There was laughter all round. They all left the bar very jolly. So much for the desire of naked black flesh. Deep down, John and Ernie, when they had the chance, wanted to go back into the bar. The boys had made a pledge to not get killed and go to heaven without ever experiencing the mystery of the female flesh.

They were singing along holding each other up when a group of the lads entered the dingy, dirty street. As they walked down and turned the corner, it seemed to go very quiet all of a sudden then Lance Corporal Adam said, "Struth! Boys, we thought you were the police!"

Then everyone started to shout. There were women standing in the front doors and there were other troops loitering around. We spotted a group of our mates, so we asked them,

"What's up boys, what's going on Bertie?"

"Don't you blokes know nuffin'?" said Ernie. "These sheilas are pros and it's two bob for a quickie or three and six for a full strip."

Bertie and William had both the same surname of Thornton but both had John as their first name. It was confusing so they were called by their middle names.

Johnny walked up to one of the girls. *God, she was black*, he thought.

"Want to come in, Soldier?" one of the girls said. She was strutting around and her tits were hanging out of her dress. Johnny started to go red in the face.

"Not tonight, luv," he said.

"Come on luv, give you a good one. I'll be nice and gentle."

Poor John didn't know what to say. He wanted to go in, but he had been reading up on syphilis from the camp manual put out by the company medic. He just walked away, turning as he went saying, "Not tonight, luv."

The boys made it back to the Camp on their last night before leaving, still with their virginity intact.

When they arrived back in the camp, Igge was missing. The others reckoned he had decided to go back and taste some of that black flesh. They thought no more about it until the morning, when the news soon spread around the camp that Igge had been picked up by the Provos for being drunk and disorderly, but the main charge was disobeying an order. His mates were stunned. He was to be court-martialled that afternoon and he was allowed two of his mates to be in the court room, so John and Ernie attended.

Reluctant Heroes

The Military Court procedure was very strict and it was all over in a couple of minutes. Igge pleaded guilty and received a sentence of twenty eight days (confirmed by Lt. Col. Scott).

Iggie, who had enlisted with the boys from Carcoar, was a bit of a lad and he had written home to his mother on 17 May 1901.

> *Dear Mum,*
>
> *Can't complain about the food. Not up to your standard, but we are not starving. We were the first troops to be here, this place is called Pietersburg Transvaal. The British own the lot of South Africa now. This is a railway terminus. We got one Boer train here yesterday and blew up a big gun and lots of ammo. It exploded all night. I shouldn't tell you this, but I got the ink, pen and paper from the station before we blew it up.*
>
> *Love, your son,*
> *Igge.*
>
> *PS. I got into a bit of trouble, locked up for 28 days. You know me. You can't keep a good soldier down. It was the Carcoar connection, Jack, Ernie and that Fox's fault. And is me horse ok, and me dogs?*

Next morning on parade they were told their orders were to saddle up and be prepared to ride out at noon.

Most of the lads had signed up for twelve months and would be glad to get back to Sydney. The war had taken on a new phase as the Boer would not surrender or stand and fight, so the orders from High Command were to burn and starve the enemy out. The Bushmen went for days at a time without seeing anyone. Their orders were to burn fields of maize, wheat and oats.

The Boer women and children were taken prisoners and put into Concentration camps.

There had been reports of some of the more zealous troops taking delight and destroying property, smashing the homesteads and even on one occasion, burning a Church.

The months marched on and they knew they would be off home soon. The Carcoar boys had gained a reputation for sticking together and their Commander, Lt. Col Airey, let them go off leading a scout party. It was getting late in the afternoon and they didn't spot anything as they rode across the veldt. They entered a thickly wooded gully, and were following a worn track when, there in front of them lying on the ground was a Boer soldier with blood pouring out of his chest. John and Igge quickly dismounted and raced to his assistance. He was in a pretty bad way. John rested the Boer's head on his lap.

"God, Iggie, he's only a lad," said John and tried to give him some water from his canteen as they tried in vain to stop the flow of blood. The other troopers stood guard in case it was a trap, but the Boer was fading fast. He was mumbling something to John in Afrikaans, but John didn't understand what he was saying.

Then John said, "The battle is over mate," as he died in his arms.

The Bushmen gathered around, and it was decided to take the dead Boer back to the camp. They placed him on his horse and they rode back into camp.

They buried the Boer soldier and Lt Avery asked John to say a few words. He had become a bit of a poet since landing in South Africa, so they all gathered around the grave and John recited his verse.

THE DYING SOLDIER

The Soldier's Funeral.
The muffled drum rolled on the air,
Warriors with stately step were there.
On every arm was the black crepe bound,
Every carbine was turned to the ground.

Reluctant Heroes

> Solemn the sound of their measured tread,
> As silent and slow they followed the dead.
> The riderless horse was led in the rear,
> There were white plumes waving over the bier,
> Helmet and sword were laid on the pall,
> For it was a soldier's funeral.
> That soldier had stood on the battle-plain,
> Where every step was over the slain:
> But the brand and the ball had passed him by."

A letter by Jack Fox from Flank Fontispa, South Africa, 16th January 1901:

To the Editor of the Carcoar Chronicle.

Sir, I arrived at this place a few weeks ago and have been garrisoned here ever since, but we have now received word we are leaving on the 23rd for Brookhorst spruit. We are surrounded with Boers and they won't make an attack. There are about 4,000 of them and only 1,900 British (42 NSW Bushmen) so you will see they have had the dead wood on us. We have a fight every two or three weeks. There was a big fight here on the 29th November. We had 21 killed and 91 wounded, the Bashies (Author note - I assume he means the Bushmen) *were very lucky, not one wounded; the New Zealanders copped it heavily. Five officers killed, and several men wounded. They were too plucky. There were about 300 of them and they got within 300 yards of the Boers who opened fire on them and fairly paralysed them. Then the Boers cleared. There were 3,000 Boers, about the same as the British, but we had no cover so we could not get near the Kopjes. They were in possession and we could not shift them out. Botha sent us word that he was going to make an attack that night, but when morning came, there was not a Boer within miles of us. They had all cleared out. So much for that day!*

Reluctant Heroes

We went into the railway station with a convoy to Bronoospruit. All went well going in, but when we were within seven miles of the camp, we were charged by the Boers. There were about 300 and we had only 60 men all told, so we could see they would have the best of it. We out flanked them and spread over the veldt and started cutting at them. We were fighting for three hours and kept them at bay but some damn fool put up the white flag. We had lost one man and five were wounded, but there were twenty of us Bushmen and old, Pretorius, the Boer Commandant told us we fought like demons. I am glad to tell you that none of us put up the white flag. A West Riding man is blamed for it and I'm sorry to tell you that they took the convoy from us. There were £2,000 on board and a lot of rations, so the Boers will be able to have a good feed when they get home. I will give the name of the Bush Contingent that were killed, and wounded. Jim Finigan from Forbes was shot dead. Trooper Fagan was shot through the groin and died the day after. Sergeant Major Weir was shot three times through the face and once through the neck, so he had a narrow escape, but he is getting on very well. Corporal Davenport was shot through the two thighs; he is having a very bad time of it. I cannot find out the other men's names. We never heard how many Boers were killed, but I think there were about as many as on our side.

We went out and had a cut at them the next day and killed two of them. They did not take any of us prisoners. They took the officer, of West Riding a prisoner, but when they came to take Captain Thomas, our officer, he would not go. He told them that he was a doctor, and they could not take him, so he got off. I think we will have a lot of fighting next month. Kitchener is going to play the devil, after the 26th, so we can expect something.

Yours Truly, J.S. Fox. No. 504

(Author's note: Jack Fox received a score of twenty-seven for his shooting test and passed his riding test. John was invalided to Australia on 11th June 1901 after about fifteen months service. He was discharged on 26th June 1901.)

John was interrupted by gun fire. The lads scattered and the funeral came to an end, but some of the lads spotted two riders racing off over the hill. No one was injured, but the word soon got around that they would be on the move again. The Bushmen would be heading back to the Cape to return to Sydney. There was jubilation as the real war had subsided into a mopping up campaign. This form of warfare did not go down too well with the majority of the Australian troops and they were glad to get back to the Australian Bush and their loved ones.

A lot of the blokes were glad of the pay and some had arranged for it to be sent off to their loved ones at home. Most of them had no work to go back to and some of the men were thinking of signing up in the Australian Commonwealth Light Horse, when they arrived back in the Cape. They were to depart on the 9th May.

Chapter 62

The loyal citizens of the Cape had organised a send off for the fighting lads at the Town Hall. There were over five hundred boys in total from New Zealand, (who had been given the nickname, the "Rough Riders"), Canada and Australia. There was dancing and everyone had a good time as the dignitaries of the City were there and the Governor gave a speech. He gave thanks to them for repelling the dreaded Boer. He mentioned battles in places such as "Mafeking and Pieter's Hill and 'let us not forget the battle at Eland's River to name a few. The list goes on. The city thanks and salutes you and we wish you a safe journey back home to your loved ones and perhaps you might visit our proud land in a more peaceful time."

Then our Commander jumped up on the stage to thank the people of South Africa for their kind words. He then introduced Trooper George Essex Evens, who had written a poem called *"Eland's River."*

The boys had heard it a dozen times but waited till he had read the five verses.

As the Bushmen were leaving the next morning, their Commanding Officer got them back to their barracks all present and correct. They sailed off into the southern ocean en route to Sydney via Fremantle, Adelaide, Melbourne and finally to Sydney. As the ship came through the Sydney Heads, there was much jubilation from the troops on board as they were greeted by hundreds of small craft in the harbour. It was an emotional scene. It was 11th June 1901, they had been away for fifteen months and the boys were glad to be back on Australian soil.

Reluctant Heroes

They marched through the Sydney Streets to Victoria Barracks where they were discharged; services no longer required. The Carcoar boys enquired about re-enlisting and were told to go home as they would be notified in writing if they needed to be recalled. Waiting for them was Jack, sporting a limp. There was a great get together that afternoon.

Some of the troops went straight to Central Railway Station to catch trains home. The Carcoar boys went into Sydney by tram and booked into the People's Palace then they walked down to Martin Place to the boozer, as Bertie called it. When they got down there, the place was packed with Bushmen, all in their Khakis. The beer was flowing and it soon become apparent some were itching for a fight, all that anger and fatigue had taken effect. The Police were called and some of John's mates were taken off to spend the night in the cells.

The Carcoar Boys were walking out the door when Bertie said, "You blokes looking for some fun?"

Iggie replied, "What do you have in mind?"

"Palmer Street," said Bertie. "We're going up there to get laid. Wanner come?"

Johnny knew that this was wrong, but why not. He was going on twenty five, he had never been with women and before he knew it, he was dragged along with the rest of them up William Street. Although it was only a short walk, they jumped onto a tram, then got off and walked up Palmer St and around into Oxford Lane. There were dozens of blokes, mainly soldiers, milling around. A door would open and a soldier would leave with his coat pulled up around his ears, trying to remain inconspicuous. Then a prostitute would come to the door, fag in her mouth and would stand there, her tits pushed out, and slowly turn around, sway her curvaceous hips and say "Who's next?" There were a few to choose from, some old, some young, a couple of Abos and one Chinese to pick from. Then Spud went in. He was from Cowra. John had played football in a combined country team with him.

Bertie came up to John and said, "Well Johnny. Is you going in or are you going to go home a bloody virgin?"

The little smart arse had been picking on some of the lads so John just let him have it. Bertie was out laid out cold. The remaining lads were around the soldier lying on the ground and one of the boys said, "Struth! John, you've killed him."

Iggie chimed in. "Nar, he'll be right but let's get the hell out of here."

As the boys raced around the corner and into Palmer Street, they could hear the Provos blowing their whistles in the distance. The lads did not stop till they reached the cover of Hyde Park. Although the notorious red light area was supposed to be out of bounds, the Military Police turned a blind eye but each week they would raid the lane. Usually someone would have prior notice that it was going to happen. So the boys from the country, still with their virginity intact, found the first pub and drowned their sorrows.

Next morning, glad to get out of the City, they caught the train over the mountains to Carcoar. The boys finally had a chance to let their hair down and there was wild singing as the train made its way down the Zig Zag railway into Lithgow and onto Bathurst, where it stopped for two hours. The troops from the train were given a civic reception from the local dignitaries. The town band played and there was a march past of school children.

The train then moved on to Blayney. As it came down the hill and onto the plain, it was a scene of white. There had been a snow storm and it looked like a picture out of an English winter. As the train pulled into the station, the Blayney town band was playing and all their friends and relatives were there to meet the local boys returning home. The boys were not aware that the train line was blocked owing to the ferocious snow storm that covered the line further down the track.

Chapter 63

Matthew and Sarah's ship docked in the Thames after arriving from Africa. They stood on the deck of the steamer and gasped over the London scene.

"Matthew. How it has changed!" said Sarah.
It had been fifteen years since he had last been in London.

"Yes," was all he could say.

They were to catch a train to Manchester from Paddington in the morning so they caught a cab to the closest tavern. As the cab was going along the avenue, Sarah said to the driver, "Stop! Stop! Look! *The Pig and Whistle*." It brought back memories of 1864 when she tried to seduce Matthew's father. (Refer to my previous book, *"Curse the Bells"*) So after some coaxing, they stopped the cab and spent the night there. Sarah, as she held Matthew in her arms after they had made passionate love, whispered in his ear that she loved him more than life itself. They both slept naked, which was something they had got used to in the hot Sydney climate. The moon was just coming over the river and city buildings and the night was quiet.

After breakfast they hired a cab to take them to the station. The train sped through the countryside and before they knew it, the train stopped at Piccadilly Station in Manchester. Sarah's son Patrick, and daughter-in- law Janice, met them. Sarah had not seen her son or daughter-in-law for close on fourteen years, so they had a lot to catch up on. Patrick was a successful Solicitor and they were soon in his motorcar, off to his country estate. However the foremost thing on Matthew's mind was to see his mother.

Sarah had made arrangements to get Mary, Matthew's mother, into the best private care possible. They would go to see her. It was early in the afternoon as the motor vehicle travelled through the serene country side and finally pulled up outside the Eventide nursing home on the banks of the Irwell River, near the Waterloo Bridge, Manchester.

Matthew had purchased a huge bunch of flowers and chocolates. The matron ushered them into the ward. There were only two old dears there.

"Mother, it's me," said Matthew.

Mary opened her eyes and looked at Matthew. "Is that you, John?" she said.

Sarah looked at Matthew and she quietly said to him, "She thinks you are your father."

"No Mother! It's me, Matthew."

"John was coming in to see me," said Mary. "He will be here shortly. He said he would come. Who is the lady?" Mary looked concerned.

Matthew introduced Sarah but it did not make any difference.

"Don't you know me, Mother?" said Matthew.

"O! Matthew. He was such a good boy."

As they walked out of the ward the matron called Matthew to one side.

"I am so sorry Mr Grieves. She just lies there and talks about when her Johnny is coming."

"Yes Matron. He was my father but he has since passed away in New South Wales, Australia, some fifteen years ago.

"She is very comfortable Mr Grieves and we have all the latest medicines to treat her," said the nurse. "The doctors say it is a form of dementia."

Chapter 64

Welcome home to the Carcoar boys.

The boys were unaware that the welcoming committee had been driven into Blayney by the new form of transport, the automobile. It was the first in the valley to meet the train, as the rail line had been snowed in and the train could not go any further. The boys recognised the eager crowd waiting on the platform. A procession of motor vehicles all decorated with Union Jack flags and red, white and blue bunting slowly made its way back down the Cowra Road. The Mayor, Mr C.J. Derwin, was leading the way back to Carcoar. The cars proceeded down Combing Street, past the churches and into the township of Carcoar. The main street was packed with well-wishers all waving the Union Jack. Iggie's father who owned the Stokes Hotel, had prepared a banquet to welcome home the Carcoar lads, and because the train was snow-bound, he gave the lads who lived further down the line a free bed for the night. All were cheering their boys home. The town band was there and they played *"When Johnny Comes Marching Home."* There was red, white and blue bunting everywhere.

All the Morris family were there, Ellen with her two sisters Alice and Katherine and her brothers William, Francis and young James. Ellen was all grown up, all of thirteen and Katherine was nineteen. Ellen had driven the family mad over the last twelve months since the Carcoar boys had left on their tour of duty in South Africa. Johnny Layburn, still a shy lad, greeted his mother and swung her around. There was to be a welcome home reception at the new School of Arts on the Saturday night. The crowd dispersed and all went off to their homes. The boys, with their families were greeted at the entrance of the Stokes Hotel by the staff and they all sat down for the banquet. The boys had had a long day and after a magnificent meal they wandered off to their homes for a good night's sleep.

They were kept busy next morning with all the pubs in town shouting the lads drinks and they finally ending up at the Royal Hotel later in the afternoon. The hotel was full of people. It was a cold winter's day but there was one consolation, it had stopped snowing. The news was that the train to Cowra was running again and would be on time to pick up the lads to take them home. Again there was a huge crowd gathered on the platform to see the lads off. The Carcoar boys were there to send off their mates with a rousing rendition of *"Waltzing Matilda"* and, as the train finally pulled out of the station, *"God Save the Queen."*

The School of Arts had been gaily decorated with sprays of bush flowers, especially wattle, along with red, white and blue bunting. There was quite a crowd expected at the hall that night and the Ladies Auxiliaries of all the local Churches had gathered together to put on a combined spread. There was even a three piece band to play, supplied by the local Orchestral Society. The town was going to let its hair down tonight to welcome the boys home. The young folk would dance and the hall was packed to the rafters.

The Mayor, Mr Derwin, got up on the stage and after he quietened everyone down said, "Welcome to The State member, Mr Waddell and his lovely wife, Mrs Waddell, members of the Town Council, distinguished guests, Ladies and Gentleman and boys and girls. Welcome everyone to this grand occasion. The boys have done this town proud. Some of the lads could not make it here tonight as they have stayed in Sydney seeking further employment. We also wish them well."

There was a roar from the crowd.

The Mayor raised his hands. "Citizens, I am sure you are all aware that some of the boys were involved in the Siege of Eland's River. Heavily outnumbered by the enemy, they held their ground till reinforcements came to their rescue and, as this nation of Australia in time looks back, the name of Eland's River will be up there along with other famous battles."

Reluctant Heroes

The hall was overflowing with people spilling out onto the footpath.

The Mayor went on to say, "Tonight, Ladies and Gentleman, it gives me much pleasure in bringing to the stage our brave fighting boys, our reluctant heroes."

The four lads were fidgeting and trying to escape to the bar.

The Mayor continued, "Can you put your hands together for the Carcoar boys from the New South Wales Citizen's Bushmen?"

With some coaching from the crowd they finally climbed onto the stage. There were only the four.

The date was 18th June 1901.

On the stage that night was the state member, Mr Waddell, dressed in the latest fashion from Sydney. His wife, Mrs Waddell, had on a black surah, buttercup bodice, covered with black lace, folded belt, tea roses and diamonds.

The boys elected John to give a short speech.

Johnny Layburn came forward, sweating profusely and nervously looking at his boots, lifted his head and said, "Mr Mayor, Mr and Mrs Waddell, Ladies and Gentlemen, err and children."

John hesitated for a moment as basically he was a shy lad, then he continued.

"My friends, Igge, Ernie, and Jack have asked me to say a few words. The other boys said to say they are sorry they could not be here tonight.

"D'ye see? We left here some months ago, and we went to Sydney and got to Africa. We did our best, we did our duty, (loud cheers from the audience) and we had hardships. We lived on bully beef and biscuits. You laugh. I know I don't look any worse.

"When we landed at Biera in Portuguese East Africa, IG, Rum, and I, we had the luck to get away. We were the first men to go through to Rhodesia. Our Captain was offered coaches to take us along, but he said, "My men will walk." We had to boot it 289 miles and I walked 250 of them. The Captain wouldn't let any man ride, that wasn't lame.

"When we got to Mafeking, I met Iggie. Our horses were lame so we got remounts and made it on to Zee-rust. I will never forget the first night at

Mafeking, it was cold, and snowing. At Zee-rust we were sleeping out with one blanket. My D Squadron was lucky as we garrisoned in town.

"*At Rustenberg, C Squadron came along. We raced through town. It was right dress there. The Boers charged us. I was a horse soldier. Our men fired and the Boers retreated and we came through the night. Baden Powell came along. The NSW men took Rustenburg, there were twenty three of us at Elephant's Neck under Lieutenant Jell. He used to like whiskey, but he was a good fellow.*

"*We were on patrol at the Eland's River depot, when out of nowhere, the Boers appeared and opened up with deadly fire. The order was, NSW to the right and Queensland to the left.*

"*We got off our horses lively or we would have been shot off. I was with a fellow named Anderson, in charge of the horses. "My word, they're coming close," he said. "Let's lay down low." Trooper Henry Burns was holding some horses near us and he let one go, a creamy, and it walked right over me and I had a sore shoulder afterwards. We let the horses go and got on the bank. Men and horses were running in all directions. A trooper came along with a horse and I got on. I could see the Boers pinking at us. We raced four or five miles. After that, we made it to Eland's River, then next morning the Boers started to shell us. We tried to get a message through to Zee-rust. We got a quick one out, then nothing, the wire was dead, probably cut by the Boers.*

"*Colonel Hoare, told us to get sconces made.*"

Someone in the hall shouted, "Was that with cream and jam, John?" and the crowd went wild with laughter.

John then explained that a sconce was an embankment. He continued.

"*But the Bushmen were tough and the ground was hard, so we gathered rocks to form a wall. That worked for a while. Then, you see, the enemy found out our position. There were some Boers about, so we were surrounded. Baden Powell tried to get to us, but he was driven back, and at first, we thought he was going to desert us.*

"*They poured a wagonload of shells into us and one Queensland officer behind his sconce was shot through the hat.*

"That Johnny Boer means to get me all right. Next night, he wasn't so lucky. He got a direct hit and it cut him clean in two. We owe a lot to Trooper Sandy Butters. He was guarding the water supply and it was through his bravery we stood so long. You see, he held his post. He had a Maxim gun and they rushed him on many occasion, but time after time, he drove them back. Sandy was a brave soldier. Later he said that the gun was at times, so hot, he could hardly load it.

"At last Lord Kitchener came along with a lot of troops 20, 000 to be exact. He could not believe we had held our position for so long. We went onto Zee-rust with Lt. Gen. Methuen. We went on and finally after further adventures, we arrived in Cape Town. We thank you for your kind welcome, here tonight. Finally we would like to thank our local member for supplying the money for our fares to Sydney."

It was later revealed Mr Waddell refused to accept the money.

There was loud cheering and the boys were the toast of the town. When the dancing started, there was no shortage of partners for the Carcoar boys.

Sally rushed up as John stepped off the stage and threw her arms around him.

"Welcome home, soldier," she said, and then she introduced him to her husband George Evans.

Ellen, was a little jealous of this woman as she was all over her Johnny, planting kisses on him in front of her husband. Ellen was excited that Johnny had returned home. She walked up to John, hoping he would ask her to dance, but he walked right past her and asked Ellen's older sister instead. Catherine was an attractive blond, nineteen years of age. She had on a frock of pink pongee (Chinese silk) with cream lace trimming. Ellen in her new pinafore raced up and said, "Catherine, I'd like you to meet Johnny."

John put his hand out, and before he knew it, they were dancing around the floor.

Catherine's mother, Mrs Morris, walked up to Mrs Layburn, looked and said "My, they look good together, Jane."

John and Catherine danced the night away; all the waltzes, the Lucille, the Destiny the Maxine and the Varsovienne.

Reluctant Heroes

    Marsetta and Jane had become good friends since Ellen's infatuation with John, but they both thought it would not last and Ellen would get over it. She was now thirteen and the boys in the Convent School were falling over each other for her attention but she just was not interested. Finally, Mrs Morris coaxed the young couple outside and they all walked home. John desperately wanted to hold Catherine's hand but he was too shy. The two families said good night. John walked with Catherine up the garden path, but young Ellen lingered back. Her mother beckoned her inside and left the young couple to say good night. John seemed stuck for words and finally said, "Arrr, that was great night, I hope we can do this again." He wanted to take her in his arms and shower her with passionate kisses but his inner self came out instead, and he said "Good night, Catherine." As he held her hands and drew her to him, Catherine moved towards John to kiss him, but John just broke away and said, "It's been a big day," and turned and left her standing there.

    They were going to meet the next night after church. Alarm bells started to ring. Jane, being a staunch Catholic, did not want the relationship between John and Catherine to blossom so she wrote to her late husband's relative in the railways to get John a job away from Carcoar. John had worked in all the main hotels in the village and he loved the work. He was strong and rolling the beer barrels around was easy work. His mates had gone off to find work, Igge in the coalmines at Lithgow and Ernie to Sydney to work in one of the big hotels. Johnny Fox had gone west boundary riding for a big cattle property, owned by some bloke called Kidman. In Fox's last letter, he explained to John that if you rode all day you would not reach the other side of the property.

    Jane had not told John of her intention to write to Freddie's uncle who worked in the railways, but true to his word the letter came and John was whisked away to work with the rail maintenance gang on the Zig Zag line, east of Lithgow. Before John knew it, he was on the train to Lithgow. All his family were there to say goodbye, but Jane did not let Catherine get too close and as the train turned the corner, Catherine waved and had a tear in her eye.

John worked on the line for three months, coming home every weekend. On his first trip home, he got into Carcoar at 8pm and Catherine was there to meet the train. The School of Arts was holding regular dances every Saturday nights and there were plenty of their friends there, all having a good time. They danced the night away, tripping the light fantastic. They slipped away and walked down the railway track behind the shops and the village. He stopped and kissed her as it was the first time they had had a chance to be together since he had arrived back from the war. Catherine spoke first.

"John, do you love me?"

John had been reading books about the great lovers, *"Romeo and Juliet"* and he had been putting together some love poems that he wanted to read to her, but Catherine was not interested in talking. She was kissing him and he was kissing her. She wanted all of him there and then. She had also been reading books, the *"penny dreadful"* and she was getting excited, but John stopped, took control and walked her home into Collins Street. Kissing her at the gate, he made arrangements to meet after Church.

Next morning at breakfast, Jane gave him a letter. It was marked Private and Confidential and was from the Dept of Defence.

It was addressed to Mr John Layburn. It read, *"You are hereby requested to report to Victoria Barracks, Sydney, at your earliest convenience. You have been selected to report for duty in the War in South Africa with the 3rd Battalion Australian Commonwealth Horse."*

John just looked at the official letter and said to his mother, "What should I do?"

Jane could not hold back her glee. One side of her said she did not want her son to go back to the war, but the other side said it would break up the possible marriage to Catherine.

"You will have to go John," she said, "but come back to us; I don't know what I would do without you. We are so proud of you."

John caught the night train and was back at work on the Monday at the construction site for the rail extension of the western line. He gave his notice to the gang leader. John's work mates gave him a rousing send off that night at the bar tent. They still managed to get him onto the night train and he staggered down from the Carcoar station to his house and to his family.

Jane, with the help from the church ladies, organised a send-off party for him in the church hall, and all his friends were invited. At the last moment, she invited Catherine and all the Morris family. She had said to her best friend, Mrs Stammers, that she liked Catherine even though she was not a Catholic. Mrs Morris, Catherine's mother come from good old Ireland and had married out of the Catholic faith. Nevertheless, John and Catherine escaped into the night for some privacy. It was a warm October evening and they walked down to the rail bridge. Catherine was chatting about their future, how many children she wanted and of the house and garden she had planned. They had wandered down the lane and finally she looked into John's big blue eyes and said, "John, hold me and kiss me, please, before we go back to the party. They will be wondering where we are."

He started to kiss her and she was co-operating and encouraging him to put his hands on her breasts. She started to undress but all of a sudden, John heard the voice in his head of Sister Maria lecturing him in school about being impure. *"It is a mortal sin, you will go straight to hell."*

John called out, "No Catherine! No please don't. We can't. We have to wait till we are married!"

He untangled his arms from around her and they slowly walked back to the church hall. He walked on back down the lane to give Catherine time to adjust her dress. He turned and Catherine walked toward him. Poor John was confused. He kept thinking of his upbringing and the teachings of the Catholic faith, but when he took her in his arms and they embraced. She was crying.

"Don't cry, don't cry Catherine," said John. "Will you marry me?"

"Yes, Yes. I will," Catherine said as she started to cry again.

They stood there, locked in each other's arms, when John finally said, "But Catherine, my love, we must keep it our secret until I come back from this confounded war. You know my mother will object because of the religion."

Catherine continued to cry and although she was happy, she had some reservations as she knew that their difference in religion would play a big part in their happiness. They slowly walked back to her house. The light was on in the kitchen and someone was playing the squeezebox. They opened the door and entered the kitchen.

Ellen rushed up and said, "Guess what, Catherine. Will and Grace are getting married."

Catherine embraced her brother and John shook his hand and in a deep voice said, "Congratulations, Will. When is the big day?"

Will went red in the face and his mother Marsetta stepped in and said, "It will be a quiet wedding down at the court house in Bathurst."

"Grace. Can I be your bridesmaid?" said Catherine.

Then Ellen chimed in, "Can I be one, too?"

Marsetta said, "All in good time. Now that your father has regained his strength and has been given his old job back in Bathurst, we are going back to live at Devonshire St."

There was silence, then old Will said, "Have a drink, John."

The room broke into laughter and their next-door neighbours, the Cummerfords, started to sing, *"For they are jolly good fellows."*

John said, "Good night!" at the gate to Catherine and out of the corner of his eye, he spotted Ellen at the front door.

John travelled to Sydney and reported for duty at Victoria Barracks. In July 1900, John Layburn received the special Imperial War Gratuity of £5, under Army order No 150, for his service in the New South Wales Citizen Bushmen.

He was promoted to Corporal as he had already served in South Africa. They were given orders to leave in late March. He was to serve in the 3rd Battalion Australian Commonwealth Horse. They went on light patrols south of Sydney as the area around La Perouse was ideal; it was thought by the senior officers to be similar to the terrain they would experience in Africa. The new troops were soon drilling up and down sand hills, digging trenches, constructing sconces and performing mock attacks.

John advised his superior officer that the sand hills were different from the savannah hills in South Africa, but at least it was as close as they could get to the real thing. John's leadership ability soon became noticed by the officers and he was quickly promoted to the rank of Sergeant.

Reluctant Heroes

They soon gained the reputation as the boys from the Bush. As their departure date was drawing near, the lads, on their night off, haunted the regular back lanes of Darlinghurst. Most of the lads had never been to the city before and the red light district was a major attraction as it was considered forbidden territory. They all wanted to go into the houses of sin but would back out at the last minute. John accompanied them on these nights however when they sailed away to duty, he was still a virgin. Just before their departure day, he visited his step sister who was living at 183 Liverpool Street, Sydney, near Hyde Park and she promised to come down and see him off when the ship sailed.

The press was starting to get a different picture of the war. The news was now filtering back to the cities of the Commonwealth how the allied forces were burning and destroying the Boer villages and placing the women and children in concentration camps. John was surprised to read an article in the Sydney Bulletin written by his newfound brother. It went on to say how the public opinion back in Britain was disgusted at what was happening. People were marching in the streets, calling for an end to hostilities. Not that long ago, names like Mafeking, Rustenberg, Bloemfontein and Eland's River were where the magnificent fighting men of the British and the Commonwealth forces had fought battles, but, lately it was coming out that the British Generals were inept and were not up to the task. It went on to say that if the colonial troops, the Canadian, Australian and New Zealand forces, were given a task to do, they did it without fuss and went in and got the job done. Matthew Grieves signed the transmission from Durban after arriving back in Africa with his wife Sarah.

Chapter 65

Matthew and Sarah returned to Cape town after seeing his mother; and realising she was in good hands, realised there was nothing more he could do. It did not take long for him to realise that although they were both in their 60s, the call of the surf and sand at Manly beckoned them. But he had promised his editor back in Sydney that, he would have one last look in at the war which was coming to a close.

There had been an incident involving three Australian soldiers who were on trial accused of murdering a group of Boers. As a top line reporter, Matthew Grieves had been sent to cover the court martial. It was an interesting case as it was thought that no Australian could be executed for war crimes. The Australian papers were full of letters to the editor, mainly disgusted at how the army officials could let this happen.

Pietersburg, 16th January 1902.

The Court Martial of Henry Horland Morrant better known as Breaker Morrant, Peter Joseph Handcock and Lt George Witton.

Shock waves reached around the Empire when the verdict of guilty was brought down and Morrant and Handcock were to be executed by firing squad. But, as the truth unfolded, it was revealed that Breaker Morant was discharged from the Second South Australian Contingent in South Africa on 31st July 1900. He had proceeded to England and returned to South Africa on the 1st April 1901 where he was commissioned in the Bushveldt Carabineers; a newly raised corps of irregular horseman.

Similarly, Peter Joseph Handcock, a farrier Sergeant with the First NSW Mounted Rifles, was discharged in South Africa and also travelled to England where he signed up and joined the Bushveldt Carabineers on 22nd February 1901.

So the official line was in both cases, that after discharge they had no connection with the Australian Military Forces.

Although the Australian military petitioned the English, nothing could save the two Australians. They were to face the firing squad and were duly executed. A third soldier, Lt. George Witton, was sentenced to imprisonment in England and released after two years. This created a huge outcry in Australia and this case and one other, were responsible for the Australian Government declaring it would never place Australian infantry under foreign legal command again.

Matthew had prior notice of the troop movements from Australia, so it was no surprise when John and his fellow officers and men walked down the gangplank of the transport ship *Manhattan* at Durban on 30th April 1902, to be greeted by Matthew. Matthew organised to meet up with John later that day after they had settled in to camp. Their orders were to proceed to Kitchener's Kop and set up camp outside the town and await orders to proceed to the Transvaal, where they were joined by Queenslander and Tasmanian Squadrons.

The war ended on 31st May 1902 after the signing of the treaty of Vereeniging.

War over, 31st May

It is estimated that 23,000 Australian and 6,057 New Zealand troops served in the South Africa campaign with 606 Australian and 232 New Zealand deaths.

The soldiers fought in many campaigns and engagements which were recognised by the issue of clasps. Each was embossed with the name of the battle. Australians qualified for eighteen clasps and the New Zealanders thirteen. During the Boer War, six Australians and one New Zealander were awarded the Victorian Cross.

The troops had hardly unpacked their bags when they were told that the hostilities were now over. The boys in John's squadron were jubilant and glad it was over before it had started. They were to report back to Durban and await passage back to Australia. The transport ship was the *Drayton Grange* and was to depart on 11th July.1902.

Sydney received notice that the War was over on 2nd June 1902. The people of the Australian cities greeted the news without much enthusiasm. The reports that had come through over the last six months of women and children being placed in concentration camps did not go down well. There were letters to the editors of all the major papers around Australia condemning the British generals for allowing the war to degenerate and allowing the slaughter of women and children, who were herded into hell camps where disease was rampant.

John could not wait to get back home to Catherine as they were going to announce their betrothal. They arrived back in Durban camp, which they had only just left a few weeks before. After roll call, there was mail from home. Most of the boys received something and there were two letters from home for John, one from his mother with all the local news, but nothing from Catherine. The other one was from her sister Ellen and he opened it slowly as he had a feeling this was not going to be good news.

It was as bad as it could have been.

Dear John,

I know you will think badly of me taking up my pen to write to you but I felt I just had to let you know that Catherine has run off with Ivan Connelly. They caught a train last week for Sydney. Mum and Dad are upset but I don't care. I will always be there for you when you come back. John, I love you. I know you think I am only a kid, but I will be sixteen soon, so look after yourself and come back to Carcoar soon. John, I love you. Stay safe, and John, guess what? Since you left, I have been taking instruction in the Catholic Faith from Father Kelly each Saturday afternoon.

Sincerely Yours,
Ellen Layburn.

John's mate Eddy Logan came up to him.

"Penny for your thoughts, John," said Eddy. "You look as miserable as a bandicoot on a burnt ridge."

John just stared into space.

"Hope it's not bad news John," Eddy said.

"Aah, me fiancé has run off. It was never going to work. Religion! She is a Protestant. I am Catholic."

"Fair dinkum!" said Eddy. "What we need John, is a drink. A bloody big schooner."

That afternoon, the boys went off into the city of Durban which was alive with boys from all the Commonwealth forces. The local hotels were doing a roaring trade. As they brushed past the local Indians heading for the nearest pub, the shouted out that they knew where the lads could get a good time. They were also harassed by shop keepers trying to sell them everything from new clothes, suits, silk shirts, dirty post cards and women. They arrived at the hotel that had been recommended by their officers, but they were told to stay in groups and not to venture down any back alleys as they could get your throat cut as quick as you could say the word. John felt like getting drunk, but deep down he felt relieved that it was all over between him and Catherine.

John and Eddie soon found themselves as drunk as Lords and it was late when they left the hotel. As they were walking past an alleyway, they were accosted by some low life who were starting to bash them up. Fortunately, the military police turned up just in time to rescue them, put them on the back of the pickup wagon and take them back to camp with the rest of the drunks.

Next morning John reread the letter again and he tried to bring young Ellen into his mind. At first he could not remember her but then it all fell into place, the football match all those years ago and she was always around at his mother's place. But she was only a kid and she was going to become a Catholic. Why?

Although the war was over, there was still some resistance in some outlying pockets, so the orders were to go out and spread the word that the war was over. John's patrol set out. It was only going to be for a short time as the ship was leaving on 11th July. They had gone about ten miles from the main camp and they stopped at the first homestead which, surprisingly had not been burnt to the ground. The lady of the house came out with three young children. One of the officers, who could speak Afrikaans found out that her husband had been away fighting for seven months and she had not heard from him. The captain explained to her that the war was over and asked if they needed anything. It turned out that there was no food in the house, so he promised her he would return with supplies in the next few days. A section of men returned to the camp with orders from the captain to return with a wagon full of supplies. They distributed them to the farms and returned back to camp in time to board the transport ship back to Australia.

The night before they left, a group of Aussies including John and Eddie were having a great time in the boozer at the docks and they were drunk on the local millet beer. The bar was packed with soldiers and itinerant workers and the smell of unwashed bodies soon overpowered the place. The shrill of the whistle the provosts blew sounded in the distance. It was the call for all enlisted men to return to their barracks. There was a mad panic as men in khaki sculled their drinks and rushed the doors to escape. John and a couple of others slipped out the back way down a lane. That night John was determined to get a woman regardless of all the talk he had heard from the doctors and officers. They soon entered a lane with black women hanging out the doors. Some had only just come out of the bush.

John stopped outside the second door. She was only a girl and her dress was hanging off her. In the half light he saw the shack had iron roof and hessian walls.

"You like to come in, Soldier?" she said. "I give you good time. You like young black girl?"

She pulled her blouse down to expose her uptilted breast. "You like to touch black tit, Soldier?"

Poor John didn't know where to look, but he knew his other mates were watching him.

She went on. "Only two shillings, Soldier. You will like nice young black cunt."

John was embarrassed by the language so, as if he had been hypnotised, he followed her into the room. She quickly let her dress drop to the floor. All of a sudden, John rushed out into the lane. He shot past Ernie and didn't stop until he reached the corner and raced into the side door of the tavern. Ringing in his ears were his local priest's words, *"Hell Fire and Damnation! That's what you are in for, if you touch the forbidden flesh."*

Ernie met him and they walked back to the camp. Deep down, John was glad it didn't happen. His mates had told him that the waiting game was on to see if he had picked up the pox. John was so naïve he thought that because he had entered her shack, he could pick up the dreaded disease.

As John's division left the Camp in Durban, they passed much worse squalor of the black native camps and he soon was reminded what he had nearly done on his last night. What was he thinking? He just wanted to forget the near experience and, at his first chance he wanted to get to a Priest and confess.

The ship berthed in Sydney on 11th August 1902. There was no fanfare and no great crowd of people to greet them and, as they marched up the streets of Sydney to Victoria Barracks, people were actually booing them.

There were even people calling out, "Child killers!" This was not true as the Australian soldiers had acquitted themselves most honourably. They Australian Troops were not involved but it was true that the high command had given orders to destroy all Boer property and send women and children off to the camps.

As soon as he was discharged, John went down and left his pack with his stepsister Kate and, after a quick cup of tea and lunch, walked across Hyde Park to St Mary's Cathedral. As it was Saturday there was a priest on duty hearing confession. There were a few Parishioners in line so he joined the queue and nervously waited. When the red light flashed on, he entered the confessional and the priest asked him how long it was since his last confession. He quickly told the father that he had just returned from a tour of duty in South Africa.

The priest, who was not in a good mood, repeated the question. "How long has it been since your last confession, my son?"

John told him it had been some months, when he was last in Carcoar.

John, after much hesitation, let it out that he thought he had committed a sin of the flesh. The priest, shaking his head and sweating profusely, wiped his brow with a handkerchief, advised him to avoid women who lurked in dubious places of temptation, and to sincerely recite the Act of Contrition, then he instructed him to say, ten *"Our Fathers"* and ten *"Hail Marys"* as his penance. John knelt down and prayed for forgiveness.

After doing his penance, he left the church feeling as if a great burden had been lifted from his conscience. On leaving the church, John turned and followed the road down to the wharfs in Woolloomooloo. Street kids were playing cricket on the road, belting the rats that came out of the drains. He quickly moved on down back lanes, finally coming out at the wharf where he sat for awhile and started to worry if the pain and the irritation would return. He was starting to doubt his faith in the church. John did not want to return to Carcoar, so he spent the next few weeks staying with his step-sister Kate near Hyde Park. Each day he would wander around the park, sit, talk and feed the pigeons.

He befriended a chap that had fallen on hard times and when the man started talking, he explained to John how he had travelled to the Sudan with the New South Wales force and served under Gordon. John was enthralled listening to his tales and the trouble he had got into. The man told John that war was an unnecessary evil and he would end each time asking John for money for a meal. John more than once would relent and give him some money knowing only too well, that as soon as he left, he would be off to spend the money on drink. However on this occasion he talked the old timer into having a meal, so they both wandered off. His mate knew all the good cheap eating places, so they walked up to Central Railway Station and stopped outside a place called the *Hole in the Wall*.

"Good tucker, here matey," said the old timer. John followed him and sat at a table. John could not believe his eyes, as the knives and forks were attached by chains to the tables so no one would pinch them.

"Pies and peas for seven pence. If you want sauce, it's an extra penny," said the other. He chatted on for some time about the state of the nation and admitted he had had a good education, but at the Sudan fighting, something had cracked and he had to have a drink to stay alive. John gave him some money and he went off to the nearest pub.

John nervously looked for the tell tale signs but eight weeks after he arrived back from South Africa, there were still no signs of the pox virus. But it never happened. John was terrified and he did not know what to think, but did not go to the hospital. He suffered in silence, and was in a state of depression. And a couple of weeks later, although he felt tired, and had headaches, he started to think it had passed him by.

The Sydney Bulletin paper reported that the South African conflict had cost thousands of Boer and Allied lives from disease, much more than the war itself. Soldiers lost their lives through disease and lack of proper sanitation. The loss of livestock, horses, donkeys and mules ran into the hundreds of thousands. There was also the loss of farmers' livestock, slaughtered for no apparent reason. It was also announced that none of the 16,357 Australian horses, called "Whalers" would return, and most would be destroyed in South Africa. Some found homes, but, because of strict quarantine regulations, they could not be returned to the Australian shores. This caused an outcry from animal lovers in Australia, so the army relented and allowed one horse to return.

Chapter 66

David and Hannah Inch travelled down from Hill End to welcome home their son Richard, who was returning home from the conflict in South Africa. They had received a disturbing letter from his superior officer Lt. Col. Williams, DSO.

Their son, who had distinguished himself in the field of battle, had been found dazed and wandering, suffering from severe sunstroke. He was attached to the 3rd NSW Bushmen. His parents were anxious to get him home to their new property at Blayney.

The band was playing in good form, and the wharf was packed with well wishers waiting for their loved ones to return. The Union Jack was fluttering in the winter breeze. Then someone on the loud hailer announced that the troop ship *Manila* had just passed Pinch Gut. Someone started to sing, *"God Save the Queen"* as the ship turned into Sydney Cove and finally docked at the wharf. The boys of the 3rd NSW Bushmen were finally home.

Richard's parents had left home and travelled to Sydney, staying with friends before going to the wharf. They had not been aware that an urgent telegram was waiting for them at home. It read,

URGENT- STOP – TRAGEDY – STOP – RICHARD – DROWNED - ON WAY HOME - HOBART - STOP.

There was much yelling and shouting as the lads called out to loved ones. David searched for his son to no avail and started to be concerned as he did not appear to be there. As the gang plank was lowered and the boys started to disembark and line up on the wharf in some form and order, David called out, "Look! There's James Fenton and William Goodie."

The three lads had been inseparable as lads and had joined up together. When they easily passed the shooting and riding tests they were excited to be going off on a great adventure to fight for Queen and country.

Then James broke rank and, with what looked like an officer, walked over to David and Hannah and introduced his superior officer.

"Welcome home James. Where's Richard?" David asked.

"Thank you Mr Inch. I'd like you to meet our Senior Officer, Lt. Col. Williams."

"Thank you, trooper Fenton. You can rejoin the other lads."

Now David could sense that something was seriously wrong and he now realised that Richard was not coming home.

Lt. Col. Williams relayed the story of how their son Richard had jumped overboard when the ship docked in Hobart, and he just sank like a stone.

"By the time we realised what had happened, it was too late. One of the lads threw him a lifebuoy, but he just ignored it and went under. You would think he had a death wish, but he was a brave soldier. I have recommended him for a Queen's Medal and three clasps. Mr Inch, your son was a daring and fearless soldier."

Later that day, David met up with the lads at the People's Palace, where the boys had organised a small get together to explain what had happened.

"Mr Inch," said one young soldier. "Back last September we were pursuing the enemy up the Toolangi Pass when we captured Boer wagons and 600 cattle and 1,000 sheep. We were in luck, some of the boys thought they were home. We soon had the stock rounded up and penned, and mind you, that night there were growling noises coming from the surrounding hills."

"That's fine lads," said David. "But what has this to do with my son, Richard?"

"Well, it was late October when we were scouting down this gully," said the other. "It was stinking hot just like home, when all of a sudden, Richard fell and passed out for no reason."

"Well, then what? Look, my son, Richard, was always the life of the party, full of life. Always ready to help a cobber."

"We thought he was just skylarking but he just lay there," said the soldier. "When he didn't get up, our sergeant detailed two of us to help him up. James and I could not believe how he was in another world. He was helped back to our barracks and placed in the sick bay. Sunstroke, it's hard to believe but he had copped a dose of it, so he was confined to light duties and he never saw any more action."

The men went on to say the transport ship *Manila* looked impressive as it lined up at the wharf at Durban. The lads from the Third Bushmen contingent had just returned from the holding paddocks to farewell their mounts as quarantine regulations forbade them to return with their beloved horses. James and William, along with their mates, shielded Richard as the medicos wanted to keep him in Durban. They told the officers in charge that they would look after him.

"He wasn't insane," said James, "just had a little bit of sunstroke. God he was as tough as old boots, worked down the mine in Hill End in a hundred degrees, sweat pouring off him. We thought he'd be okay. But Richard wasn't okay. When the ship docked at Albany, we had twenty four hours, and we'd been told of a pub down by the docks, that had beaut sheilas. So we all left the ship and as we approached the *Southern Arms*, we turned around, but Richard was nowhere to be seen."

James took a deep breath.

"I said I thought he'd appear and snap out of it," he continued. "But as we climbed the gang plank, Richard was nowhere to be seen. Finally the Provos picked him up down at the whale station. He had tried to stow away. We didn't know what to think as the ship entered the Derwent and glided up to the wharf in Hobart. There was a gala atmosphere at the wharf and on the dais the Mayor and Premier were there to greet us.

"Then out of the blue, Richard jumped. We were stunned, but finally someone shouted out, "throw a life-buoy" but Richard just sank. It was so sad. He was a brilliant soldier. It was so sad."

Chapter 67

The End of the Boer War

Lessons were learnt from the war that would change conflicts well into the next century. The distinctive advantage of the modern rifle rendered it all but impossible to cross the fire zone of two to four miles without exposing the besiegers to almost certain destruction. A well equipped, entrenched force enjoys a comparative immunity from danger that a few years ago would have been thought impossible except behind regular fortifications. This was strikingly illustrated in the case of Ladysmith, Kimberly and Mafeking where immensely superior numbers were kept at bay for months, defeating every attack made upon the besieged towns.

Rapid movement had become indispensable, and for this the horse would be increasingly in demand. The invisible soldier will in future, be in as much demand as the smokeless powder. In the opening days of the campaign it was soon made obvious the British uniforms and the bright coloured tunics and helmets of the soldiery led to disasters.

Chapter 68

There was no big announcement, but in the Bathurst Papers on 28th July 1902, it was noted that Catherine Cott, aged eighty-five, nee Disney from Sligo, Ireland passed away, death caused by Bronchitis. She had been living with her daughter Catherine Arrow, in Busby St. Bathurst.

Poor old George, aged eighty-three, was taken to Sydney to stay with his son from a previous marriage. The funeral procession left the Catholic Church in Bathurst and Catherine was buried in the Catholic section of the Bathurst Cemetery. The mourners who gathered on that cold winter's day felt the temperature, as it was near freezing and snow was starting to fall.

Her daughters placed her Irish linen apron in her coffin, (Catherine had brought it all the way from Ireland and although it was threadbare, she wore it all of her life). The families had agreed to raise enough money to place a head stone and, when it was finished, it read.

**HERE LIES OUR LOVING MOTHER
LORD REST HER SOUL IN PEACE. WE MISS THE SOFT
CLASP OF HER HAND
AND HER BREATH WARM ON OUR CHEEK.**

AMEN.

At a gathering after the funeral, her meagre belongings were distributed amongst her daughters. Marsetta received the family Bible. As she opened it, although she could hardly read, there were no entries, just a few scraps of paper.

John Layburn finally arrived back in Carcoar with none of the fanfare of his previous return. He spent a week with his mother. He spent the day sitting on the back veranda staring into space, seeming to drift off in a dream. He finally announced to his mother that he would spend some time down with Alfred, his half brother at Woodstock. So saddling up his horse, he set off riding into the bush and did not return for weeks. He wrote to his mother explaining he wanted to be alone for a while, but would help Alfred work around the big cattle and sheep station.

Alfred had married Mary Friend. John had been at school with her and he loved to visit their children, Gladys and Harold who was just three years old. He would stay there for a few weeks helping Alfred around the farm, and then he would get restless and move on. He eventually ended up at old Johnny Fagan's property, Sunny Ridge. Johnny was getting on, he was now sixty and would spend his days sitting on the veranda.

They talked about old times. Johnny Fagan still had a clear mind and would tell the story over and over, about the time back in 1862 when he was held up by the Gardner gang while driving escort for the gold. It became the famous Stage Coach hold up at the Eugowra Rocks.

John Joseph was fidgeting and said, "Johnny, I thought I had this problem. I visited this girl in Durban down this back lane but nothing happened. I've been too embarrassed to see anyone about it."

Johnny replied, "Did you pick up a dose of the pox over there?"

John Joseph shuffled and finally said, "Mr Fagan. No I don't think so. You know I avoided women right through the war. It was only the last day, before we came home."

John went on to tell him about the letter he had received from young Ellen, telling him that her sister, Catherine, had run off with another fella.

"Look John," said Fagan. "Go and see a doctor."

So John took Johnny Fagan's advice and promised he would go and see the new doctor in town when he returned home.

Over the next few weeks, John became withdrawn. He was always quiet, but his friends thought it was because of his time in South Africa. He went on getting work here and there when in 1905, on returning home, his mother said, "There is a letter for you, John."

The letter read, *To Sergeant John Joseph Layburn No. 1711. Report to Victoria Barracks on the 25th April 1905, to receive a medal.*

Jane was all excited about the chance to go to Sydney and see her daughter Kate Cassidy, as well as see her son accept the Queen's South African War Medal & Clasp.

The medals were for action in Rhodesia, The Transvaal, the Orange Free State and the Cape Colony, South Africa 1901 to 1902. He would also receive the Imperial Gratuity of £5 under A.O. 160 in September, 1902.

Ellen was now eighteen and more determined to get John than ever. So she pleaded with her mother to let her go with Jane and John to Sydney to see him get his medal. They all boarded the train from Carcoar and travelled down and across the Blue Mountains to Central Station where they caught a tram down George St. and walked up to Liverpool Street to the Peoples Palace. It was a beautiful autumn morning as they crossed Hyde Park and caught a tram up William Street to Victoria Barracks. John was in his khaki uniform, especially pressed by his mother. As Ellen stepped from the tram, John held out his arm to steady her. She never said anything, but John had a look in his eye that she had never seen before.

Almost immediately, he bumped into all his old mates, Iggie, Jack and Eruie. All the parents were there and they were treated to morning tea.

At eleven am, the sound of the bugler announced that the ceremony would start. They all formed into ranks of the New South Wales Bushmen, and John, who served twice, was also in the Australian Commonwealth Horse. They were called out one at a time to receive their medals. When "John Layburn" was called out, he smartly marched up to receive a Queen's Medal with four clasps.

After the ceremony, John and the boys were going down to the pub for a drink. Ellen looked disappointed, but she realised she had waited this long and she could see that he needed to get something out of his system. She did not know what it was, but she was patient.

Jane and Ellen went around to Kate's flat to wait there for John to return. Kate Cassidy was the daughter of Jane and Michael Cassidy who fell to his death in the main street of Carcoar. Kate was not married and was working at Mark Foys department store after first working for the Government Railways.

John had a few drinks with the lads. None of them had taken the plunge and married. Ernest was going steady but had not yet named the day. They wanted to go on up to Kings Cross but John declined, as the memory was still vivid in his mind of that black girl back in Durban He was going to wait now till he was married. He was keen to get back to his sister's place too. Young Ellen had grown up in the last year and she was what the boys would say, "A good looking sort."

He knocked on the door and was greeted by Ellen, who at eighteen, looked lovely. John picked her up and twirled her around and then he went red in the face and placed her back on the floor.

John always seemed to be embarrassed around young women. "My, you have grown up Ellen," he said. "It was only a year ago that I saw you last!"

She curtsied with a smile. "Thank you, sir," she said flirtatiously.

Next morning they made their way back to Central Railway Station and caught the Cowra train. John sat next to Ellen and she talked about everything, how she now had been accepted in the Catholic Church and had taken her first communion.

When they arrived home in Carcoar, John took no time in asking William Morris for his daughter's hand in marriage. John decided that they should not rush into it and they planned a long engagement. William, although keen for the couple to be married, wanted his daughter to reach the age of twenty-one. Ellen was so excited she could not contain herself. All that year she worked two jobs up to the wedding in November, helping her future mother in-law Jane, who was in her sixty-fifth year and had finally retired from her cleaning duties.

Chapter 69

Sarah's sister had been given the task of organising builders to construct the dwelling in the new part of Manly near the beach at North Steyne. It was to be built in the new style which later became known as Federation.

Matthew had settled into the new house in Manly and was having a quiet morning coffee on the veranda. He had received a letter from the Port Jackson Steamship Co. advising him that he was receiving two free passes to travel on the ferry as he had built a house in Manly.

The side gate opened and running up the path was one of the kids next door. He came racing up the front stairs, shouting, "Mr Grieves, Mrs Grieves. Come quickly."

Matthew dropped the paper he was reading and called out, "What is it Jimmy? Slow down."

"A big ship, Mr Grieves. Down at the beach." Jimmy had a vivid imagination.

"How big, Jimmy?" asked Matthew.

By this time Sarah had come out to see what the commotion was. Jimmy was jumping up and down and then he went racing back down the path and out the front gate. All he could say was "Big Ship! Big Ship!"

Matthew and Sarah decided to go and see what it was all about, so they set, off arm in arm down Pine Street and through the pine trees. There it was. A ship practically on the beach and by this time, there was a huge crowd all looking at the giant vessel. Strong seas had blown it on to the beach through the night. Matthew could make out the name, *Vincennes*.

"What sort of ship is it Matthew?" asked Sarah.

Reluctant Heroes

"It's a Barque, a big one too, about 1,900 tons."

Matthew had been experiencing chest pains and was going to see his doctor and, as he crossed Ocean Parade, he stumbled but quickly regained his balance. Sarah was worried about him but he smiled, held onto her arm and continued to cross the road. Sitting on a bench was a fellow with a faraway look in his eyes. Matthew stopped and said, "Why, it's Henry, Henry Lawson. Well, I'll be damned!"

With that, the fellow got up and staggered down the road towards Manly.

"Poor Henry. I am sure that's who it was, Sarah," said Matthew.

Matthew quickly contacted his old newspaper and that afternoon, a reporter was on the scene. The date was 24th May and they were going to celebrate Empire Day that night with fire crackers in the back yard. All that week, two tugs, the *Hero* and the *Advance* tried to pull the ship off the sand bank. Finally, on 2nd June on the high tide, it was pulled into deeper water and towed into Sydney Harbour for repairs. It was reported in the newspaper, the *Manly Daily*, that over 70,000 people came to visit the stranded ship. Although the paper was not to be launched till July, the publishers got an exclusive one page scoop on the story and it was on the streets before the bigger Sydney papers. Also in the exclusive edition was a poem, written by the poet Henry Lawson, called *"The Stranded Ship."*

Matthew and Sarah would walk in the late summer afternoons along the beach, returning home down Pittwater Road and calling into their local shops for supplies. They were always fascinated by the shop next to the butcher, as it hardly ever opened, and when it did, you could hardly walk inside for all the stock. The two old spinsters had everything from fire crackers to Manchester. It was chock a block with goods. On the odd occasion it was open, they would wander inside, but when Matthew, on one occasion wanted to purchase something, he was politely told that it was taken or reserved for another customer.

As the weeks went by, life in Manly returned to normal and in July, with the publication of the first *Manly Daily*. Young Jimmy who earned a few bob each week doing odd jobs for Matthew and picking up the Sydney paper, came in all excited. He had the first edition of the local and on the front page was,

"Sly Grog and SP Shop Exposed"

"Well, I never," Matthew said to Sarah that night over their meal. "I always thought there was something fishy going on, behind all that clutter.

Chapter 70

Back in Carcoar, John had been seeing the local doctor and was receiving treatment for depression. The doctor knew that there was something playing on his mind but John would never let it out. Then the doctor advised him that he thought it would be okay to go ahead with the wedding.

Marsetta had taken her daughter aside and told her the truth about her Grandfather James Fines and how he had arrived in the Colony back in 1823 as a convict. She had told her how he had worked as a shepherd and how she was raised in the village of Limekiln. She said she was never to forget her Irish ancestors and, although she had married her father in the Protestant Church and they had strayed from the Catholic Church, she was proud that Ellen was returning to the good and true Catholic tradition.

"Ellen, I have my mother's Bible, she brought it with her all the way from Ireland and when I go, I want you to have it," said Marsetta.

The big day came around on 28th November 1908. As Ellen walked down the aisle with her father, she looked radiant in her white wedding gown, her two sisters Catherine and Alice, as her bridesmaids. Catherine wanted to explain to John why she had run off with Ivan Connelly and how it didn't last. They had parted and she now thought she would never get married.

After a short service conducted by Father James Kelly, they caught the train to Bathurst and on to Orange for their honeymoon.

When John and Ellen arrived back home, there was a letter from a Solicitor in Manly. It was addressed to Mr John J. Layburn.

Dear Sir

My Client Mr Matthew Grieves, formally of 27 Whistler St. Manly, has passed away and has left instructions for me to advise you that, as his wife has passed away, he is leaving the above house to you on his death. He has instructed me to tell you that you are his sole benefactor.

I await your instructions.
Yours Faithfully
James Kline Sol.
Raglan St. Manly

John thought long and hard about the property in Manly, and what a country boy would do with it now he and Ellen were happily settled in Carcoar. Matthew had come into his life nearly twenty years ago. He turned up just as his father had died. He had liked Matthew and was sad when he had heard he had passed away.

John advised the Solicitor in town, Mr Harold F Morgan, to advise the Solicitors in Manly to go ahead and dispose of the property.

Life carried on in Carcoar, and the newly wedded couple moved into the family home in Stokes Lane. His mother Jane would spend her days sitting on the veranda. She had taken up knitting. Her stepson Freddie, had gone to live with his brother in Woodstock. Although he was wheelchair bound, he had become an expert craftsman with leather and would spend his days repairing and making bridles. John went back to work at the Royal Hotel and they became one big happy family.

Ellen was having her first child and John, being a good husband, was home after work and into his garden. Old Charlie Wong had gone back to China with his wife. His son Larry had taken over the veggie and egg run. John and Larry had been at school and were about the same age

"Mr Wayburn." In all the years, he had been around Carcoar, he never could get his tongue around the letter L. "Mr Wayburn, I like to buy a shop in town. What you think?"

"Well Larry, knowing you, you will do all right," replied John.

John did not like to say, but there had been some opposition to the Chinese in Bathurst and in Sydney. But Larry's family had been in Carcoar for over thirty years and he knew if he wanted something, he would make a go of it.

Ellen was not aware of John's health problem and she thought his lack of interest in sex was because he was just shy. It was the morning of 12th April 1910, and Marsetta had been worried as Ellen had already had two false alarms for the birth of the baby. The doctor had advised Ellen that she was not due until early May, but after visiting the City Bank where the Layburn's deposited their money, she was crossing the road in front of the old Bakers Hotel when a horse was spooked by a dog and she slipped and fell. A crowd soon gathered around and their family doctor, Dr Hawthorne was called. He decided to place her in the upstairs of the old Bakers Hotel which was closer than trying to get her to the hospital. Later that night, John and Ellen were blessed with a daughter. They had agreed to call her after Ellen's mother, but in the confusion, she got called Marcella, instead of Marsetta.

Mother and daughter soon got over the ordeal and before long, Ellen was pregnant again; another girl this time. John took no chances and she was born at the Hospital. They named her Philomena. The family was very happy. Dad in his garden, the two grandmothers looking after young Marcella, when for no apparent reason, Philomena died one night in her sleep. A death notice was placed in the Carcoar Chronical.

The death notice was also placed in the Chronical for John Fagan, age seventy-two. It stated that he passed away at his home at Sunny Ridge on 16th September 1912. The funeral was to take place at Lyndhurst and he was to be buried in the Lyndhurst Cemetery.

John was waiting at the station for his friend who was returning from Cowra. As John approached the carriage door to greet his friend, there was a loud noise and shouting coming from the front of the engine. As John and his friend strolled down the platform there came a loud call.

"Ambulance, someone get an ambulance, there has been an accident."

Alfred Green who was working at the station as a cleaner died after being lodged under the front of the engine. The train was held up while the local Constable Haynes held an inquiry into the accident. He found that, in his opinion, the deceased had lain down on the rails and the guard bar in front of the engine had struck him and thrown him clear of the rails.

The Coroner, Mr T. Fitzpatrick, found that the deceased met his death by being run over and killed by a train driven by Alfred Arnold. However, there was no evidence to show whether it was accident or otherwise.

The Royal Hotel held a brief wake in the hotel the next day as there were a few old timers there. Little was known of Alfred Green only that he had lived at Sheet O' Bark

This was all considered part of life. The families had had their fair share of miseries but, like clockwork and being good Catholics, young Enid was born in 1913. Finally in 1914, to keep with tradition, a son John Joseph, later called Jack, was born to the loving couple.

John, with his two young daughters, Enid and Marc struggled up the hill to the village cemetery to find his father's grave. The girls had picked flowers to put on their Grandfather's grave, lilacs and dahlias from his garden. It had been playing on John's mind for some time to have a proper headstone erected at his father's grave site. The grave took some finding in the long grass. It was near the Church of England section and, with the help of his daughters, John spent the afternoon pulling the weeds away and erecting a rough wooden cross so the stone masons could identify it later on.

The children attended the Convent of the Sisters of Mercy. The three children seemed to get on very well with their lessons. Young Enid was always used to getting her own way and her father he used to spoil her rotten. Enid at a school concert which was held in the School of Arts at the end of the year, after the students had been given their new readers for the coming year, bold as brass, told the Sister that she thought she should have been given a prize. So before the end of the night, the Sister made an announcement that a special award was to be given to Miss Enid Layburn for her help with the Sisters.

On another occasion the town had gathered at the railway station to meet the Prince of Wales, the future King of England. The train stopped and the Prince got out and made a prepared speech to the large gathering to much cheering. As he was about to board the train and continue his journey onto Cowra, the crowd went quiet and at the top of her voice young Enid said, "He hasn't got his crown on."

The crowd went very still for a moment, then the Prince smiled and waved goodbye. The next day in the local 'Chronicle', the story of the Prince's visit was on the front page and at the bottom of the page was young Enid Layburn. She was the toast of the town.

The Layburn family seemed to strike trouble down through the ages and young Jack was becoming a bit of a handful. Even at the age of six he would run away from his sisters and get into no end of trouble. One evening, it was dark and the Station Master, Neil Daley knocked on the Layburn's door.

"Sorry to trouble you, Mrs Layburn," he said, "but I found the young rascal hiding in my office, said he was going to catch the eleven pm to Cowra."

Ellen thanked him, dragged Jack into the kitchen and sat him on the kitchen chair. He just grinned from ear to ear. Ellen who had been the rock whilst her husband was sick, just had to go out into the back yard and down near the creek to weep.

John's illness was not getting any better and finally he had to leave work. The doctor said it was war wounds from the Boer War.

Some of the lads from the Boer War had re-enlisted in 1914, so John shuffled up to the station to see his mates go off to war. There were places no one had heard of in the Far East and France. He read stories in the Sydney papers of the casualties and he reminisced about the raids on the Boers, about places that were starting to fade into history, but he always remembered The Battle of Eland's River.

Chapter 71

William Layburn, 1887-1918

William John Alfred Layburn was born in Dunedin, New Zealand. He was the eldest son of John Layburn and grandson of John Joseph Layburn. He joined his father's wool and hides business and went to Australia in 1909 to obtain orders for his father and to gain experience as a wool classer. He travelled through New South Wales, Queensland, South Australia and Victoria. In 1915 he enlisted with the Australian Infantry Forces and was sent to France with the 22nd Battalion as a private. He was awarded the Military Medal in October 1917 for conspicuous courage and devotion to duty as a runner under heavy shellfire at the battle for Zonnedbeck in Belgium.

January 1917, Letter to his mother.

> *I don't think I will be long single, when I get back to Australia. No doubt the young lady I left behind is well on her way to being a Converted to our religion, so don't worry about me in this respect, Mother Dear.*
>
> *After the war, I would like to know if you want me to come home first, before I go to Melbourne and perhaps get married very shortly after I get there. I am very much attached to this young Melbourne lady, for I consider her to be one in a 1,000.*

Reluctant Heroes

24th May 1917. Letter to his mother.

My fiancée has a school at Shepparton in Victoria and she writes to me once a week with nice cheerful letters. Gee! She is a fine girl and I'm not sorry about my choice, for I am certain that I have done right and not made a mistake. That, I have absolutely made up my mind about.... Her name is Mabel Bliss...

Whilst he was staying in hospital and convalescing in England for a knee injury, William's fellow mates started to sing a popular song about *My Mabel Waits for Me* (song taken from a well known Australia poet). He was later transferred to the Australian General Headquarters.

William returned to the Front Line in mid-1918, where his Battalion was joined by the newly arrived 129th American Regiment. It was noted that the untested US troop's admiration for the Australian soldiers and deference to their judgment was almost embarrassing.

For two months William was involved in several fierce battles as the Australian forces pressed on to their target, the strategic town of Peronne on the Somme River. Getting close to their objective at the small village of Herleville, so depleted was the Battalion's fighting strength, that only with difficulty could a total of a hundred and twenty bayonets be raised. Of these, thirty had to be held back to be retained as reserves and the remaining ninety men were faced with the task of assaulting the German line on a front of over half a mile. Wave formation was obviously impractical and thin section groups were formed for the attack.

On the road which led into Herleville a few hundred yards to the right of the village and about four hundred yards in front of their posts, was a crucifix. The village and crucifix were connected by a sunken road, crossed in places by trenches and boarded on the far side by a high bank which served as a parapet for a strongly held trench. Around the crucifix there was a simple trench system.

William's Battalion orders were to occupy the sunken trench.

Taken from William's diary….

"Went over the top at 4.15 am. Big resistance from enemy machine guns….Ran the gauntlet of machine gun fire back to our lines and reported to Captain Pollington."

Taken from a letter to his mother dated 21 August . William explained what took place.

"Last Sunday morning, we went over the top and Fritz was waiting for us with dozens of machine guns. There were nine in our little party and we fought our way past a wood that was a nest of Hun machine guns. We got to a sunken road where we done a lot of damage. I killed four Huns myself and, as we were getting surrounded, we were forced to retire hurriedly and fight our way back. I was the only one of our platoon to come out alive and only four of our party got back. There were eleven of us left out of the company. The officers all reckon I was very lucky to get out the way I did. I strongly recommended our Lewis gunner for a decoration and I hope he gets it.

The O.C. of our company has promised me promotion.

The 22nd Battalion History states, *"Of the ninety men who took part in the attack, sixty were killed, wounded or missing."*

But William's good fortune was about to run out. He wrote:

"On 25th August 1918, after a few days rest on the banks of the Somme River at Vequemont to re-equip and re-organise, the Battalion departed in motor buses. After a wet ride we de-bussed near some newly dug reserve trenches, about four miles from the firing line. The next evening we took over the freshly captured positions, just beyond the ruined village of Cappy. The Germans were fighting a rear-guard action, depending mainly on isolated machine-gun posts, established in some of the old trenches which were abounded in the area….there was little time for careful scouting…This constant advancing was terribly fatiguing as sleep was a luxury and the nerve strain constant… we engaged the enemy, wherever found, with bayonets, and we lost seven (killed in hand to hand fighting, in the dark)."

The Australian Commander, Lt. General Monash, determined to push the Germans backwards to the Somme River and capture some of the bridges. He ordered "aggressive patrols."

Setting off at six thirty am, William was part of a group sent forward to sort out the village of Dompierre, *"where a few Germans made a little show of resistance. They were soon mopped up,"* as he later wrote.

Monday 26th August. William wrote the final entry in his personal diary. *"Having good rest in trench. Hop over tomorrow morning. It is going to be a "big stunt."*

The ultimate object was the town of Peronne.

22nd Battalion History. A further advance of 2,000 yards, was made on 28th August, when Black Wood, on the outskirts of Herbecourt was reached. During the day an advance party of twelve was vigorously attacked by a number of Germans belonging to the Kaiserin Augusta Guards Regiment. They were splendidly led by a very brave officer who shot William through the head.

According to a report from the Battalion Adjutant, William Layburn *"was buried where he fell and a cross bearing his name and Battalion colours, now marks his grave."*

Records show his body was disinterred twice and then somehow lost.

The letter of condolence from his superior officer reads in part, *"He was taking part in the great advance and on the above date, when just outside Herbecourt, he was shot through the head, by a German Officer."*

It was a severe shock to all his family back in New Zealand and his relatives in Yorkshire. William was a gentleman and he often spoke to his fellow mates of how he was going to return to Melbourne after the war and marry his sweetheart Miss Mabel Bliss.[8]

Over the next couple of years, some of John's mates came back with terrible stories about the *"War that was going to end all wars."* Some had experienced mustard gas and other horrors too ghastly to mention. There were times at the Royal when some of the lads would gather and reminisce

---

[8] Post script. By Wilf Layburn, Wellington NZ. 2002 See page 379

about the good times. One of the stories that got a laugh was the times spent in Cairo, and places that to speak about would shock the good folk, the strip joints, the acts of women with donkeys, shocking things but they all laughed and would drink to forget the other times that were too diabolical to talk about.

Once Billy Smith got started you couldn't shut him up.

"Yer, all for six bob a day."

Then a young lad you was too young to join up chimed in. "Sound like a fortune, that's over two quid a week."

Billy Smith got back on his high horse. "Yer, that's right, but those bloody froggies would put the price up, so it was not that good. The girls in Paris, wow they were terrific, great if you were a Frenchman but the moment we opened our mouths they knew we were from Australia and up went the price."

One day the lads were having a quiet drink at the Royal, when Bazza just fell to the ground and was shaking uncontrollably. His brother and the lads helped him to a chair and one of the boys got him a stiff drink. Larry, his brother, told the story of his brother's time in the trenches at a place called Ypres in Belgium, where he put up with constant days of shelling and had returned home with what was now being described as "shell shock."

Then Bazza opened up.

"Gee! There was this Pommy mate, Harry," he said. "Can't remember his last name. He was on report duty. He had just returned from a short spell in the infirmary, so they put him on carrying messages from the front line back to the command post. You know fellas, it was supposed to be light duties. Light duties, be buggered! He was out there, risking his life every time he went over the top. So, one morning, he just refused to carry on. God! Do you know what the pommy generals did? He went on trial and they shot the poor bastard for failing to carry out an order."

With that, he went into another fit.

Thank God it was over. Some of the able bodied lads would help the boys to their homes who had injuries, loss of limbs and sight. There were now new place names that would go into the history books, *"The Somme," "Gallipoli"* and some beach called *"Anzac Cove."* It was just plain stupidity. Thousands of Australian and New Zealand troops lost their lives, along with many more allied troops. John, who read all the Sydney papers, could not believe that it had all started in 1914 when Archduke Franz Ferdinand, the heir to the Austrian throne, was assassinated.

Chapter 72

It was a summer's night in 1917, and the townspeople of Carcoar were all gathered around the Post Office to experience a major event, the turning on of the first electric street light. As the sun set in the west and it became darker, the town clock struck eight pm. At first nothing happened and then there was murmuring in the crowd. Someone shouted, "Turn the lights on" and the lights came on. The town went wild, there was dancing in the street as someone brought out a squeeze box and another started to play the piano in the Royal Hotel. Everyone had a grand time, no one wanted to go home.

In 1921, John's mother, Jane Layburn died at the age of eighty-two. An announcement was placed in the Carcoar Chronicle of the passing of a dear friend and long time resident of the village. The funeral was to be conducted in the Roman Catholic Church in Carcoar.

From the Church of the Immaculate Conception, the funeral procession moved off to the town cemetery and she was buried next to her second husband, Michael Cassidy. John walked down to his father's grave. The weeds had regrown and he mumbled to himself, "Must do something about this, one day."

Ellen took young Jack, with his father John to Stanmore in Sydney so he could attend the best hospitals. Marcella and Enid went to their Nanna Marsetta in Devonshire St. Bathurst.

The Morris family lived near the Chifley's and Marsetta, after her father's death, took on selling some eggs to the Chifley family to earn some extra money. (Author's note - Young Ben, who was a train engine driver, later went on to become the Prime Minister of Australia).

John was in and out of all the major hospitals in Sydney but he seemed to get worse. Finally, in February 1924, Ellen made the long trip back to Carcoar. John was now an invalid in a wheelchair and he would rave in his sleep that he wanted to go home to die. He wanted to talk about Durban and how he resisted the temptation but God called out to him and he ran off. He had never been with a woman and he wanted to keep himself pure for his wife. But the girl, she was young and black. When she lifted her blouse, her breasts stood out, and he was mesmerised and wanted to touch them.

Enid now age eleven, would push him down to the Royal and the barman would give him a drink out the backdoor. Easter that year was a sad occasion. Enid had been to Mass on the Sunday with her mother, sister and brother and the family prayed for their father to get well. Young Enid said special prayers for him but on Easter Monday, 19th April 1924, John Joseph passed away, age forty-seven. Was it Boer War syndrome? There had been letters in the Sydney Morning Herald of other Boer War soldiers dying at a young age. He was buried in the Carcoar Cemetery next to his mother who had passed away in 1921 at the ripe old age of eighty-two.

There were letters written to the Sydney papers of how the Government should pay compensation to war veterans who had been permanently wounded or incapacitated, but nothing ever came of it.

With a heavy heart, Ellen made the journey back to Sydney, with her son Jack and youngest daughter Enid. Her eldest daughter, Marcella had been accepted at the Hospital at Carcoar as a probationary nurse at £30 per annum. On her first day at the hospital, she was given the ten rules for nursing.

She had been on the job for about one week, when a patient, a Chinese man, came running down the corridor shouting out, "Clean the sheet on my bed."

The matron, who was quick to reply, said, "You do, you dirty bugger and I will rub your nose in it"

"No! No!" He repeated. "Clean sheet on my bed."

Nurse Layburn, not wanting to be left out of it, said "Well sir, why didn't you say that?"

Before Ellen had left the town of Carcoar, she had been talking to the new Doctor O'Hallaeran. He told her he was impressed with Marcella Layburn and he had recommended her for the position at the hospital.

After John Joseph had been buried, she decided that what she needed was a fresh start. The good Father had given Ellen a letter to be presented to the local Church in Sydney. Jack was accepted in the local convent but it was soon apparent that the school was not big enough for him and he was expelled. He ended up at Plunket Street Public School.

The head master called Ellen in one afternoon to give her the bad news that Jack had been picked up wagging school by the police down at Broadway. The police had to report it as this was not the first offence and if he did not behave he would find himself in Long Bay. Ellen was distraught and visited the Church. She took the good Father O'Brien's advice and had young Jack, at the age of eleven, placed in the Boys' Home at Redfern for uncontrollable youths.

But his stay there only made matters worse. Before long, he was involved in activities that sent his mother into a nervous state and she spent some time in Callan Park, a hospital for the mentally ill. Young Enid, who was working in a factory in Balmain, was trying to hold the family together. She visited her mother every weekend, but she had her hands full trying to keep her brother out of trouble. Finally she sat down one night, tears in her eyes and wrote to her elder sister, Madge, pleading with her to come to Sydney. So Madge (Marcella), reluctantly left the hospital in Carcoar and moved to Sydney to be with her sister and get her mother out from the mad house, Callan Park.

Ellen arrived home. Times were tough as the country was in the grip of a depression. She went back to work cleaning and earning a living as best she could. They saved string and brown paper, and the family licked envelopes at three pence for a hundred. They would work late into the night to earn a few extra bob but there was never enough. When they weren't licking envelopes, they went to bed early (practical in winter), to save power.

Jack was in and out of trouble but finally got work helping on a milk run and he seemed to be happy. He was in his element as he loved horses, especially at Randwick race track. There was an SP bookie at the pub for placing bets. He would still get up bright and early and help old Charlie Wilcox with the milk run. He would take charge of the reins while old Charlie delivered the milk. He was soon responsible for taking the horses to the stables and feeding the two draft horses.

But soon he got tired and bored and over the next few years he drifted in and out of various labouring jobs all over Sydney. He was cautioned on several occasions for drunkenness and rowdy behaviour and his mates wanted him to go into boxing as he had a wicked left hook. He tried this but soon got tired of it.

He met Joan Boothe at a dance at Paddington Town Hall in 1937 and that night, when he arrived home, he told his mother he had met the girl he was going to marry. Joan was good for him and he even gave up drinking. Old Charlie retired and sold Jack the milk run on the "never, never" and Jack was doing very well. He made some payments to old Charlie, but then his mother got a letter from a solicitor saying that, with the passing away of Mr Charles Wilcox, his contract with one Jack Vincent Layburn was terminated. The first thing Jack did was go to the pub to celebrate and drink to his old mate, Charlie. The happy couple tied the knot in 1938. The bride's parents, family and Jack's mother and two sisters and their husbands were there. Jack and Joan were blessed with the birth of Patricia, who was born in 1939. Ellen, their second daughter was born in 1941.

Ellen, young Patricia and their father would visit Nanna Layburn on a Sunday afternoon and catch up with their cousins. Uncle Jim and their father would be down the back to have a beer.

"How is the milk run going there, Jack?" said Jim, in his country drawl.

"Are! Gave it up, sold it. Got a good profit," said Jack.

"What are you going to do now?" said Jim.

"Me mate, we're going into selling clothes props and rabbits. Me mate, Clarence, been making forty bob, just on the weekend. Every house in Sydney needs a clothes prop."

Reluctant Heroes

"Well, I suppose you are right. Enid would never let me do anything like that. I have been with Jansens' now for four years," replied Jimmy.

Chapter 73

Ellen received a letter with the news that her mother had died, and so she decided to make the train journey back to Bathurst to attend the funeral. Her eldest daughter, Marcella, accompanied her. As the train pulled into Bathurst she was met by her two sisters, Catherine and Alice. It was a quiet affair attended by family and close friends. The service was held in the Catholic Church and then the mourners proceeded to the Bathurst cemetery.

After the service, the small family group assembled back at the Violet Street residence. Marsetta did not leave anything of value except personal items and a family bible which had come from Ireland with Grandma Fines. Marsetta had promised the bible years ago to Ellen. Her elder brother, Will Morris, had written out their mother's instructions, as she could not read or write her whole life. The list was read quickly as there were few items to distribute, but when it came to the family Bible, it was given to Catherine who was the eldest. Ellen and her daughter stood in shock for she knew what this would do to the family. There had been no love between her mother and her two sisters. As they departed the family group, her youngest brother James, drove them back to the train station.

"James," said Ellen. "That Bible was promised to me, and mum said it was mine. I will never forget this day for as long as I live."

As they made the journey back to Sydney, she earnestly explained to her daughter that, when she passed from this world, she didn't want any of them invited to her funeral.

Ellen had taken a live-in housekeeping job in Manly. It was at a lovely place in Bowra Street, not far from the ocean. Her employers were Mr and Mrs Burnet. Although Ellen did her job as a house keeper, she did not meddle in the Burnet business. All she knew was his business was manufacturing.

It happened on 21st August and was reported in the Sydney Morning Herald that Mrs Burnet was alerted by a scream and, that she found her husband lying in a pool of blood. The police were called and they were mystified as there had been no break-in and his expensive gold watch was lying on the bed.

Reg, Ellen's son in law, was the first to read about the incident in the paper. He and his family were living in Lane Cove. He had called his mother-in-law and told her he would be over to pick her up and she was moving to live with them in Gardenia Ave.

When he arrived, she was shaken to the bone as the police had vigorously grilled her, and were still there investigating the affair. It was in all the major newspapers around the country.

"You don't think my mother-in-law would be a serious suspect in this crime, Officer?" asked Reg.

"Well, I am sorry Mr Wakeling, but we have to explore all possibilities."

Reg and Ellen walked her down to the Manly Wharf and they caught the bus to Lane Cove, where she remained till the day she died.

Later, there was a full police investigation and Ellen was cleared of any blame.

Chapter 74

Jack Layburn joins up for World War II.

It was a Saturday night in October 1941 and Jack was drinking with his mates at his favourite watering hole. He had started drinking again, regardless of what his mother and wife said. He arrived home late on the Monday night and announced that he had joined the Army.

"You have done what?" said Joan. "You bloody big Galoot."

"I have joined the Army," replied Jack. "I'm now Private Jack Joseph Vincent Layburn. Number NX 57179."

Jack was attached to the 34th Battalion. The Battalion was a militia and was not to serve overseas. Jack also kept his day time job as a milkman.

The 34th Battalion were recognised as the Dad's Army of coastal patrols. They were stationed up and down the coast of New South Wales. Although Joan thought he was mad, she did admit he looked smart in his uniform. Jack signed on as a cook and was stationed in the Marrickville barracks, Sydney in the General Details Ordinance Depot. Shortly after Jack joined up, the Japanese bombed Pearl Harbour and the Yanks were drawn into the war with the bombing of Pearl Harbour.

Australians went about their business thinking the War Zone was far away. They believed they were safe "down under." Nobody would touch them here in Australia, far from the battle fields. Sydney-siders were shocked on the morning of 20th February 1942 to read in the morning papers, that the Japanese had bombed Darwin. The authorities kept the total number killed a close secret and it was soon taken off the front page of the southern papers; anyway most people still considered it was too far away to affect them. It happened three days after Singapore had fallen. [9]

The locals soon had the Yanks categorised. They were "over-paid, over sexed and over here." The large numbers of American troops soon changed the Australian way of life. Most towns and cities in Australia closed down on the weekend but the Yanks had money in their pockets and soon hotels, theatres, clubs and restaurants opened on weekends. This had a major impact on the local economy. The war in the Pacific was not going well for the first part of 1942 as the Japanese were spreading forever southward and closer towards Australia.

After having had their planned seaborne invasion of Port Moresby turned back at the Coral Sea Battle on 21st July 1942, the Japanese landed the first of an eventual force of 13,500 fully trained and experienced troops, at Gona in New Guinea. Their aim was, to strike over the Owen Stanley Ranges and capture Port Moresby. This engagement was later to be known as the Battle of the Kokoda Track.

The Militia, 39th Australian Infantry Battalion, had been in Port Moresby since January 1942 to defend against a seaborne invasion and had spent their time as wharf labourers and preparing for the invasion. The average age was eighteen years with mostly WW1 officers. Having come from other militia units, they were mostly fairly well trained in weaponry but lacked experience in training together in large groups. They were badly equipped and poorly supplied, lacking base support troops and medical and logistic support. They were effectively on their own.

The 1,200 men of the 39th Battalion, outnumbered ten to one withstood a concerted effort by the Japanese to move over the Kokoda Track for a full seven weeks, until the first contingent of the 2/14th Battalion arrived to relieve them at Isurava, where they, the 39th were all but annihilated. The 2/14 was the first of three experienced AIF Battalions fully equipped with jungle green and appropriate Owen guns and artillery, base and medical

---

[9] Footnote 9: See page 380

supplies that were being held in reserve in the Atherton Tablelands. The 2/14, with the 39th held the enemy to within thirty-eight miles of Port Moresby. The Japanese had the harbour in their sights, but the enemy were stretched to the limit as their supply lines could not keep up and had run out of steam. This gave the Australian Forces time to assemble the experienced AIF Brigades (the 25th and 16th) although the Lee-Enfield 303 rifles with which they had been issued, were difficult to handle in close country because of the length of the barrel. There was the constant request for the Owen gun that was easier to handle with rapid multiple fire if required. All the troops soon suffered as the 39th had done for months, foot sores, malaria and other insect-borne problems and infections, due to the constant rain and sweat from the humid conditions.

The Army Generals back in Brisbane had no idea of the terrain and the conditions at Kokoda and the officers were constantly requested to explain why the troops could not build a road over the track.

The Japanese were forced back to three strong points on the north coast of New Guinea. They had dug in at Gona, Sanananda and Buna. The coast line was surrounded with malaria infested swamps and jungle and Kunai grass which could cut you to pieces. It rained each day and the ground turned to bog, with the snakes, crocodiles, and high humidity. There were better places to be. The Australian forces had been on the go and had just crossed the Kokoda, fighting as they went.

The initial plan was for the Aussie 25th Brigade to attack Gona, the 16th Brigade to take Sanananda and the five Regiments of the Americans to take Buna. What the planners had not taken into account was that all the Aussie Forces were, to put it plainly, buggered. Most of the Yanks were young and completely unaware of what they were getting involved in, as they were totally inexperienced.

The Australian forces eventually took Gona on the 9th Dec. 1942. The 16th Brigade did not take Sanananda and the Yanks made no progress on Buna, so the Australian 18th Brigade was transferred from Milne Bay. The allied forces had just built two air strips and the 2/9th Battalion, which was attached to the 18th Brigade, did in one day what five Battalions of Yanks could not do in four weeks. That is, they broke the Japanese defence. The 2/10 Battalion then took over and made further progress and the 2/12 had the job of cleaning up Buna, and finally, on the 20th January, 1943 after further heavy battles, they took Sanananda. The campaign took a heavy toll. The Australians lost 2,400 killed and over 4,000 wounded, but there were also over 14,000 evacuated through illness; Malaria, Cholera and Psychological problems. The Americans lost 671 killed and 2,172 wounded.

The American forces took over Buna and Sanananda as occupying forces, after the Australian Battalions had cleared the area of Japanese.

The Japanese also landed on the Southern tip of Papua New Guinea in mid August 1943, at a place called Milne Bay. This was to be part of a Japanese pincer movement to take Port Moresby but the CMF and the experienced AIF 7th and 18th Brigades were there to defend it. They arrived just before the Japanese landed. The Japanese advanced at a fast rate westward to the main concentration of Australian Forces, where they met their first opposition from the 9th and 61st Battalion of the 7th Brigade. They were involved in a fierce battle in early September which lasted four days and forced the Japanese eastward, then the 2nd/9th Battalion took over and forced the Japanese to evacuate. This was the first time in the Pacific Campaign that the enemy had been defeated on land, and although it was only a small battle, it was significant.

March 1942

One night, Jack Layburn was assigned for Guard duty at the Marrickville base but failed to front for duty as he got involved in a two-up game at the local hotel. He was charged with being Absent Without Leave and brought up before his Commanding Office.

"LEFT RIGHT, LEFT RIGHT," the sergeant yelled out as Jack was escorted into the office..

The CO read out the charge.

"Private Layburn Number 57179, AWOL, Sir," replied jack

The room went quiet as the CO looked over Jack's previous record.

"Have you anything to say for yourself, Private Layburn?" asked the CO.

"No, Sir," Jack replied.

"Fined £2. No weekend leave," snapped the officer

Jack was marched out.

This was not the first time he had been reprimanded. Jack had been fined for staying out after curfew and also for selling his bayonet on two occasions, but he was what you would call a bloody good bloke. He would give you the shirt off his back and he wasn't bad in the ring either as he was the undefeated champion of the Battalion.

The boys were on five bob a day which didn't go far, so they were into gambling, mainly two up. They were frequently at Wentworth Park Dogs and the Trots and there was always a game on at some back street in and around Marrickville. You had to know the bloke on the gate who was called the 'Cockatoo' to get in. The game was never held in the same place twice so as to give the gaming police the run-around. There would be a bunch of blokes standing in a circle with the banker in the middle, controlling the game and taking his cut on the money. The two pennies were placed on a piece of wood called a kip, and then tossed in the air. Hundreds of pounds were won or lost on the toss; there was mad shouting from the winners and grumbling from the losers. Part of Jack's pay would be sent home to his wife but he always had enough for 'roleys' (roll your own cigarette) and a beer.

Talk about beer! When they had the chance, they made their own. Any kind of fruit, add a little sugar, let it ferment and you got home-made beer.

Jack's platoon was stationed at Collaroy headland on the Manly Peninsular. Late one night in May 1942, it had started to rain and the clouds covered the new moon. It was pitch black, there were sounds of thunder, and it was bitterly cold. Jack and Bluey had become inseparable. They did everything together and were on patrol, checking for enemy invasions. It was a cow of a night and their army coats were pulled up high around their necks.

"What's that?" whispered Jack, as the small moon came out from behind a cloud.

Bluey said, "Don't know, Jack. Could have been a whale or a sub."

"Nar! If it was a sub, it must be a small one."

"Anyway, gee that livened up the night"

But later on, Blue decided to report it anyway as you never can tell. Jack looked around the area along the beach front it was in total darkness all windows were blacked out. All you could here was the sound of the waves lapping the shore, then in the distance beyond what he thought would be Narrabeen a light was flickering like someone sending a signal. Jack called out to their Sergeant and it was noted to be investigated. There had been rumours of a German who was operating a gunpowder factory in an area behind Narrabeen around the time of World War 1 could be responsible.

The local authorities were onto it straight away and investigated the said property early next morning. The place was locked up and it looked like it had not been used for some time. The surrounding property owners were interviewed and no luck. The responses were all the same. The powder works factory closed well after the First World War. The local police would keep an eye on the area just the same. A local farmer told the police that they did hear a car around 9pm he said he mentioned it to his wife that it was strange as they never had traffic in the day time let alone late at night. [10]

The first implications of the Ingleside activities were not revealed until the outbreak of the WW1. It was then discovered that the Narrabeen venture was not a mere swindle by one person but one nation of another.

The mysterious buildings in a secret gorge, contained two huge drying chambers, had also a central work room, large laboratories, and several offices in effect the building had been an official sub branch of the German Government

They reported both incidents back at headquarters however no one appeared to be interested

As they climbed into the back of the army Blitz and travelled back to town, young Smithy talked about the trots on Friday night. He knew one of

---

[10] Footnote 10: See page 381

the stable hands who worked for one of the top trainers at the park, and all the talk was about the trotter, *Blue Adieus* that was even money to take out the Magic Mile race on Friday night. Blue had a mate who was an SP Bookie who could lay the best odds around.

As the Blitz crossed the "Coat hanger" as the Sydney-siders called the Harbour Bridge, Jack said, "Hey fellas! Look down there, over at Garden Island. Looks like one of our ships has been hit. What's goin' on?"

Young Smithy said "Aah, you know, the navy always has some manoeuvres, but it looks pretty real to me."

As the truck ventured down into the city and up Broadway to take them back to the barracks, young Dougie, who having conned one of his mates to get him a "ham radio," listened to John Harper on 2KY.

"Hey! Listen guys. Harper is going to do his stunt and 'break' a new record, The Andrews Sisters. He usually played it first, then in a loud blast, over the radio, came, "For you folks out there, especially our boys in uniform, I don't see what you see in them, but here it is, the Andrew Sisters and *Boogie Woogie Bugle Boy*."

Next morning at the Barracks at Marrickville, the place was abuzz with activity as the news filtered down to the rank and file. The morning papers were delivered by a lad, just after six am, and the front page said it all: [11]

Jap Submarine Sinks Ship In Sydney Harbour. Twenty-One Killed

It went on to say how the sub got into the harbour in the dead of night.

When Bluey saw the paper, he woke Jack up.

"Struth Bluey!" said Jack. "It must have been a sub we saw last night. Just as well we reported it."

In fact two midget subs managed to sneak into Sydney harder in the dead of night.

---

[11] Footnote 11: The sinking of the HMAS Kuttabul, Friday 29th May 1942. See page 381

People around Sydney Harbour where frightened and started a selling boom. There was an exodus of people selling up to move to the Blue Mountains west of Sydney. Flash places around Double Bay, Watson's Bay and Rose Bay saw the price of real estate drop to a ridiculous level as speculators came in and brought up mansions for a song. They were punting on a quick sale after the war.

There were further attacks on 7th and 8th June and more terror as shells rained down on Sydney and Newcastle. [12]

That night the 10:15 pm train for Goulburn, south of Sydney, was packed with late passengers all leaving the city for safer places.

The lads were called on parade and were informed that they were off to North Queensland for jungle training. They had just returned from Rutherford army training camp near Newcastle where they had been on more route marching and drill.

Jack said, "Gee lads! Jungle training, sounds like we could be off to New Guinea. We will have served overseas."

Then Private John Duffy chimed in. "Sorry to disappoint you, but you're wrong. New Guinea is not classified as overseas. It's classified as an external territory."

But Bluey would not let go. "Hang on, fellers! You have to get there by boat. Isn't that overseas?"

"I'm afraid not. You could say Tasmania is overseas, but it's still a state of Australia," John chimed in.

The notice board that day had a few announcements:

1. Lost bicycle No 22075. Please return to Barrack Seven.

2. Attention all ranks. All communication to any parent or loved ones, of a military nature, is an offence under the Defence Act, punished by a fine or imprisonment, or both.

---

[12] The Bombing of Sydney: See page 383

3. It has come to notice that some personal have been seen wearing sandals around the parade ground. This will cease immediately.

4. Found. One pair of waterproof trousers. Owner please reply at Battalion Headquarters.

Chapter 75

Sport was a major ploy of the Army to keep the troops active and their morale high. Football was the main sport and there was Rugby League and Aussie Rules ("Aerial ping pong" as the locals in Sydney called it) played between divisions, but all the talk was the big fight between the local boy from the 34th, Jack 'Slugger' Layburn and a lad from 14th Heavy Anti Artillery, Jack Connelly. The fight was well organised and was set down for 6th June. At first it was going to be held at the Barracks gym, but as the fight came closer, it was decided to transfer it to the Leichhardt Stadium. They had arranged a fight between a Yank ranked in the top ten in the world, and an Australian middleweight yet to be named. The local fight between the two Jacks was to be the first preliminary bout. It even made the back page of the afternoon papers. The main fight did well, as there was no love between the American soldiers and the local lads. The 14th were on leave in Sydney, when Jack Connelly's manager, Private Hector Noel Spicer, made a statement to the paper that his boy was undefeated and he would put these smart arses from the 34th Battalion on the canvas in the second round.

It was the Friday night before the big fight that the four lads got talking about the Japanese attack on Darwin.

Bluey said, "Not much happened according to our papers. There were a couple of Jap Zeros dropping a few bombs and that was that. We heard the Post Office copped a bit of flack."

Noel looked at Jack and he started into him. "Nothing happened? You don't know the half of it. A few bombs! There were over 240 people killed, untold ships sunk in the harbour, and it was complete chaos."

"Now Noel, you know we weren't supposed to say anything," said Jack.

"They can bugger off, the truth should be told," said Noel as he downed another schooner. He was just getting wound up. "Look you don't know the half of it. You see mates, we were camped at the Darwin football oval with the 14th Heavy Anti Aircraft Battery and we thought our Ack Ack guns were top of the heap, but when these Jap planes came in from the north east with the sun in our eyes, we had little hope; smart little bastards. We were not allowed to have any firing practice, and our ammo was WW1 vintage. "

Someone yelled out, "Would someone shut that bastard up before I deck him!"

"Another four beers, please luv," said Bluey.

Everything was okay, then Hector jumped onto the bar at the local Exchange Hotel. It was about ten minutes to six pm and the grog was flowing but the pub was about to close. Florrie, the barmaid, at the top of voice, called out, "Last drinks, gentlemen." Hector had spilled his schooner on the bar, Florrie mopped it up with a cloth and squeezed it back into his glass.

The young barmaid had a bit of a reputation, as on most days she wore revealing, low cut blouses. She was notorious and, on some occasions, she would place the change on her large exposed breasts and the patrons would, if they were game, get it out with their teeth. This usually drew a large crowd of drinkers to cheer him on. The lads had been there most of the afternoon and Noel was drunk as a lord. He slipped and fell, then unceremoniously, he picked himself up and said he made a mistake, his boy could knock the slugger out in the first round not the second. There was laughter all round.

The pub was crowded with boys in army uniforms who were not supposed to be there. The boys from the 34th started a riot there and then in the local, the Royal Exchange. It was on for young and old. The Provos barged in through the front door and there were bodies everywhere. Florrie, who had a soft spot for Bluey, quickly summed up the situation and whisked the four lads out through the cellar and made a quick getaway, out the back gate and down the lane

They were briskly walking down the lane when out of the dark a voice called out, "Hey wait there. I want to talk to yu. Don't run! I am from a newspaper, *The Truth*."

At first they thought it was the police or the Provos but as they reached the corner the four lads slowed down.

Noel called out, "What you want to talk about?"

As the reporter finally caught up with the lads, he said, "Look! I'm from *The Truth*, Brian Lane's my name. Can you tell us what really happened in Darwin?"

Noel said, "We had a couple of mates that were stationed in Katherine two hundred miles south of Darwin. One night they were coming back from the pub with a couple of Yanks drunk as skunks When all of a sudden a plane came zooming in and created a massive wind gust that would have blown a dog of a rusty chain. We dived into the ditch beside the road, when the coast was clear we made it back to camp. As we walked through the entrance there was this bloody big crater.

The reporter sneered. "Come of it, mate," he said. "The Japs never got down that far!"

Well Noel was back on his soap box, "What's it worth? No names, no pack drill."

Brian agreed that any information would be kept confidential, so Noel and Jack gave their all and kept nothing back. Brian finally left the boys and promised drinks all round after the fight. With that, the lads dispersed and melted into the night. [13]

---

[13] Footnote 13: The Bombing of Katherine, in the NT Australia. March 1942. See page 383

Chapter 76

The Big Fight

The Leichhardt Stadium was packed. The main bout was between an American, Alf Houseman who was the US Army South Pacific Champion, Heavyweight Division and an unnamed Australian. The American had already fought seven fights in Australia, winning five by knockout and two on points. The Australian Army was trying to find a suitable opponent. As Bluey and Jack arrived at the stadium, the entrance was plastered with posters of fighters who had fought there over the years and the list was impressive. On the wall was advertised tonight's preliminary fight:

JACK 'SLUGGER' LAYBURN

V

JACK 'PRETTY BOY' CONNELLY

Both fighters were in the welterweight division and both tipped the scales at ten stone seven pounds. The fight to be over five rounds of three minutes. The referee was Mr Joe Wallis, entry was five shillings, men in uniform had free admission.

The sign went on to say that the preliminary fight would be between two lads from the 14th and 34th Battalions. The two Jacks would soon be off to fight the Japs, so tonight they were here to let off a bit of steam.

Jack and Bluey laughed their heads off.

"Pretty Boy! He won't be pretty after I've knocked his head off," said Jack.

Some of the pugilists displayed on the posters were
- Keith Francis – Bantamweight;
- Stumpy Butwell – Flyweight;
- Spider Tymms – Flyweight;
- Mickey Miller -- Bantam. Held both Feather and Welter Divisions;
- Teddy Sprouster;
- Billy Watson. Popular – Featherweights; and
- Up and coming Vic Patrick — Lightweight and National Welterweight.

Lastly, the sign said that appearing for the first time tonight is a singing group, the McKenzie Cousins who will be singing popular war songs for the boys.

Jack was in awe of the names and wondered if there was a future in boxing after the war. He thought to himself he would have to give up the grog and train, but it all seemed too hard. He was going to get in the ring tonight and knock Jack Connelly's head off.

Before the war, Jack Connelly had been an up and coming Lightweight and had fought a few fights as an amateur in the town of Bangalow where his father who had also been a boxer, owned a pub. After the fight, the two fighters would shake each other's hand and go to the pub for a few schooners. Tonight would be very different.

As they were ushered down the back to the dressing rooms for this major fight, his Commanding Officer spoke to him, wished Jack well and told him that the mighty 34th was looking forward to a good winning fight. All of a sudden Jack's legs went to jelly but Bluey got him into the dressing rooms, gave him a slug of whiskey and brought Jack down to earth. Hector came in and spoke to Bluey about who was supposed to win but Bluey told him to bugger off. It would be a clean fight and the best fighter would win.

Hector gave his boy some last minute instructions and a light sparring session.

"Lead with the left, Jack, now the right, now come in for the kill" yelled Hector. Jack came in for the kill all right. He connected with his right and Hector went down, out to it, but their second threw some water on him and he bounced up. Five minutes later he was a little shaken but ok. He was not going to miss this for love or money.

Jack Layburn looked like the real thing as someone had loaned him a fighter's dressing gown and last, but not least, he combed his hair, just in case the press was there. Joan had come to the fight and had been given ringside seats. She tried to make her way back to Jack's dressing rooms but the crowd around the door was too great, so she made her way back to her seat to cheer her fella on.

The young singing group were out the back and were being introduced to the fighters and John Harper of radio 2KY.

He said, "Who is the leader of the group?"

Sianna, the eldest of the group introduced her three cousins and sister to Mr Harper.

"What sort of songs are you going to sing young lady?" he asked.

"Well, for a start, we are going to sing all the Andrews sisters' songs."

Poor old John nearly had a heart attack. He hated the Andrew Sisters and would smash their records on air in his radio program. But every time he did it, his audience following would go up.

"What's the problem Mr Harper?" said Sianna. "Don't you like the songs? Because that's what we will be singing."

With her arms folded, Sianna, followed by the rest of the group, left the dressing room and they made their way to the centre ring.

The ring master climbed through the ropes and announced, "Ladies and Gentleman. It gives me great pleasure to bring into the ring, the one and only, your favourite and mine, from 2KY, Mr Gravel Voice himself, Mr John Harper, who will be introducing the next act."

The ring attendant lifted the ropes and helped the young ladies into the ring. John Harper stepped forward, raising his hands to quieten the huge crowd and said, "It gives me great pleasure to introduce an up and coming sensational singing group, who have put together a selection of songs including my favourite group Ha, Ha, the Andrews Sisters. Ladies and Gentleman put your hands together for the McKenzie Cousins."

He turned to the singers. "What's your name, young lady?" said Gravel Voice.

"My name is Sianna and these are my cousins Madde, Emma, Erin and my sister Teah and we are the McKenzie Cousins."

"Ah, thank you, young lady and you're not going to sing those songs by the Andrews Sisters, are you?"

"Ah, yes, we are," said Sianna firmly.

Then someone called out from the crowd. "Get off, you mug."

"Ok! I give in. Well, a big round of applause for the young ladies, fellas," said John Harper as he lifted the ropes and left the ring.

The boys went wild. They loved them, especially when they sang, *"We're in the Army Now"* and they shouted for more. Finally when they left the ring, they were mobbed by the press for photos. Young Peter McKenzie who was acting as their manager, assisted by Lang and Luke McKenzie, called out "Now, gentlemen, this way for photos, please."

The press were there all right, but they had come to see the main event between Alf Hoosman and a fighter yet to be named, not the McKenzie Cousins. The fight organisers were frantically trying to match up an opponent for the American but it was not looking good. It looked like the boys from the Army were going to be the main bout. Bluey ventured out into the Bleachers, came back and told Jack the place was packed to the rafters and all he could get was even money on a win.

Then from the door came the announcement "Jack Layburn, you're on."

As Bluey led Jack down the aisle to the ring, the announcer shouted at the top of his voice, "Tonight, ladies and gents and members of the Armed forces, we have two fighters, representing the 34th and the 14th Battalions."

Young Douglas Jordan O'Malley was Jack's second, but he was only a lad of seventeen. He was standing in the corner of the ring waiting for the bout to start, helping Bluey sponge Jack and apply ointment to his eyes. The gloves were on and they were ready.

The McKenzie group had been given ring side seats and were making eyes at Jordan. Young Emma said to her cousin, "Doesn't he look gorgeous in his uniform?"

"Who are you looking at?" cried Maddie.

The announcer called out: "JACK 'BRUISER' LAYBURN, in the Red Corner, from the 34th Battalion and JACK 'PRETTY BOY' CONNELLY in the Blue corner, from the 14th Battalion."

There was a roar from the crowd, and then the cheering died down.

The referee ushered the two fighters into the middle of the ring and said "Now boys, I want a good clean fight, no hitting below the belt and when I say break, I mean break."

The two Jacks went to their corners, stripped their gowns off and paraded into and around the ring as the crowd went berserk; the girls in the crowd were calling out and there was whistling.

The bell went for Round One and Jack Layburn raced out, arms flaying in all directions. Pretty Boy just kept his distance and danced around him. It was obvious that Connelly was the better fighter. He was fitter and he caught Jack with a vicious left to the chest. Jack heard the bell ring for the end of round one and was glad.

Bluey tried to instruct Jack what to do, but Jack, after he regained his breath, just nodded, took a swig of water and was on his feet as the bell went for Round Two. Jack, the southpaw came at Connelly with a rush and caught him with a hard right to the jaw, then Connelly got Jack with a right to the body and Jack went down but bounced back just as quickly as he hit the deck. Jack stayed out of trouble and the round ended. Pretty Boy was just ahead on points.

In Round Three, Jack rushed Pretty boy with aggressive punching but Bluey told him in the break he had to do more. The two fighters fought toe to toe and the crowd went wild. They were locked in a clinch. Jack whispered in Pretty Boy's ear that it was shame about his mother working down in Palmer Street to make ends meet. Well, Pretty Boy let fly with a series of left and rights to the mid section, but Jack was too quick and swerved and dodged most of them. Then he let Connelly have vicious right hook, right on the bell. Jack thought that he had done enough to even up the points.

In Round Four, Jack never stopped trying, slugging punches left and right and then he caught Pretty Boy with a left hook and Connelly went down for a count, but he picked himself up and was not hurt at the end of the fourth round.

In the break, Bluey said to Jack, "You've got him, Jack, but don't drop your guard."

And so it was Round Five, the last round. The bell rang. The two fighters came out, shook hands and you would have to say they were even on points, but then Jack did it. He waved to Pretty Boy to come and get him. Well, it was on for young and old. Pretty Boy came inside Jack's left and got him with a big right to the jaw. This would have put any good fighter on the canvas but Jack shook his head and countered with a heavy right and left combination to the body. Finally the bell rang and the crowd leapt to its feet, yelling and shouting for more. But it was the end of the fight.

The referee came to the middle of the ring, raising both hands of the two Jacks. The fight was declared a draw. It was a good result, so the boys left the ring and returned to the dressing rooms.

The main fight was cancelled as they could not find a suitable opponent for the Yank.

There was a loud roar from the mob to bring back the singers so the young lasses returned to the ring and had the service men dancing in the aisles but finally, after three encores, they left the stage.

Good looking young Douglas Jordan O'Malley, known to his mates as Dougie, was mobbed by the girls.

The police had anticipated a riot but the mob were satisfied they had got their money's worth. At the end of the night, the crowd surged to all the local watering holes around Leichhardt, Marrickville and Balmain. The two Jacks with their seconds and hangers-on jumped on a tram and made it back to the Royal Exchange in Marrickville. It was way past closing time and the publican had closed the doors but on seeing who it was, let them in. There was much shouting and laughter as the patrons relived the fight blow for blow as the drinks started to flow. It was eight o'clock but the local Sergeant turned a blind eye and gave them till ten pm to return to their barracks. That night, drinking at the bar were two characters that had just dropped in for a quiet drink after a day at the dogs (Greyhound dog racing). They had been known to bet on two flies crawling up the wall and they soon were told of the fight result.

They wanted the two Jacks to fight in Melbourne the next week, and they were guaranteed twenty quid each if they did, but the Army had other ideas. The Battalion was moving out and going north to prepare for jungle training. After the four lads realised that they would have to go AWOL, Hector Spicer who was the spokesman and had now sobered up after being KO'd by Jack Connelly back at the stadium, quickly told the two characters to get lost and this nearly started another brawl.

As Jack and Bluey, along with their merry mates, staggered back to the barracks, (God only knows who was holding whom up), singing at the tops of their voices, Jack fell and was out cold, Bluey sobered up and some other stragglers helped him get Jack back to their barracks.

Jack started to dream of how he got to where he was today.

His mother and younger sister Enid were on the train, heading for Sydney, his father had just died, he was ten and he had been expelled from the convent in Carcoar, so his poor Mother in desperation had decided to try their luck in the big smoke, Sydney. (Ellen Layburn had nursed her husband who had died from war wounds from the Boer War).

Marcella, her eldest daughter, had been left behind as she had been accepted as a nurse at the Carcoar Hospital. So Jack, Enid and their mother settled into a semi-detached house in Stanmore, it was rat and cockroach infested but it was near the Catholic Church and Convent, so on the next Monday morning, Enid and Jack were packed off to school. All went well for a while but about three weeks later, Enid came home with a note for her mother to visit Sister Marie that afternoon.

Ellen was working, doing domestic work at the Public School, so she trudged along to the Convent. Sister ushered her in and asked her if she would like a cup of tea.

"No, thank you, what is the trouble Sister?" asked Ellen.

Reluctant Heroes

Sister looked at her for a moment and could see she was a woman who was suffering from stress and had been through a lot.

"Look, Mrs Layburn," she said. "We can't control young Jack. He will have to go somewhere else. I am sorry."

Ellen left the Convent, saddened and about to cry. She pulled out her handkerchief when Jack came bouncing along.

"What's up, Mum? What did the old sister say?" said the young devil.

Ellen replied, "Don't be disrespectful, Jack! The Sister said you will have to go to another school," and she burst into tears.

Jacks eyes lit up "Great! Me mates go to Plunket Street. They have got a great football team and they go down to the Domain Baths for swimming lessons."

So, against Ellen's better judgment and her Catholic upbringing, Jack transferred to Plunket Street Public School. Although he came home with the occasional black eye and tears in his pants, Jack kept himself out of trouble until one day the Head Master summoned Ellen Layburn into his office.

"I am sorry to trouble you Mrs Layburn," he said, "but young Jack has got himself into serious trouble. The Police picked him up in school hours with some other lads down at Broadway, shop lifting."

So Jack spent the next twelve months in a home for uncontrollable boys. His mother had a nervous breakdown and spent some time in Callan Park Mental Asylum.

Round three, Ding! The bell started ringing in Jack's head.

"Wake up! Wake up!" Bluey shook him. "We're on Parade in twenty minutes."

The boys in the 34th were available to do all types of general duties and they found themselves down at Garden Island loading the navy ships and liberty ships. The war effort in Australia had been busy making prefab huts, warehouses and hospitals to be shipped out to the Pacific Islands and New Guinea. The work was hard yakka but his mates were there. Bluey and Jack made the most of the situation, the wharf labourers were always good for some cheap cigarettes, you name it, it was available on the docks.

"I really hate doing this shitty work," said Curley. "It's not what we signed up for."

Bluey said, "God I don't know, as long as we get paid who cares what we do."

They were having a quiet drink in the Bell's Hotel down near Garden Island in Woolloomooloo when Bluey was confronted by a bloke who wanted Jack to get in the ring with Vick Patrick Lucca (later he would be better known as just Vic Patrick).

"Look," said this bloke. "Your boy Jack Layburn put up a great show at Leichardt stadium and we're looking for a fighter to go ten rounds with Vic before he fights Rush Millings at the Sydney Stadium. We will put up fifty quid if he goes the distance."

Jack was dumb struck. "Look mate," he said. "It sounds good, we will have to get back to you, can't say what's happening but we could be pulling out soon, can't tell though, we are the last to know."

That was the last they heard from the promoter.

Saturday night, young Jordan contacted the McKenzie girls and was looking forward to meeting them, especially that young brunette. The lads had decided to go to the Paddington Town Hall, the place would be packed. The girls had got permission from their parents on the proviso they got their uncle Brett to chaperone. The band was one of Sydney's best, the *Jack Daniel All Stars*. Young Jordan who went under the nick name of Dougie, hogged all the dances with his new romance. She had him standing on his head in the jitterbug and they looked great in the jazz waltz. Young Private Patrick White was not being left out of it either, he had his eye on young Maddelyn and they cut a mean rug.

"Attention Ladies and Gentleman," called out the band leader. "We not only have our boys in uniform here tonight but an up and coming song and dance group. We have persuaded them to sing a popular song for us tonight. Can you put your hands together for the McKenzie Cousins?"

The group again brought the house down and were mobbed by the boys in uniform.

Reluctant Heroes

The solo vocalist and leader of the group Sianna, was asked to sing a song by Vera Lynn, *"The White Cliffs of Dover"* and there wasn't a dry eye in the house when she had finished. Then the requests came in, young Peter was up there collecting the money from the boys who had some, ten bob and the odd shilling.

Jordan got a brief chance to talk to Emma before she was whisked away by her elder brother. He handed her a note, which read, "Meet me on Central Station platform three, one week from today at three pm."

It was against Army regulations for personnel to be handing out classified information on troop movements but, if you knew someone that knew someone, any form of information could be obtained.

The lads were given one week's leave to spend with their families. Jack caught the tram to Lane Cove to spend a few days with his sister and his three nephews. His relationship with his wife had hit a sour note and she had decided to spend a couple of nights with her sister, but she had promised Jack she would be back to see him off at Central Station. Jack walked from the terminus to Gardenia Avenue and, as he passed the paddock at the top of the street, the Lennon's Circus' crew were putting up the big tent. The elephants were being unloaded and the lions were roaring. When Jack arrived at the front door with his kit bag, he was greeted by his nephews.

"Uncle Jack, will you take us to the circus please?" they begged.

"Well boys, I just might do that tomorrow night," he replied.

All the next day he helped his brother in-law Reg, and his neighbour Ken dig an air raid shelter in the back corner between the two properties. It had reached the required depth of seven feet and they were putting a roof on it to keep out the rain. They had a rough wooden floor and a ladder to get in. The two families had worked tirelessly to complete the shelter. Ken's eldest daughter kept up a steady supply of lemonade to the men who both worked in clerical jobs and were not used to hard yakka, but with Jack and his eldest nephew Peter's help, they put the finishing touch to it. It was Jack's suggestion that they should go up to the Junction Hotel for a quiet drink to finish off the afternoon. Ken had a '37 Pontiac and, because of his job, he had petrol ration cards. Jack's sister was apprehensive about the three men setting out for the hotel because she knew what her brother was like when he had a few drinks aboard

Her good friend and neighbour said "Aah, don't worry, Wake, (she always called her Wake) what they deserve to have is a bit of relaxation. I know my Ken deserves some. He and your Reg have been working hard, all those hours he does down at the docks with the Customs. They will be all right."

It was after six o'clock when the merry trio returned home, and Jack and Reg practically fell through the front door. Before John went to bed, he wanted his uncle to give him some sparring practice in the lounge room.

"Come on John, hit me. Lead with your left, then right, and again." John hit him right on the nose and gave him a bloody nose. Marcella came running in with a towel, and Jack was left on the lounge, snoring away to see out the night.

He woke next morning with a giant hangover. Reg had gone to work as he wasn't feeling the best. It was a school day, so the two eldest boys walked up to Burns Bay Road and got the school bus to Chatswood. They had left early so they could get a glimpse of what was going on at the Circus. Peter, the eldest, had got a job after school as a Telegram boy but he was always home before dark. They eagerly waited for the time to pass, they had their supper and it was 6:45 pm, but still no Uncle Jack. Their father had been called to supervise the unloading of a super ship, the *Queen Mary* up at Port Stevens, north of Newcastle. A taxi pulled up outside 13 Gardenia Ave and their Uncle rolled out of the cab, three sheets to the wind. The three boys met him at the gate.

"Don't worry boys," he said. "I said I'll take you and take you, I will."

After a quick bite to eat he escorted the lads with their mother up the street and, as they arrived at the tent, they saw the sign which heralded *"Lennon's Circus, still going strong since 1895."*

Because he was in uniform, he was directed to the best seats. The lads had a great time and John got to ride on the pony in the ring. Jack carried the youngest lad Douglas, home, as he had fallen asleep.

Next morning before he left, he had a long talk with his sister about his marriage and his love for his two daughters.

"Will you look after them for me, Marcella, if something happens to me?" he said.

"Of course I will, but you will be okay. You street smart blokes, it's the likes of you that survive. Just keep your head low and don't drink too much," said his sister.

Marcella waved him off at the gate and assured him they would be there to see him off at Central Station.

All the lads from the 34th were lined up at Central Railway Station, although it was not certain where they were off to. The word was Cairns, Northern Queensland, then by ship to Port Moresby, New Guinea. John was given the letters NX to go with his service number 57179. John did not know it at the time, but his brother-in-law Reg, explained to his sister that 'N' was for New South Wales and the 'X' was for AIF.

Chapter 77

It was a pleasant spring day in September 1942. All their loved ones were there; to wish them well and the wives and girlfriends were crying their eyes out. Bluey and Jack had secured a good carriage on the train and had put their bags into the luggage racks. They were on the platform having a cigarette, and Joan was there with young Trish, crying her eyes out.

"Don't go, Daddy, don't go," Trish sobbed. The tears were rolling down her little face when Joan started crying.

All Jack could say was, "Don't cry, now."

Bluey stepped in and saved the day pulling Jack onto the train.

It was September 1942. The war in Europe was not going well, but the papers were putting on a brave face for the public.

The McKenzie Cousins also turned up at the station. Jordan was the life of the party, with kisses from all the girls. Emma, who was sixteen going on seventeen, pulled Jordon away and, as she flung her arms around his shoulders, she said, "Jordan, I'll write to you every week, please be careful and comeback to me in one piece. I think I love you."

Jordan was going red in the face. He had never had so much attention.

"Come on, Dougie!" came a yell from the train. "Or you'll get left behind."

As the train pulled out, packed with Aussie troops, hundreds of voices rang out from Church choirs that had assembled. Sydney had rallied to send off their beloved boys who were off to fight the dreaded Japanese. By the time the train had reached Redfern Station, a card game was in full swing and someone brought out two pennies for two up. Bluey got out a bottle of whiskey and it was on. The trip took forever, picking up troops at Gosford, Newcastle and throughout the Hunter Valley.

The train was chugging along. They had gone through Armidale in the early hours of the morning, and then a short stop at Glen Innes, then off again. Someone shouted, "Next stop Tenterfield." The train chugged into the station and the lads of the 34th were told to move out with their kit bags and line up on the platform.

"What's going on?" said Bluey.

The top brass came forward and read out a statement that the line was down with a derailment just south of the border. The troops were formed into platoons and marched off down through the town and out to the army barracks at London Bridge. This had not been a planned stop but they reached the camp and set at ease.

It was soon realised that just to the east were the tank traps that had been erected to stop the progress of the enemy if they broke through from Brisbane.

Frank then burst out, saying, "I read in last Sunday's *Truth* newspaper, that it's all Pig Iron Bob's fault. Not only did he sell scrap iron to the Japs, but he wanted to sell us out to the Japs and give them all of North Australia."

"Nar! That can't be right. It was all Eddie Ward's fault. He hates Bob Menzies guts and will say anything," remarked Bluey.

"Jack, why don't you talk to your cousin, the Premier William McKell? He should know the real truth," said young Frank.

Jack never had anything to do with his second cousin, Will McKell. In all his life as a kid in Carcoar, he never mixed with the McKell family. He overheard his mother say one day, "We just aren't good enough for them." After a few minutes Jack replied, "Remind me when we're back in Sydney, we might go and visit him in Macquarie St."

There was a short pause and they all burst out laughing.

Then Frankie said, "Are you really related to him Jack?"

Someone up front called out to stop the talking in the ranks and get in step.

That afternoon the boys were allowed to inspect the tank traps and see Thunderbolt's cave which was right next to the traps.

Frank was curious about why the tanks would not just go around the barrier. Jack turned to Frank and commented, "I wonder why they put them there and why they didn't think the Japs would just go around.

"Struth, I don't know either" said Frank. "Guess some engineer thought it was a good idea at the time."

Finally they were marched off back through town and up to the railway station. The men of the 34th were spread out along the platform and card games were in full swing. Although it was early October, it was freezing cold, and the Station Master had rigged up forty-four gallon drums loaded with wood, which took off some of the chill. The train got the all clear around one am and the engine was fired up, the whistle blew and the men of the 34th boarded at two am. The train shunted about four hundred yards from the station along a spur line and stopped. The line was a single track to the border and they were delayed for a few minutes until a south bound train passed.

The rail gauge was different between New South Wales and Queensland. This went back to the 1860's because the states and territories could not agree on a uniform rail system.

At about six am, the train finally pulled into the station at Wallangarra on the Queensland and New South Wales border, everyone piled out onto the platform, as there would be a short wait for the Brisbane train. [14]

As the weary troops emerged from the train, they were greeted with strong winds and a light snowfall. It was hard to believe that here they were, just on the border of sunny Queensland with snow coming down. Some of the more adventurous troops jumped down and were throwing snowballs, acting just like kids. There was a rush to the Red Cross tea stand for refreshments, while others were lucky standing around the fire place warming their frozen hands. A young Red Cross nurse at the refreshment stand said that it was not unusual to have this bleak cold weather so late in the year.

Then the whistle blew and they were back on board and off. Finally they arrived at South Brisbane Station

The troops marched over the Brisbane River to Roma Street, as the men turned into Turbot Street, a bunch of American servicemen started cat calling out to the Aussies. The officer in charge tried to settle the men down. Some broke ranks but were soon herded back into line. They made their way to the Roma Street goods yard where every available spot was taken up with tents.

They were to catch the Sunlander Express to North Queensland, but the train was so slow they reckoned that if you planted a packet of seeds at the front, by the time the whole of the train passed the plants they would be in flower. At the station they were addressed by the Commanding Officer, and given their orders. It was no surprise that they would be leaving Cairns for New Guinea. But first they had to get to Cairns. The train was to leave Brisbane for Cairns on the Monday morning and the estimated time of arrival was Wednesday or Thursday, depending on the time spent stopping at small sidings to deliver mail and everything from live chickens to frozen meat.

The Commanding Officer went on to say that they had leave of thirty-six hours, to stay out of trouble and don't leave Brisbane. The train would leave

---

[14] Footnote 14 The Brisbane Line. See page 384

at eight am Monday morning from their temporary camp site in the Roma Street goods yard. The lads, Bluey and Jack, and some of their mates took no time in sprucing themselves up, found a gap in the back of the goods yard and were off walking down to the Valley, as they had heard of some great joints down there.

They had been walking for about twenty minutes when Kenny said, "God, I'm thirsty. I could die for a schooner. Anyone else?"

None of them could pass up a hotel, so one of the boys suggested they call into all the pubs on the way. No need to rush things. They had thirty-six hours before the train left.

The Victory Hotel was full with servicemen both Australian and American. Everything was quite normal until a Yank picked on Frank Jarrett, so Jack said, "Outside."

Bluey tried to break them up but this big black Yank stuck his frame in and smacked Bluey in the face. Then it was on for young and old, there were bodies everywhere. The Military Police siren was heard in the distance so the Australians, Jack and the boys dived down the next back alley. It was dark but they had entered a dead end, and the whistle could now be heard at the end of the lane way. The boys thought that this was it, they would be caught for sure, but half way down, a door opened and in the light, a woman stood in the doorway.

"Going anywhere, boys?"

Well they all piled in. Outside they could hear loud shouting as the police ran down the alleyway.

After the introductions, Sally said, "It's ten bob each for a quick time, fifteen shillings each and I will throw in a case of Four-x beers."

"Luv, do you have any Carbine Stout?" said Frank.

Sally just looked at him and said, "Who's first?"

Bluey went back for a second time.

They all left Sally's place early in the morning and walked back to the City, where breakfast and a cup of tea was being served in the Salvo's Citadel, then they staggered down to the Botanic Gardens to sleep it off until lunchtime.

Reluctant Heroes

It was Sunday afternoon and as they had to be back at Roma Street railway yards by five pm, so the four blokes picked themselves up and brushed the grass off. Bobby Williams went to walk into a pub but Bluey dragged him out. At the Gardens entrance, they passed an ice-cream vendor. It was a brand they had never heard of McNiven's. There was a queue, so like school kids they joined at the end and treated themselves to a big double header. They passed a newsagent and out the front, the *Courier Mail* announced, *"Yanks hurt in street brawl in the Valley."* It went on to say that at about nine pm last night, the Army Police from Australian and American Forces were alerted to a brawl that started in the Valley. The publican stated members of the Australian Forces had started it. Three of the Americans were admitted to the Army Hospital at Enoggera.

They quietly returned to the station and when Sergeant Noel Gray, the officer at the gate looked at the bruised face of Private Frank Jarrett, he casually said "Tripped and fell Private Jarrett?" as he winked at them.

"Yes, Sir." Private Jarrett responded

Emma McKenzie was in Sydney with her brother and Mum, as they had been evacuated from their Queensland home because of the threat of an invasion from the Japanese forces. It was referred to as the *Brisbane Line*. She was attending an arts course at the Eastern Suburbs Tech and was doing a course in fashion design. Her cousins happened to be in Sydney and were being considered for a song and dance show that would tour the country, so they were all excited. She had sent Jordan a letter each week as she said she would. Jordan was not a good letter writer and he tried, but it was hard to write in the heat and jungle.

Chapter 78

As the train was packed to the rafters with service men, the train would not pick up any passengers. It was early on Tuesday morning when the Sunlander Express broke down outside the seaside town of Bowen. The train was soon bombarded with locals trying to sell everything from booze to mangoes and even the odd girl got on board trying to sell her wares. A quick one could be had in the mail carriage for five shillings. There was a steady stream of soldiers all wanting to get the dirty water off their chest. Some were thinking it may be their last chance, as they could be killed. The rumour later on was that the Engine driver and the guards had arranged it with the local girls to stop the train and they would get a kick-back.

On Thursday, at long last the train pulled into Cairns and the men waited all day to catch the train that would take them to the tablelands for jungle training. None of the boys had been in Far North Queensland before and as the train made its slow journey pass the cane fields, it climbed up through the Barren Gorge. They were allowed a short stop at the station at Kuranda. Bluey could see the pub through the trees, but soon found an Army sergeant guarding the entrance. Although they had been told it was cooler on the tablelands, it was still going to take some time getting used to the tropical heat. The camp was near Mareeba. The tablelands were cooler than the coast but it was still hot and sticky. Jungle training consisted of getting up at dawn and marching to god knows where, and then marching back again. Eventually they were introduced to the real jungle which included snakes and spiders. It was not for the faint hearted as they would spend days camped under a bit of canvas. It never stopped raining and it was infested with leeches.

Finally they got their first weekend off. The local Saturday night dance in Mareeba was packed and some of the boys were venturing out to a place called Dimbulah. They had met some of the lads from the 31st Battalion and they reckoned that this was the place to go, great sheilas. It was out of town so the boys piled into a taxi and made the twenty-four mile trip.

"Struth! where are you taking us?" said Bluey to Bert, the taxi driver.

Bert knew everything, so he told them about the Japanese invasion at a beach called Cromarty where a hundred and six Japanese had landed.

Bluey thought for a moment and said, "Come on Bert, are you on the level or having a lend of us. Japs landing on Australian soil?"

Bert carried on. "Fair dinkum and I'll tell you something else, the American Negroes who were based nearby saved the day and killed a few. But that's not all that has been hushed up. Down near Townsville at a place called Upper Ross River, members of the Australian 11th brigade, my brother was there, manned a road block at a place called Corbeth's Water Hole. About 250 Negro soldiers were on the rampage and were heading for Townsville to play merry hell as they had been drinking. They were firing at the white officers who retaliated. The story never made the Cairns Post. [15]

The bitumen soon changed into dirt and meandered through paddocks with kangaroos and stray cattle. As they entered the small town of Dimbulah and drove down the main street, they could hear the music blasting out of the town hall. The main street was packed with army trucks and motorbikes, there were two pubs doing a roaring trade. They decided to get a taste of the local beer to get the dust out of their lungs so they pulled up outside the Junction Hotel and barged straight in.

---

[15] Author's note - There have been many stories over the years after WWII regarding Japanese landing in Northern Australia off the coast of North Queensland but there has never been any positive proof.

"Schooners all round, mate," said Bluey.

The barman just looked and one of the locals said, "What's a Schooner, you mug lair?"

Well, that started it. Bluey grabbed the first one, "king-hit" him and the cowhand landed on his bum. It just seemed that when Jack and Bluey were in a pub, trouble soon followed. Then it was on for young and old, three cowhands had Jack bailed up in the corner, he gave the first one a left hook and he went sprawling out through the door. He knocked the second one out with a right cross and the third gave in and ran. By the time the Provos arrived, the place was a mess with bodies strewn across the floor. So much for the dance! The boys from the 34th were rounded up, transported back to barracks and spent the rest of the night behind bars.

Jack had lost some hair on top from the fight and they gave him the nickname of Curley, so the pair became "Bluey and Curley."

The pair spent more time in the lock up than out, so finally they were put into the kitchen as the Battalion commander thought his staff could better keep an eye on them. They couldn't get into too much trouble peeling potatoes.

Finally word came that the lads were moving out as they had completed their jungle training. They marched down through the Atherton Tablelands to the Myola railway siding to board a train. When it finally pulled into the siding, they all climbed aboard, but it was nothing more than cattle trucks used to transport cattle from the Gulf to the Cairns sales yard. They were finally on the move down the mountain through the picturesque Kuranda railway station which was covered with ferns and tropical plants. The train moved slowly passed the Barron Falls, which was putting on a spectacular show with thousands of gallons flowing over the falls and down to the sea. They crossed the Barron River and finally stopped at Redlynch where the orders were for them to march into Cairns. As they crossed down through the sugar cane fields, the cane cutters all lined up along the road and gave them a great cheer. There were men from all over Australia who came to far north Queensland to work in the fields, some Italians who were interned, some

Kanakas from the Solomon Islands and the odd person escaping from the law down south.

The cane cutting was in full swing, one field had just been put to the torch and the men were covered in ash and cinders. The wild life was scurrying out of the cane, rats, snakes and wallabies all running to get out of the way of the flames. The birds were in their hundreds, scooping down to catch their prey. As quickly as it started it was over.

They finally reached Sheridan Street when Dougie called out, "There it is, Hides Hotel. Good grub, good beer and good sheilas."

They marched all the way down to the Cairns Wharf to board the steamer that would transport them to Port Moresby.

When they arrived at the wharf, it was full of all sorts of craft anchored in the harbour, but the steamer that was going to take them to Moresby was nowhere to be seen. They later found out it would be alongside the wharf in the morning. The men, who mainly came from Sydney, could not believe their eyes. The harbour was nothing but mud flats, and as they would have to camp overnight, the battalion was formed back into some order and, as they marched again down to Cairn's Parramatta Oval where the sergeant read them the riot act.

"No soldier, I repeat, no soldier is to be away from the oval after Twenty Hundred hours and certain pubs in town are out of bounds, namely the Hides and Barrier Reef. Do I make myself clear?"

It was late in the afternoon, and most of the troops were buggered from the forced march down from the tablelands. Even the ride in the train was uncomfortable, so most of the men decided to rest up, but by six pm, a small group led by Bluey and Curley were walking back into town.

The Barrier Reef Hotel was the first pub they passed and they were all dying of thirst so they walked straight in. There were only a few Yanks drinking at the bar, but when a Yank started to mouth off regarding how many women he had had, Bluey let him have it.

"Who do you think you are, you over-sexed, overpaid bastards?"

Curley, who was usually the aggressor of the two, grabbed Bluey and pulled him out the door. The usual lot were there and Smithy said he had been given an address down the back of Trinity Lane, which was close to the wharf. After awhile they decided to give it a miss and return to the barracks, so they ran back to the oval just as the clock struck twenty hundred hours, the guards on the gate just let them in.

Next morning, the Sergeant came into the barracks and roused them to get up. "The steamer leaves at seven hundred hours," he said, so there was a mad panic. A regular force manned the canteen, and after a quick meal, there was to be a special parade, so the troops all lined up, some bleary eyed, to hear the top brass give them a lecture about King and Country. The officer in charge went on to say, "Men of the 34th. I wish you well. Do your best look after yourselves and your mates. God speed and we will look forward to seeing you, when you return."

Chapter 79

The Battalion was on its way, marching down to the docks, all singing the latest song on the radio - "I don't want to join the army. I don't want to go to war."
Then someone yelled out "Don't you know any more of that bloody song, for God's sake?"

"Oh, well how about, *"It's a long way to Tipperary. It's a long way to go?"*

"God! I hate that song," cried someone from the back.

Some of the troop ships were nothing more than coastal tramp steamers, commissioned by the Government for the purpose of transporting troops to New Guinea, but the 34th were to go on the troop steamer *Kanimbla*. The date was 24th November 1942. As it quietly slipped out from the pier, they were in a convoy of mine sweepers and other ships, there was no fanfare, no crowds waving them off, only a few sea gulls and two wharfies to throw the ropes. As the vessels moved out of Cairns Harbour and past Green Island, a breeze sprang up and it was a pleasant day.

By late afternoon, storm clouds loomed on the horizon and drenched those who elected to stay on deck. The next morning the ship passed the tip of the Cape and passed Horn and Thursday Islands on its way across Torres Straight. There was no relief from the oppressive heat; it was over a hundred degrees on the deck. Some of the troops were scrubbing the deck and their officers had them clean and polish their rifles and buckles. Their boots shone in the sun.

The troops landed at Port Moresby, New Guinea, where their orders were to set up camp, and then they were on unloading duties for the ships that were lined up with supplies.

They had worked their guts out for a couple of weeks, when on parade, they were told that they were off on a sightseeing march for a few days. They were to ascend the Owen Stanley Mountain Range. It was then that they realised that the jungle training would come in handy. The troops started to ascend the range, and a quietness come over them as they hacked their way up and down the steep slopes, crossing flooded creeks. Their thoughts were with the brave boys, just lads of Commonwealth Military Forces, known as the CMF that formed the 39th Battalion. They had been christened "Chockos" or Chocolate soldiers, but they had kept the Japanese tied down for ten weeks. Although they retreated back to the Moresby hills where they held the Japanese off, but eventually, they were forced back to the west coast where the experienced AIF routed the enemy.

The boys of the 34th soon realised that this was not going to be a picnic. They had very little protection from the mosquitoes and little to eat but bully beef. It was late afternoon and they were erecting their tents when it started to rain. It came down in torrents and the next morning, as they climbed the next hill it was so slippery, it took them all morning to reach the ridge. It soon became apparent to the boys of the 34th that the 39th were heroes, not only for being shot at by the Japanese but for handling the conditions. As they were slipping their way across the track to Kokoda, it became a nightmare; a living hell, with dysentery, poor food, constant rain and the threat of malaria. As well, Dougie had been severely bitten by the dreaded red ants.

The boys had been out for three days and were glad to return to Moresby. As they trudged down the last hill Bluey said to Curley, "God, mate, it could have been us, we were Militia."

Two days later they were picked up by DC3s and transported to the East Coast. They were to be attached to the 2/9th.

Bluey and Curley were on kitchen duty in the army hospital. (all major medical cases were transported by Air Ambulance from there to Port Moresby). The main force, 34th Battalion arrived in November 1942 and was mainly on unloading duties at the airfield and the docks, as well as general duties around the coastal area. The Japanese offences had finished late in 1942, but some pockets of resistance had been reported, so the troops were kept on full alert. It did not take long for Curley and Bluey to get into the swing of things, and at every opportunity they were into card games down at the dance and beer hall, generally making nuisances of themselves.

It was late on Saturday night, and some of the boys had been to the Americans base camp for a dance. The Yanks had rigged up a mess tent and somehow they had gathered enough timber for a dance floor. Out of nowhere, they had a six piece band playing all the latest tunes. The boys let their hair down and the Australian nurses were there and in big demand. The jeeps had left to take the men and nurses back to the Australian Hospital, but four of the lads, including Bluey, Curley and Dougie decided to walk as there was a defined track. Although it was after midnight, they were skylarking and singing out loud when the shot rang out, and Dougie fell on the ground holding his stomach. Curley quickly took control and stood guard with his rifle.

"Can you see anything Bluey?" said Curley.

"Can't bloody well see my hand in front of my face," replied Bluey. Then another shot rang out, nicked a palm tree close by, so the boys lay on the ground, they were lucky enough to have fallen behind a log. Dougie started to moan.

"Be quiet, Dougie," said Bluey.

From the corner of Curley's eye he noticed a flash about fifty yards in front of them then the heavens opened and it started to pour.

Although the boys from the 34th had some basic jungle training, none of them had expected to come into contact with the real enemy. Some of the boys who were in the hospital said the fighting was over and the Japs had retreated back to the Bismarck Sea. Three more shots rang out. When Curley finally fired (he had seen some movement as the moon shone on something silver), he heard the enemy cry out in pain.

The rain had stopped and the air was still as the four boys lay there in the rain-soaked undergrowth. It seemed like they had been lying there for about one hour, and there was a cacophony of frogs and crickets making such a racket that the boys could hardly hear themselves talk.

Then there was a cry in Japanese from the enemy position. Bluey fired again.

"How many of them are there, do you think?" whispered Curley.

"I can't say in this light," replied Bluey.

Just then the moon came out from behind a cloud and one of the enemy jumped up and ran off into the bush. Curley and Bluey both fired and, from a distance, thought they winged him. Slowly they advanced up to the two Japanese bodies lying on the ground, their guns aimed and ready to fire.

With Dougie a casualty and Smithy holding him up, Bluey said to Curley, "Don't touch the bodies. They may be booby-trapped."

Curley raced back the short distance to the American camp for help and returned with stretcher-bearers who soon had Dougie back at camp and in good hands. The orderlies later said to Curley as they put him in the chopper, "His injuries were internal and as long as no major arteries were damaged, he will be okay."

They returned to the scene and spotted a military haversack in the long grass. At first, the temptation was to leave it as it could have been a trap, but after close examination, they finally picked it up to hand it in. They eventually made it back to camp but they were covered in leeches, a regular nasty that had to be confronted in the jungle. They stripped off, and with the help of one of their mates, burnt the leeches off with a lighted cigarette. They knew that if they were not removed carefully, the wounds could become septic.

Next morning the three lads, Bluey, Curley and Smithy were to present themselves to the Camp Commander for what they thought would be disciplinary action, as they had been out after curfew. Dressed in their smart army khaki parade uniform (they had polished the boots), they were marched into the officer's tent. But they got a pleasant surprise. There were handshakes all round and congratulations for their fine bravery in the face of adversity. They had forgotten about the bag they had handed in until the commander said, "Men, come over here and have look at what was in that bag you found." The contents were on the table and at first it looked like a heap of maps and bundles of papers, but then the sergeant pulled out one map in particular. It was a map of Australia in Japanese.

"Bloody Hell! Take a look at that. The buggers! They had it all worked out," said Bluey.

"Yes, but look at these bundles of bank notes with the Jap Emperor's face and an outline of Australia on them," the sergeant pointed out.

"Struth! Sarge, can we spend them?"

The top brass just looked and said, "Don't be stupid boys. These will be destroyed, but we will keep some to go back to the mainland. Anyway, great work. Thanks to the lads of the 39th, the Japs were turned around. If they had reached Moresby, anything could have happened."

Bluey and Curly directed a platoon back to the area where the incident had taken place. Although it was less than twenty-four hours, the jungle had swallowed up the path and they had to slash their way through. When they finally arrived, they found evidence of a cave that had been dug into the earth and camouflaged. They searched the site for any more evidence but found nothing. It was later revealed that the enemy had distributed the maps and fake money to selected troops. Over the following months, evidence of the fake money was found on dead Japanese soldiers who lay on the Kokoda track. The boys found a stack of pushbikes all covered with grass. It was later revealed that the Japanese soldiers were going to ride them over the mountain range.

The 34th were scheduled to leave New Guinea and the lads were skylarking around and getting up to all sorts of mischief. Their sergeant yelled out at the top of his voice, "You lot, follow me." As they formed into some sort of order, they were given shovels and picks and marched out to a spot where the Sarge ordered them to dig a trench. The Yanks had great delight in harassing them and one Yank yelled out, "Hey, that's why they call you Diggers."

Bluey shouted back, "I'll shoot the next Yank that calls us Diggers."

The Sergeant also mentioned that Dougie, who had been airlifted back to Moresby, was expected to make a full recovery.

The mob from Marrickville only lasted four months in the Milne Bay area; they had been attached to a tent hospital that took in cases until they could be transferred to the Hospital Ship moored at Milne Bay, which took all the serious cases back to Moresby. Curley had just about had enough by the end of February and was glad to hear the news, they were returning back to the mainland. He had been working in the kitchen at the field hospital as a cook for most of his time in the army. Most of the cases that were now being treated were malaria, dysentery, dengue fever and a host of other tropical diseases that came from the oppressive heat and continuous rain. The troops' clothes were never dry, they could never get a cold shower and they were always on constant lookout for snakes, crocodiles, spiders, tree ants, green flies, scrub typhus and a host of other nasties. The boys were glad to be heading back home to the mainland.

At the American base at Buna, one of the Yanks got to hear about Curley "Bruiser" Layburn, (he had been in Sydney at the Leichhardt Stadium when Curley had his fight with Jack Connelly). The Camp Commander of the 2/9th put his foot down and said that because of an ugly incident in Brisbane, there would defiantly be no fight. He was worried that there could be a riot regardless of the outcome of the fight. They received word that the mighty 34th was to pull out in the morning and the troops were to make their way back to Port Moresby.

It was in the early hours of the morning, when the camp started to stir. Bluey pulled the blanket from Curley, and in the half-light, he sensed something was wrong. They were to be on early morning kitchen duty.

"What's wrong, Cobber?" said Bluey.

Curley was shivering uncontrollably and finally stammered, "I think I've got it."

Bluey said, "What have you got?"

The two privates had gained a reputation for skylarking and acting the fool, but finally Curley said, "Malaria."

Bluey was about to say, "Stop fooling around and get up," but Curley was sweating profusely, his teeth were chattering and he was shaking violently. He had all the symptoms, so Bluey left him and raced to the sick bay to report his condition. The medico was quickly on the scene and Curley was moved into the wards for malaria cases.

Curley's superior had received information that Private Jordon Douglas O'Malley had died suddenly the previous night, from complications caused by a blood clot. Curley was stunned as he felt responsible for Dougie. As he lay there on his hospital bed drifting off to sleep, an image of a young brunette flashed in front of him. It was the girl in the singing group. He tried to think of her name.

"She will be devastated," he thought. She had written to Dougie every week.

There were a few other boys who were left behind as the 34th flew back to Moresby to meet the transport ship the "Willis Van" that was to take them back to Cairns. The medical staff worked on Curley for nearly three weeks before he finally turned the corner. The nursing staff, especially nurse Shirley, sat by his bedside, night after night while Curley talked in his sleep about his childhood, his father, the milk run, his girls, young Trish and finally, his wife Joan. Was she pregnant again? He went on about her, what a good looking sort she was, how he could not wait to get back to Sydney, and -- and-- and – strangely, he never finished what he wanted to say, but as his condition improved, he would pester the nursing staff for a beer and a fag. It rained each afternoon, and it was steamy and hot. Some of the men in the hospital, would wake in the night and start screaming, and then there would be a panic to quieten them down. As Curley became stronger, he started to exercise, and with help from one of the nursing staff, he would walk down to the bombed out beach. The palm trees had started to regenerate and everything looked green.

Shirley said, "Gee, Curley. In six months you wouldn't know that there had been a war here."

Curley and Bluey had befriended a native family that lived in the mountains about a half day's walk from the hospital. On occasions, they would venture down to trade with the soldiers. There was hell of a commotion as Curley and Nurse Shirley walked down among the palm trees, as there was a group of seven natives, yelling out and shaking their fists. Shirley, who could speak "Pidgin English" walked over to them to find out what was happening. When she returned, she explained to Curley that one of the men, who was employed as a stretcher bearer, (they were called "Fuzzy Wuzzy Angels" by the troops), had been killed in an ambush on the Kokoda Track. Shirley arranged for the widow to call at the hospital the next day, as she had arranged a collection of goods to give to her.

On the beginning of the fourth week, Curley was considered out of danger. He was the old Curley and was giving cheek to the nursing staff. He would spend late afternoons, sitting under a canvas awning with some of them, bottle of beer in hand and a kero lamp to fight off the "mozzies" (mosquitoes). Curley would tell them about his wife and his girls and end up in tears. His favourite nurse had prolonged his stay but he finally said goodbye and was moved back to Moresby. The nursing staff all cried when he left. As the campaign was virtually over in Milne Bay, the Australian troops would soon be off to places more important in the fight against the Japanese.

Curley spent the next six months fighting a war of depression. The medical staff called it war fatigue. He would have an attack and break out into a sweat and shake, he would be cold one minute and hot the next. The doctors said it was the after-effects of malaria and he could have the symptoms for the rest of his life. Curley had always liked a drink but in Moresby, he drank at every opportunity. His superior officers did not know what to do, and they send him to every medical officer available. The psychologists diagnosed him with depression. Finally he was passed physically fit for duty, so he re-joined the 34th Battalion in North Queensland at Mareeba where they were on standby to return to New Guinea if needed.

As the men lined up on the parade ground, there were only a hundred and twenty-one men left in the 34th. They were brought to attention and addressed by the Commanding Officer.

"Men of the 34th, this Battalion has had a proud tradition," he said. "It was formed in 1916, saw action in France and, one of our officers, Captain

Jeffries was awarded the Victorian Cross. The Battalion then saw action in the Somme. Yes, it has a proud tradition."

The men were starting to get agitated.

"What's this all about?" Bluey said to Curley.

Then the Brigadier told them. "As from 12 December, the 34th has been amalgamated with the 20th Battalion and you will now wear the 20/34th Battalion patch."

No other explanation was given.

As the men walked back to the Barracks, Curley said "Struth! Bluey, what do you make of that?"

The boys made their way back down the coast, and as the train pulled into Roma Street, the troops tired and weary, (the train had stopped at all the sidings down the Queensland coast) were tempted to visit the Valley, but they were quickly informed that they would be moving out early the next morning.

The train stopped off at Rutherford near Newcastle, and they spent three days at the nearby army barracks.

Chapter 80

The Battalion finally made it back to Sydney, but Bluey could not understand Curley's behaviour. He was not his usual devil-may-care self. Curley was disappointed that his family was not at the station to greet him, but standing there, was a young lass from the McKenzie Cousins, with her mother. She had tears in her eyes as the Battalion officer consoled her. As Dougie had no living relatives, he handed her Dougie's hat and promised to send on his medals once they were issued.

Zero Shot Down

It was reported in today's afternoon paper, the *Sun,* that a Japanese Zero fighter was shot down in Gona in New Guinea, on 26th January 1942.

"Struth! Gona, fellers, we were only just there," yelled Blue as he downed another schooner.

They had decided to front the bar and have a drink for Jordan, so they made it back to the Royal Exchange in Marrickville where there were many blokes from all the units of the forces.

One afternoon, Curley and Bluey were holding up the bar, and it was getting on to six pm, the official closing time, (after the war, it would be referred to as the six o'clock swill), but the publican had been ignoring it. He would close the doors and let the boys drink on. As for the local constabulary, as long as there was no fighting, everything was ok. Just before the doors closed, young Barry Fifer came in with his cry of "Paper! Sun! The Mirror! Get your copy." The publican would turn a blind eye.

"Ah, fellows, look at this. A damn Wirraway shoots down a Jap Zero," said Curley.

It was front page.

"The Jap pilot must have been drunk," Curley added. [16]

There was always someone who wanted to talk about the big fight. They had got talking to three boys from Western Australia, and after a while, it was revealed they had served in Timor in the 2/2 Battalion. They were attached to a signalling group, and all were in Sparrow Force but now on their way home to Perth. They introduced themselves as Frank, Keith and John. They didn't want to reveal their rank or surnames. This didn't worry Bluey and Curley as they thought they were undercover Military Police. After a few schooners, they told the story of Sparrow Force, how a few hundred specially trained Australian diggers who worked undercover with the help of their Timor mates, attacked the Japanese with hit and run tactics, and how in the end, they were ordered back to the mainland. (It was later reported the Japanese slaughtered thousands of the peace loving Timorese). The boys were last seen arm in arm walking down Marrickville Road towards the station. They were going to see the lads onto the train and back to the barracks at Ingleburn. As the train pulled away from the station, Bluey yelled out, "Go on you buggers. Back to the West. Sparrow Fart was it?"

A voice from the train called out, "No! you boof head, we were in Sparrow Force."

The two boys left the station and wandered back to their barracks, but as they passed a laneway, Bluey said, "What do you think, Curley? Is it two up, or those couple of good looking sheilas down in Murdock Lane?"

Curley spent the next twenty-four months in and out of hospital and was never out of trouble. His malaria would flare up and he would be back in hospital. He was given shore patrol up and down the east coast of New South Wales.

---

[16] Footnote 16 See page 385

Finally John Joseph Vincent Layburn was discharged from the AIF, on the 23rd November 1945, having served 1,464 days, with one hundred and nine days overseas.

Jack Layburn received four War Medals, The Pacific Star, 39-45 Star, War Medal A143492 and the Australian Service Medal.

Jack Layburn may have been a bit of a larrikin but he was a great bloke. He would give you the shirt off his back. He may have only obtained the rank of private, but Jack Layburn, like a lot of other soldiers, went to war, not knowing what to expect in the trials and tribulations of war in the tropics. Some went off to the Middle East. ("The Rats of Tobruk"), to the Burma Railway, Changi and the death march of Sandakan. All those returning after the war suffered deep hidden depression and troubles. Some recovered, some became alcoholics, some committed suicide and some just never forgot the horrors. But some of the stories revealed from the POWs included how only six survived out of about 2,500 prisoners who were forced to march, in what has been recorded in the history books as the death march of Sandakan. The list of other stories goes on.

Although word had got through on 6th October 1945, that Jack's mother had died, Jack could not be contacted by his superiors. Ellen Layburn had been visiting her daughter's home in Lane Cove, Sydney. It was a sad day when Nana Layburn died, and the family gathered around the home in Gardenia Ave.

Ellen Layburn died during the night, of a heart attack. The funeral had been scheduled for Friday, and it was Tuesday. Marcella's sister and brother-in-law, Enid and Jimmy Gair, had been notified and the call went out for their brother, Jack who was still in the Army. At his last visit, he was at Ingleburn Barracks, but by Friday morning he had not been contacted. Enid was livid and vowed she would never talk to him again.

Aunt Enid said "I will never forgive Jack for not being there for his mother's funeral."

Her eldest daughter, Marcella kept her mother's wishes and did not contact any of her mother's other relatives.

The small family group were gathered round the grave site in the Roman Catholic Section at the Northern Suburbs Cemetery, and as she was finally laid to rest, Marcella, with a tear in her eye, placed some flowers on the grave, red roses (They had been nurtured by her mother, who had been a keen gardener). As she laid the flowers on the grave, she cut a piece and placed it in her mother's bible then the small family returned to Gardenia Avenue, Lane Cove.

Jimmy broke the silence and said, "There, she was a good stick, never a bad word to say about anyone."

"That will be enough, Jim," said Enid.

Jimmy Gair had had a few drinks and was outspoken. "What about her brothers and sisters, Marcella?" he remarked.

"Jimmy, shut up. Leave them out of it," said Enid.

But Jim went on. "She had a hard life, what with your father getting sick and she had to look after him before he died. The Boer War had a lot to answer for, you know."

When Jack finally returned to civilian life in Sydney, his marriage to Joan was soon over, involving a messy divorce.

He finally arrived at his sister Marcella's home in Lane Cove late the next week. His breath stunk of beer and when he sat on the lounge, Marcella held him in her arms and he broke down and cried.

"Be good to me, Marcella. I never meant to be away. I only got the message on Friday morning as there was no way to contact me," he said.

Jack stayed on at Lane Cove and went to work at Corbett's Chemical factory. Then he was off to Wagga Wagga.

Jack married again, a Norma Woodroffe in Wagga Wagga, and in 1950, he fathered the last John Layburn.

Jack Layburn became a reformed drinker but his health started to deteriorate from the effects of the war and malaria. His heart gave way and on 6th September 1969, Jack Layburn died peacefully. It was a sad occasion, and his wife, Norma, never informed his sisters in Sydney till after the funeral.

Remarks by Lt. F.J. Wells VX 88362,
2/43 Battalion 24th Brigade 9th Division about the war in New Guinea

"The American military high command, General McArthur, in Melbourne, at the time of the New Guinea campaign, criticised the Australian troops, ordering them to attack, not retreat. Never having been in New Guinea, he had no idea of the conditions. Major General Morris, in charge of Port Moresby, told Bert Kienzle to construct a road over the Kokoda track for ease of movement so heavy artillery and tanks could be deployed if needed. Kienzle knew it was an impossible dream. He was chosen, as he had military experience with the native troops; he had joined up as a Captain. It is worth noting that neither Morris nor Blamey went past Owens Corner in New Guinea.

"Even now 63 years on, there is still no road."

Remarks by Lt. Clive Boorman 2/12 Australian Infantry Battalion
QX4985 (Q199866) about the New Guinea campaign

"On the 21st July 1942, the Japs landed the first of an eventual force of 13,000 at Gona. Their aim was to strike over the Owen Stanley Ranges and capture Pt. Moresby. This fighting was to be called the Battle of the Kokoda Track. At first, the Australians only had an inexperienced Brigade, the 39th, consisting of CMF troops, to resist the Japanese advance. The experienced 21st AIF Brigade joined, but was unable to prevent the overwhelming force of Japs from reaching a position, thirty-five miles from Port Moresby. The Japs later revealed they could see the lights in the Harbour. By then, the enemy supply lines were stretched to the limit and had run out of steam, and the Australian forces had delayed the enemy sufficiently to assemble two experienced AIF Brigades the 25th and the 16th, so the Japs were forced back to three strong-points on the north coast of NG. This coastline was surrounded by malaria-infested swamps and jungle with Kunai grass which would cut you to pieces. It rained every day, the ground turned to ankle deep mud, and with very high humidity, there were better places to be. The

Australian 25th and 16th Brigades crossed over the Kokoda Track fighting as they went.

"The initial plan was for the 25th Brigade to capture Gona, the 16th to capture Sanananda, and the five regiments of American troops to capture Buna.

"What the planners had not taken into account, was that the Aussie forces were buggered, the Yanks were young and inexperienced, poorly led and had no idea what they were getting involved in. The result was that the initial attempts to capture the three strong-points failed. (The Aussies eventually took Gona with the help of the 21st Brigade). On 9th December 1942, the experienced Australian 18th Brigade, that had recently taken Milne Bay was called in.

"The 2/9th Battalion of that Brigade did in one day, what the Yanks could not do in one month. They broke the Japs' defence at Buna. The 2/10th Battalion took over and made further progress and the 2nd/12th Battalion then cleaned up Buna on 1st January 1943. Finally, Sanananda fell to the 2/12th Battalion, on 20th January 1943.

"Whilst the above was going on, the Japs landed on the south eastern tip of New Guinea at a place called Milne Bay. This was to be a pincer movement in the capture of Port Moresby. The allies had built two airstrips there, and were constructing a third when the Japs invaded. At first, the inexperienced 7th CMF Brigade defended Milne Bay and, just before the Jap troops landed, the experienced AIF 18th Brigade arrived. The Japs, at first advanced at a fast rate westward to the main concentration of Australian forces guarding the airstrips. They were delayed on the way and were stopped in a fierce battle at the third airstrip by the 61st/9th Battalions of the 7th Brigade. The 18th Brigade then took over and the 2/12th Battalion forced the Japs to retreat in a fierce battle over four days. They were relieved by the 2/9 that then took over and forced the Japs to evacuate. This was in early September, 1943 and was the first time that the Japs had been defeated during the war on land. The second time it was defeated was in the battle for Kokoda, Gona, Sanananda and Buna described above. These battles were significant as the threat of invasion of Australia had been defeated.

"All these battles took a heavy toll. The Australians lost 2,400 killed, over 4,000 wounded and a further 14,000 evacuated through illness such as Malaria, Cholera and Psychological problems. The Americans lost 650 killed and over 2,000 wounded."

The 39th Australian Infantry Battalion 1941-43 existed as a unit for only twenty months. Their story is one of the most unusual and proudest in the annals of Australian military history.

Formed in haste from disparate Victorian militia (home defence) elements, in October/November 1941, initially officered (except for platoon commanders) by WW1 veterans, its ranks largely composed of eighteen and nineteen year old boys armed with WW1 weapons and designed for passive garrison roles in administered Papua. The 39th Battalion was, in the full sense of the term, a scratch unit. (The war in the Pacific changed with the devastating aero-naval attack against the United States naval base at Pearl Harbour). The Battalion, other equally scratch elements of the 30th Brigade, embarked on the *Aquitania* for Port Moresby, where it was to fulfil a much more significant and historic role than was ever contemplated at the time of its formation.

The Boys of the 39th were described as "The Moresby Mice," "Those Ragged Bloody Heroes" and "Those Chockos." Whatever they may be called, the fact remains we owe them a great deal of gratitude.[17]

---

[17] Footnote 17: See Page 385

Many thanks to the following "Reluctant Heroes."

To the families of Noel Hector Spicer, Service No. NX160560, and Jack Connelly, Service No. NX137526, for their part in this book. Both men served as gunners in the Royal Australian Artillery in the defence of Darwin. Jack Layburn service No NX 57179 Born 22- 12 -14 Erskineville Sydney Served in the 34th Batt.

Joe Dawson obtained the rank of Sergeant, Service No. V56140 and VX117313 in the 39th Australian Infantry Battalion. –

Geoff Smith of Bathurst, author of "100 years of the Peal" –
Jeff McSpedden, Lagoon — Mrs Tobin, Bathurst -- Martin Tobin, for allowing the photo of his dwelling, the old Lime Kilns Hotel -- Garry Tobin, Glenn Innes and Mrs Beryl McLain from Lime Kilns -- John Douglas Layburn, Maryborough, Queensland.
-- Graham Murray, Wauchope.
-- David Alexandra, Riverwood, Sydney
-- Eileen Szabados, for the use of her late husband's pencil drawing.
June Matthews, Nambucca Heads for early editing.
Pencil drawings, by Harris Redford, Blayney.
Weatherboard Inn supplied by the Blue Mts. Historical Society Inc.
Special thanks to my two sons, Peter and Steven.

"The Brisbane Line." Taken from Wikipedia
Notes of "A walking tour of historic Carcoar," written by Chris Dent, first published 1999. ISBN 0-649-37783-3.

"Chronicles of a country hospital, NSW," first published 2002 by Jill Cole, National Library of Australia Cataloguing-in-publication data,
ISBN O 9581295 0 9.

"Dear Mother," published by the Blayney Shire and Local History Group Inc. Bibliography includes index ISBN 0 958 1513 0 X
Norman Stockdale Sec. 39th Australian Infantry Battalion, 1941-43 Assoc. Incorporated.
Mark Edwell, 34th Batt. AIF.
Late Jack Wells, Service No VX88362
Late Clive Boorman, QX4985 (Q199866)

The reference to the Australian campaign in Portuguese Timor is taken from the book "The Independent Company" by Lieut. Col B.J. Callinan, D.S.O. and M.C.

Notes for a walking tour of Carcoar written by Chris Dent first published in 1999 ISB NO 0-649-37783-3

Chronicles of a country hospital Carcoar NSW first Published 2002 author Jill M Cole National library of Australia
Cataloguing-in-publication ISBN 0 9581295 0 9
Research by Rhonda Jones, Blayney Library, identifying members of the NSW Bushmen from Carcoar.

The section re the Zig Zag railway taken from 'When We Rode The Rails," by Patsy Adam Smith, 1983, Lansdowne, Sydney.

I wrote to RPLA Pty Ltd. 176 South Cr. Rd, Dee Why West. NSW seeking permission to use extracts from its book on the Zig Zag railway. After receiving no response. In referenced to part of the book on the Zig Zag rail section between Lithgow and the Blue Mountains.

Records of Australian Contingents to the War in South Africa, 1899 - 1902, compiled by Lt. Col. P L Murray RAA (Ret.) printed by the Government Printer, Melbourne, Albert J Mullett.

"History of the War in South Africa" by James H Birch Jr. in collaboration with well known author, Henry Davenport Northrop, published by The Parish Publishing Co. Toronto, Canada.

Bathurst Free Press and Mining journal
Special mention to my two sons Peter Andrew and Steven for having their faith in their father.

Footnotes
Footnote 1

It is well documented that my great, great, grandfather James Fines, arrived in the Colony of NSW, in 1823. What is not clear, was whether this was James Foynes who was arrested in King's County, Ireland and may have been mixed up with 'The White Boys' or 'Molly Maguire's', secret societies (they were halfway between the Mafia and what was the IRA) which carried out attacks on, or intimidated people, such as officials, landlords and rent collectors. The Irish Chief Secretary of the day, Sir Robert Peel (later, the British Home Secretary, was cracking down on these gangs.

James Foynes was sentenced to death, but later his sentenced was remitted to transportation to NSW. The surnames Fyan, Fyans, Fynes, Fines, Foyne, and Foynes are all rare names and all stem from the original Dublin, Fyan family.

Footnote 2
Thomas Raine 1793-1860 when he sailed for Australia in 1814 as a junior officer in the convict ship Surry an epidemic of Typhus broke out and left him the only surviving officer. He sailed the ship to China for a homeward cargo. He travelled through the Great Barrier Reef and named Raine Island after himself. Confirmed as captain he made five more journeys to Australia in the Surry between 1816 and 1823

Footnote 3

It was in the year of 1856. Samuel Taylor went on to start the Mortein's Empire. In 1870 J Hagemann, a German immigrant arrived in Sydney and with the help of his French wife thought up the name (Mort) meaning dead and (Ein) meaning one. Hagemann developed a powder from crushed Chrysanthemum flowers to produce Pyrethrum extract. When first used, the powder was sprinkled about the infected area. This product was distributed by wholesaler Samuel Taylor until his death in 1895 soon after that the business went broke in 1909. The business then came into the hands of

F.S.Steer and Thomas Jackson. They revived the Taylor business and in 1937 set up a propriety company as Samuel Taylor P/L. This company played a critical role in Mortein's development

Footnote 4

Was he Myth or Legend?

He was described in a book by Cedric Emanuel, who was famous for his pencil drawings, that in the town of Sofala, his horse won the cup and he rode off with the prize money.

'Robbery under Arms' (notes on Captain Starlight) by Rolf Boldrewood. First published in 1888. National Library of Australia, Cataloguing-publication data.
Boldrewood, Rolf 1826-1915
ISBN O 858356929

Footnote 5: This is an author's note on page 140

Footnote 6

The Story of Slippery Jack

Slippery Jack was a bushranger who roamed for several years in the rugged bush land around Sunny Corner and Palmers Oakey and in the hills and ranges around Limekiln, NSW. He didn't stage any hold ups, but lived the life of a recluse, obtaining all his needs from miners' camps and sheep properties then retreating back into the bush. It was said he was a dangerous escapee from a French prison on the island of New Caledonia.

There are many newspaper reports in the Bathurst Free Press and Mining Journal from 1893 to 1896, regarding his encounters, and also his final capture.

Footnote 7

Thomas Howarth was convicted in Lancaster 1827 for cow stealing, he always believed he was wrongly convicted as he believed it was his cow. He was sentenced to death but it was commuted to life and he was transported to Botany Bay, NSW.

Footnote 8
Post script. By Wilf Layburn, Wellington NZ. 2002

Some 75 years passed without any further clarification as to the final resting place of my uncle, William Layburn. I had a chance discussion with an official at the NZ Government's Dept. of Internal Affairs, and he offered to initiate enquires through the Commonwealth War Graves Commission in Maidenhead, Berkshire. Within 48 hours, the name of William Layburn - but not his grave, was located on the Australian National Memorial at the Villers-Bretonneux Military Cemetery.

Villers-Bretonneux is a small town 16 km east of Amiens, on the straight main road to St.Quentin. The actual Memorial is on a ridge about two klms north of the town and honours Australians killed in France and Belgium, who have no known grave.

In January, 2002, as part of a personal pilgrimage to the Somme, retracing the well documented footsteps of William and my father, Ernest Thomas Layburn, who also served in WW1, my wife and I visited the imposing Australian Memorial to the Missing at Villers-Bretonneux. A total of 10,982 names "Known unto God" are engraved on the screen panels, but just one name stood out on panel 96 that held my special attention, that of Layburn W J A. MM.

We also visited the hamlet of Herleville (today Hurleville) and were amazed to find the "sunken road" and bullet-scarred crucifix, a wayside cross, still exactly as described by William, 84 years earlier.

Having personally explored the Somme and gained a much better appreciation of the carnage and appalling loss of life during the Great War, I am now satisfied that William's burial site will never be located and that he lies forever in the soil of France.

One final thought

After the 1918 Armistice, a large number of remains were brought into Villers-Bretonneux town cemetery (known today as Adelaide) from small graveyards and isolated positions stretching out well beyond the town. They were without exception, those of the men who fell in the months from March to September1918.

Their remains were reinterred at 'Adelaide' in three large plots.

Plot 111 consists almost entirely of Australian graves, 250 being unidentified. William Layburn could be one of them!

On 2nd November, 1993, following a request by the Australian Govt., an Unknown Soldier was exhumed from Plot 111 and reinterred in the tomb of the Unknown Soldier at the Australian War Memorial in Canberra. There is a possibility - admittedly extreme - that the remains of the Australian Unknown Soldier could be William Layburn of New Zealand.

Footnote 9

The Bombing of Darwin.

The first enemy attack on Australian soil in the history of the Commonwealth of Australia occurred at 9.58 am on Thursday 19th February 1942. The small Northern Territory town of Darwin suffered an air attack by 188 Japanese aircraft. At the time of the attack, the civilian population numbered less than 2,000. It was later revealed that the anti-aircraft guns used for the defence of Darwin were obsolete. The ammunition was WW1 issue and was useless as they had no effect on the Jap planes as they came in to attack. Although radar was available, (it was used in the Battle of Britain) it was not made available, and to top it all off, the gunners were not allowed to fire practice rounds.

It has now been revealed that the same planes that bombed Perl Harbour lead by Commander Fuchida were involved in the bombing of Darwin. The town of Darwin was bombed 60 times between 19 February1942 and 12 November 1943 The Japanese lost only 7 aircraft to the anti aircraft fire in the first two raids. However by April 1942 Darwin's air defence had greatly improved and Japanese air losses greatly increased. The Japanese also bombed the towns of Broome, Wyndham, Katherine and Derby.

Footnote 10

In 1884 a German by the name of Carl von Bieran had set up a factory to manufacture Gun Powder. West of the sea side village of Narrabeen in an area known as Ingleside

Footnote 11
The sinking of the HMAS Kuttabul, Friday 29th May 1942.

The Kuttabul started out its life as a ferry, transporting passengers from the city to the north side of the harbour before the Sydney Harbour Bridge was built. It ceased operating after the bridge was built and for a short time was used as a show boat. In 1941 it was requisitioned by the navy to serve as accommodation for sailors in transit and was permanently berthed at Garden Island.

5 large Japanese subs, were positioned 65klms NE off Sydney Harbour, carrying three midget Subs and one sea plane.

Saturday, 30 May 1942, 4.30. Submarine 1.21 sends float plane on a reconnaissance over Sydney Harbour. Confirms allied war ships' presence. Identifies USS Chicago, and observes submerged boom just inside the heads. On the return leg, it passes over Kirribilli.

6.30 am. Float plane returns to submarine and sinks in rough seas. Pilot dragged aboard to safety.

Sunday, 31 May 1942. During the day, the five subs move to within 6-8km closer to the Sydney Harbour Heads.

4.45 pm. Sun sets, full moon rises.

5 pm. Lieutenant Keiu Matsuo and Masau Tsuzuko set off in midget sub 1.22 at 4knots to make his way into Sydney Harbour.

5.28 pm. Lieutenants Kenshi Chuman and Omori in midget sub 1.27, the 3rd midget sub, with Ban and his navigator, Ashibi, set off.

The plan was for Chuman to enter Harbour first 20 minutes after the moon rises; the other subs to follow at 20 minute intervals.

8 pm. The first sub follows Manly ferry undetected. At 8.05 pm, he changes direction (reason unclear) and heads for west boom net and gets tangled in it. He is spotted by Maritime patrol watch, who reports it. Patrol boat drops depth charges but they fail to explode.

10.27 pm. General warning alert to all ships and harbour is closed to all outward shipping.

9.48 pm Sub-lieutenant Katsuhisa Ban, in midget sub 1.24, follows a Manly ferry in undetected.

10.35 pm. After two and a half hours Chuman, after trying to free gate, self destructs.

10.52 pm. 'Chicago' spots Ban's sub, and fires unsuccessfully. Matsuo's sub is spotted by HMAS Laurina.

11.03 pm. HMAS Yandra drops depth charges, breaking windows in houses, near shore.

11.14 pm All ships darkened.

12.25 am Ban's sub lines up his torpedoes to fire at the USS Chicago, distance 800 meters. They were 350 kg of explosives at a depth of 2.5 meters. (Chicago has a 7 meter draft).

12.30 am. Ban's torpedo fires and misses Chicago, passes under a Dutch Sub. K9, and hits HMAS Kuttabul, killing 21 naval ratings.

Ban sets out to meet up with mother sub, 29 klms south of South Head. His battery probably failed as he was never found.

2.56 am. Monday. Lookout on Chicago sights Matsuo's sub. (It had recovered from the attack by the HMAS Yandra, four hours before).

3.50 Matsuo's sub is fired upon by merchant cruiser HMAS Kanimbla, from Neutral Bay

5 am. HMAS Sea Mist spots Matsuo sub off Taylor's Bay. Dropped depth charges and the sub was blown to the surface. Matsuo and Tsuzuko shot themselves.

Footnote 12
The Bombing of Sydney

The 8th June 1942 Sydney-siders were living in fear of an impending attack from the Japanese navy. The beaches along the coast were set up with tank traps and barbwire and were heavily guarded

On the night of 8th June 1942, a Japanese sub stationed nine kilometres off the coast sent nine shells into the Waverly area. There was little damage. Bondi had a 250 mm gun dating back to 1892 but it was never used that night and missed the chance to retaliate. Once the war in the Pacific commenced, Bondi and Manly were not the desired places they were once. Residence of the beach side suburbs were in a panic. Those who could afford to close up their homes, headed for the Blue Mountains.

Sydney's defence was part of a coastal fortress system. The North Head Fortification was completed in 1937 at a cost of £2,000 as well as the lives of two civilian labourers. Other 9.2 inch Batteries were established at La Perouse and Middle Head in Sydney Harbour

Three eight-inch guns were purchased in 1893 for the defence of Port Jackson (North and South Head) and Botany Bay and were mounted on a hydro-pneumatic mounting and were known as a "Disappearing gun." They were revolutionary for their time and could fire at a rate of three rounds per minute at 30,000 yards. The guns were replaced in 1937 by six-inch guns.

Footnote 13
The Bombing of Katherine, in the NT Australia. March 1942

It is a perfect example of the stupidity of war. The Japanese pilots on a one way trip not enough fuel for the return to base. Bombing a pile of rocks in an outback town and to kill an innocent indigenous man, absolute madness The indigenous man nicknamed Dodger deserved to be remembered as the sacrificial lamb to the slaughter that followed.

Footnote 14
The Brisbane Line.

As far back as 1891, the NSW Government was concerned about being invaded by forces from the north.

But in February 1942, "The Brisbane Line" was a controversial defence proposal allegedly formulated during WW2 to concede the northern portion of Australia, in the event of an invasion by the Japanese. Although a plan to prioritise defence in the vital industrial regions between Brisbane and Melbourne, in the event of an invasion, it was rejected by Labor Prime Minister John Curtin and the Australian War Cabinet. An incomplete understanding of this proposal and other planned responses to invasion, led Labor minister Eddie Ward to publicly allege that the previous government (a United Australian Party/Country Party coalition under Robert Menzies and Arthur Fadden) had planned to abandon most of northern Australia to the Japanese.

Eddie Ward continued to promote the idea during late 1942 and early 1943, and the idea that it was an actual defence strategy, gained support from General Douglas MacArthur, who referred to it during a press conference in March 1943, where he also coined the term "Brisbane Line." Ward initially offered no evidence to support his claims, but later claimed that the relevant records had been removed from the office files. A royal Commission concluded that no such documents had existed, and the government under Menzies and Fadden had not approved plans of the type alleged by Ward. The controversy contributed to Labor's win in the 1943 Federal election, although Ward was assigned to minor portfolios afterward.

During WW2, Tenterfield, where the New England and Bruxner highways meet, was earmarked as a key battleground if the Japanese should invade the Australian mainland. Thousands of Australian soldiers set up camp around the travelling stock route, their aim was to set up tank traps to hold back an invasion as it was the only wet weather road to the south. Thousands of Australian families, who lived north of Brisbane, were evacuated to the south.

Footnote 15: This is an author's note on page 355

Footnote 16

On 20th January 1942, a message was sent to RAAF command in Melbourne from Rabaul, by Squadron Leader J.M. Lerew, *"Nos Morituri Te Salutanus"* which means. "We, who are about to die, salute you." (the phrase uttered by gladiators in ancient Rome before entering combat). The RAAF achieved immortal fame, when 8 Wirraways, including A20 - 177, piloted by Serg. W. Hewett, did battle with a force of 109 Jap fighters and bombers. three Wirraways were shot down, two crashed and 1, severely damaged. Although hopelessly out-classed by the enemy aircraft, they remained in the front line as a stop gap fighter and on 26th December 1942, history was made by the light Australian trainer, when Pilot Officer J.S. Archer and Sergeant Arthur Coulston in a Wirraway, A20-103 shot down a Zero at Gona near Milne Bay.

PO J.S. Archer was stationed at Popondetta airfield in Papua while on a tactical reconnaissance mission on the east coast of New Guinea. He was awarded the DFV for his efforts. The Wirraway is now housed in the Australian War Memorial.

Footnote 17

My mother, Marcella Wakeling, told us when we were young children, that her Grandmother, Marsetta Fines, born at Limekiln near Bathurst in New South Wales, was the daughter of James Fines, a French sea captain who sailed the seven seas. As children we were kept 'in the dark.' Nothing was ever told to us about the family's past.

It was after the sad death of our mother that we found out about our ancestors. Low and behold, James had not sailed the seven seas. The only sea he sailed was to New South Wales as an Irish convict sent out in 1823, convicted for house breaking. The term was for seven years. He was transported on the *Medina* and served out his time as a shepherd near Bathurst on the Western Plains. Smashed was the myth that he was a sea captain. We were tricked with the name Fines, as it sounds like a French name. Some of his descendants cheered that we finally had some convict blood in us, and some cringed, but that's life!

While on one side of the family, we had Sir William McKell, (the nephew of Jane Layburn) who rose to great heights and, after being Premier of the State of NSW, went on to become the Governor General of Australia. James Fines' only claim to fame in the colony was that in 1852 he was charged with operating an illegal still.

He was finally married to Catherine Disney, just before he died. It is hard to believe that after raising ten children (there is a question re Mary, Catherine's first child) along the way, he never married Catherine. There were plenty of opportunities to marry. We could only find Baptism papers for all the girls, except for Mary. The three brothers were never baptised, they had all died in childbirth.

The Defence of Rabaul.

The 2/22nd Australian Battalion, a 1,400 strong Australian Army garrison, known as Lark Force, commanded by Lieutenant John Scanlon, were deployed to New Britain in 1941. The Lark Force is perhaps the only military unit made up entirely of recruits from the Salvation Army. Also there were 80 men from the New Guinea Volunteer Riflemen. In air defence the RAAF had 24 Squadron made up of four Hudson Bombers and eight Wirraways. On about 20th January 1942, a force of about 120 Japanese aircraft attacked and destroyed or damaged all but one Wirraway. They also put out of action, the two coastal guns.

The name Wirraway means challenge, in Aboriginal. It was also called 'Australia's little wonder' and was only to be a multipurpose training plane, with a top speed of 350 mph. and crew of two, with two 7.7 Vickers machine guns.

Publicity Stunt

Early in March 1943, Flying Officer Geoff Stevenson on a publicity exercise for the war effort to drop leaflets in the Sydney CBD, with his two other pilots decided to do a fly under the Sydney Harbour Bridge. At the last minute, one of the pilots broke rank and flew over the bridge. On returning to Bankstown they were in deep trouble for their perceived act of stupidity.

By Private Mark Edwell, 3rd Battalion Royal NSW regiment

THE 34TH INFANTRY BATTALION
The Illawarra Regiment

The 34th Infantry Battalion, AIF, was formed in January 1916, and was composed of men chiefly from the Maitland area and thus dubbed 'Maitland's Own.' The first recruits for the 34th, however, hailed from the far North-West of the state and arrived at Maitland after joining a recruiting march that started in Walgett. These men were known as the 'Wallabies.'

The 34th became part of the 9th Brigade of the 3rd Australian Division. The unit sailed for England in June 1916, and after a brief period, proceeded to France, where it saw action in various sectors of the front line.

The 34th Battalion had to wait until the emphasis of the British and Dominion Operations switched to the Ypres Sector of Belgium in mid 1917, to take part in its first major battle; this was the battle of Messines, launched on 7th June, 1917.

At the battle of Passchendaele, the Battalion suffered severe casualties, and one of the officers, Captain C.S. Jeffries, was posthumously awarded the Victoria Cross for outstanding bravery.

In March 1918, the Battalion was engaged in the heavy fighting on the Somme, and subsequently took part in the general advance in August 1918, in the final assault on the Hindenburg Line.

After the 1st World War, the Battalion was re-formed in 1925, with headquarters in Sutherland, and in 1938 transferred to Wollongong.

At the outbreak of the 1939-45 war known as World War 2, a large percentage of the Unit's members enlisted in the AIF and saw service in various theatres of War. The Battalion however, was not privileged to serve overseas, and after a period of recruit training and coastal defence, was disbanded in December 1943. It was reformed in 1951 at Wollongong, and took place with sub units at Port Kembla, Nowra and Thirroul.

The Regiment's alliance with the Border Regiment, which was first established in 1935, lapsed in 1943, on the disbandment of the unit and the 34th was re-established in 1955. The alliance with the King's Own Scottish Borderers was established in 1953. The Regiment takes great pride in its links with these two famous British Regiments.

The Governor of New South Wales, His Excellency, Admiral Sir Dudley De Chair, K.C.B. M.V.O. presented the Colours being trooped in this ceremony to the Regiment in 1925. The Regiment is proud to have presented it to today's new Queen's and Regiment Colours, which are to be received at the hands of the present Governor of New South Wales, His Excellency, Lieutenant-General Sir John Northcott, K.C.V. O.C.B.

Back To Carcoar

It was 1971, the year NSW went back in time. Daylight Saving was to start on the last weekend in October, and Jimmy Gair had promised to take Enid, his wife, and his sister in-law, back to the old town of Carcoar. He had spruced up the old Austin A40. The first stop was to pick up Marcella in Dee Why. She was waiting for them at the bottom of her unit and they set off, heading west over the Blue Mountains. They stopped at the 'Hydro Majestic' for the night and set off early the next morning, arriving in the sleepy town of Carcoar. They were greeted with the banner over the main road stating that tomorrow was 'The Ben Hall Festival'; fun for all, starting off with a parade past the Royal, and the town band was to play in the new park opposite the Court House. There was to be a re-enactment of the infamous bank hold-up and a Cobb and Co. coach would be in the parade.

Jimmy had booked into the Royal Hotel. They had arrived on the Friday afternoon, so Marcella and Enid were eager to do the walk around town searching for old school friends. They walked down to the new park and were told that the old service station had gone; a truck had got out of control on a frosty winter's night, skidded on the loose wet gravel and smashed the old barn to pieces. To add to it, the overturned truck caught fire and burnt the building to scrap.

That night they had a meal in the hotel and were up bright and early the next day. One of the main reasons for their visit was to discover the grave site of their Grandfather, John Joseph, who had died in 1886. They drove up to the hospital where Marcella had worked in the 20's as a junior nurse. The hospital had closed and the building was now a nursing home, and a local doctor had his rooms there. They slowly drove back down the road and turned into Stokes Lane and drove to the end. The old house was still there, and the sisters momentarily went quiet, as they reminisced about their early childhood before they moved to Sydney. By the time they had returned to the Royal for a counter lunch, the parade was in full swing, and they had to park at the rear of the pub. They then moved onto the cemetery.

Reluctant Heroes

After parking at the gate, Enid moved down to the unmarked section, but it was no use, she was lost. It was so long ago when she had visited the grave with her father, and the area looked like a jungle; it had not been mown for some time. All Jimmy could say was, "It's a disgrace. He should have had a proper headstone." They went on to where their Grandmother's site was, next to her second husband, Michael Cassidy.

Jimmy started to laugh, "Bloody Catholics! The poor old bugger was left out of it. But he was laughing; I bet he is still 'Cursing the Bells.'" That night Jimmy had got talking to some of the locals, who were holding up the bar, he then escorted the girls up the stairs to bed.

Enid said "Don't be long now, Jimmy. We hope to get an early start tomorrow and we lose an hour with daylight saving." As the two sisters walked to their adjoining rooms, they were arguing the pros and cons of the time change. Enid had been told that the chooks would not lay. Marcella tried to explain that the sun would still rise just the same.

"Now, don't forget to wind your watch forward one hour before you go to sleep" said Marcella.

Jimmy slipped as he made his way up the stairs, as he had had a 'skin full.' He was ready for bed, but he was confused. He was to wind the clock forward one hour. "I think that's right," he mumbled to himself.

Much to Marcella's amazement Jim and Enid were ready right on the time that they had arranged for breakfast; at seven thirty. Jimmy was all in a dither.

"You know it's really only half past six here," he said.

There were three other couples seated for breakfast, but 8 o'clock came and went, with no sign of any activity in the kitchen. Jimmy said he would go to the bar and investigate, but he returned. "Nar, couldn't find a soul there."

Finally at 9.00 am, a very apologetic maid rushed into the dining room and said that she was confused with this new time. She put her clock back two hours and slept in.

As the Austin A40 wound its way up the hill, Jimmy stopped and took a photo of the view down to the sleepy village of Carcoar. In the distance they could see one of the last trains to use the Cowra branch line pulling into the station. The sisters had one last thing to do and that was to visit the cemetery. Their father was buried next to his mother who had been buried with her second husband Michael Cassidy. Time was getting on but they wandered off down through the grass looking for their Grandfather's unmarked grave but time had passed him by. It was no use, but Marcella said she seemed to remember the grave over near this rock. Finally they left with no certainty at all and it was left to remain one of life's mysteries. Jack reckoned they should ask the church. "Turn it up, Jim. He was not buried with any of the churches in town," Enid said, having the last say as they left the cemetery and returned to the car.

A Family Reunion

It is more than 100 years since John Joseph died, and on 30th November 1986, a gathering of John Joseph's descendants met at the quiet village of Carcoar, west of the Blue Mountains in NSW, involving 20 people and four generations. The families travelled from Melbourne, the North Coast of NSW, Sydney, Jervis Bay, Ettalong and the Hunter Valley, so this was the ideal opportunity to bring the families closer together. The group stayed at the historic Royal Hotel, where an ancestor, Mary Friend worked and witnessed the savage murder in the bank next door. They visited John Layburn Jnr's family home which has featured in the movie 'Let the Balloons Go.'

The reunion was highly successful and it is intended to have further reunions with descendants from the UK and New Zealand as well as Australia. The weekend was highlighted by the group planting a Liquid Amber Tree in the park opposite the Courthouse.

Carcoar is one of the beauty spots of NSW and it is little wonder J.J. Layburn decided to settle there.

THE WHEEL HAS TURNED FULL CIRCLE.

Of course no family history is ever complete. New generations are being born and more information is being found concerning the old generations with each passing month. It is my sincere hope that this brief outline of the Layburn Family will merely encourage further research.

Taken from thoughts by the Author.

On my first visit to the sleepy town of Carcoar I was taken aback by its beauty. My mother, who was born in Bakers Hotel on the main street opposite the Royal Hotel, had described Carcoar to me many times. She described the characters of the village of her younger days, 'Browns Creek' which become the 'Belubula River'; where my wife, Elizabeth and I were married in 1998 in the park opposite the Court House.

Now the main road bypasses the village and it is so quiet, you could pitch a tent in the main street. Last but not least, the Railway Station. Will we ever see trains through there again?

Thoughts from John Douglas Layburn, Great Grandson of John Joseph Layburn

I have never thought about being the last John Layburn in a line of John Layburns. I have mixed emotions of not being able to continue the tradition and of course the family name.

When I was growing up, it was a bother to me to have my father's name; I was called 'Johnny Junior.'

But now, in retrospect, I can appreciate the importance of tradition. I now refer to myself as 'John Layburn the 4th.

It is with sad heart that I cannot introduce my son as 'John Layburn the 5th', but as my father said, "What's in a name? It is the way a person lives his life and the honour he brings to the family name that matters."

Mr Nicholas Wakeling

In the State of Victoria, the Bracks Labor Government had been in power since 1999. In the outer suburban electorate of Ferntree Gully, Knox City Councillor, Nicholas Wakeling gained preselection for the Victorian Liberal party to contest the 2006 Victorian election. He was seeking to unseat the incumbent Labor member.

Nick, as he was known to his friends, was first introduced to politics in 1975 when his father served as Campaign Director for the Liberal candidate for the Federal seat of Holt during the turbulent period of the dismissal of the Whitlam Government.

Nick and his brother, Tim helped their father put flyers in letter boxes, and fold brochures, in what turned out to be a very dirty campaign, political posters were torn down all over the electorate.

Growing up in politics, Nick progressed from joining the party as a teenager to eventually being elected to local government in the outer Eastern Melbourne municipality of Knox.

Nick's local representation saw him being encouraged by many local residents to seek higher office in the Victorian parliament. Consequently, he was successfully preselected by the party as its candidate at the forthcoming state election.

For the next 18 months, Nick campaigned for the seat at every available opportunity - be it knocking on doors, standing on street corners or visiting the local sporting clubs.

He was also attending the odd bbq fundraiser to try and raise some much needed funds for his campaign.

The campaign proper went into overdrive for the six week period prior to the November poll. Volunteers filled shopping centres, door knocking continued with much fervour and the letterboxes of unsuspecting householders were inundated with election material.

Nick's family had come out in force. His wife and children were helping, so too were his parents and brother and even his uncle had flown in for the journey from his NSW Mid North Coast home.

Reluctant Heroes

The state of Victoria went to the polls on 25th November 2006, and Election Day was filled with anticipation. Up at four am, supporters were setting up polling booths. After 18 months of campaigning, the result hinged on the results of one day.

The booths closed at six pm and the campaign workers all gathered at the local church hall at Rowville. The local Liberal branch had organised a BBQ for the workers and a giant plasma TV had been set up to allow people to watch the result. At 9.00 pm the Labor Party Premier claimed victory. Shortly after, Opposition leader Ted Baillieu conceded defeat but put out the challenge that his team would take up the fight to the new Government.

By 10.30 that evening, the result in the seat of Ferntree Gully was still too close to call. Nick's uncle predicted that his nephew would win, whilst others were not so positive in their predictions. Counting of the votes continued on Sunday and Monday and the lead see-sawed with the counting of postal and absentee votes. His uncle, who had travelled from Valla, NSW, had booked a plane ticket to return home the following Wednesday, but by the following weekend, the seat of Ferntree Gully had still not been decided. The Returning Officer announced that a result would be determined by Wednesday 6th December, a full 12 days since polling day.

After a long and exhaustive delay, Nick was called at two am by his campaign chairman on the Wednesday morning to inform him that he had won the seat by a mere 27 votes.

After a whirlwind election campaign, Nick had been elected to the Victorian parliament and within a matter of days, he had taken his seat in the Legislative Assembly. Shortly after the formal opening, the Deputy Speaker called upon the new member for Ferntree Gully to rise and deliver his maiden speech. During his inaugural speech in parliament, in which he outlined his vision for his community, he also acknowledged the legacy of his ancestors - including John Joseph Layburn who had travelled from England to forge a new life in the NSW township of Carcoar.

Nicholas Wakeling was the Great Great Grandson of John Joseph Layburn who arrived in NSW in 1864. J J Layburn never aspired to the

Political arena however, Nicholas was related to Sir William McKell who was Premier of NSW and went on to be Governor General of Australia.

EXTRACT FROM PARLIAMENTARY DEBATES

HANSARD

Mr WAKELING MP
Ferntree Gully

Address-in-reply

Wednesday, 20 December 2006

Mr WAKELING (Ferntree Gully) — In this address-in-reply debate I should like firstly to congratulate you, Deputy Speaker, on your election to the high office you occupy, and secondly, to congratulate the other newly elected members of this house.

It is a privilege to be elected as the first Liberal member for Ferntree Gully. The electorate of Ferntree Gully lies to the west of the picturesque Dandenong foothills. Located within the municipality of Knox, the electorate comprises the established suburbs of Ferntree Gully and Boronia to the north. To the south, lie the suburbs of Rowville and Lysterfield, which over recent years have experienced significant growth as many young families have established their new residences within these two suburbs. I am a passionate advocate for the needs and aspirations of residents in the Ferntree Gully electorate. It was this passion that inspired me to serve this community as a councillor with the City of Knox and now as a member of this house.

I firmly believe that the Ferntree Gully electorate deserves a greater range of services and infrastructure. This community has demanded improvements to public transport, road infrastructure, law and order, education and health services. Over the next four years I commit myself to being a strong advocate for my constituency. It is clear that the Ferntree Gully electorate requires significant improvements to public transport. The Rowville community is demanding a long-term solution to solve its transport needs. As a Rowville resident I understand the frustrations of my constituency and will continue to advocate for the completion of the Rowville rail feasibility study. Furthermore, to overcome concerns about community safety, I will continue the fight to upgrade Ferntree Gully railway station to premium status.

Law and order is a major concern to my community. The Rowville police station is currently operational for only 16 hours a day. This situation is untenable and I will continue lobbying for this station to be operational for 24 hours a day. The road network throughout my electorate requires significant upgrade. Many residents complain that there appears to be no clear planning to overcome congestion on our local roads. I commit to fight for the duplication of Napoleon Road. Once completed, this will allow for the construction of the long-awaited Dorset Road extension.

Health and education services in the region also require significant upgrades. I will continue to lobby for important upgrades to the Knox Community Health Service and also continue to push for the upgrade and redevelopment of our local school infrastructure. It is not acceptable for my constituents to be educated in substandard facilities.

The Ferntree Gully community has been well served over many years by a number of highly regarded Liberal members of Parliament. Sir George Knox served the region with distinction for 33 years. In April 1927 Sir George was elected to the Legislative Assembly as the member for Upper Yarra. In November 1945 he was elected as the member for Scoresby, a position he held until his death in 1960. During his period in Parliament, Sir George served as Speaker of the house between 1942 and 1947. Prior to his tenure in Parliament he served as a commanding officer with the 23rd Battalion, which included service in Gallipoli. He also served as a councillor with the Shire of Ferntree Gully for five years. In recognition of his service to the Ferntree Gully community, the City of Knox was named in his honour.

The Honourable William Borthwick represented the region with distinction, serving as the member for Scoresby between 1960 and 1967 before serving as the member for Monbulk until 1982. During his tenure in Parliament he served at various times as a minister of water supply, lands, soldier settlement, conservation, health and also as Deputy Premier between June 1981 and April 1982.

The Honourable Geoffrey Hayes represented the region as member for Scoresby between 1967 and 1976. He also served the Parliament with distinction as a minister for planning and housing. Mr Hurtle Lupton, who would be known to many in this house, served as the member for Knox between 1992 and 2002. Hurtle was committed to the Knox community, having served as a councillor with the City of Knox for 20 years, including three terms as mayor.

I am proud of the contributions my ancestors have made to life in Australia. My maternal ancestors emigrated from England and Ireland in the 19th century. James Tomkins and his wife Maria produced 10 children in their native Dublin. Like many victims of the potato famine, the family travelled to Australia on the *Midlothian* in 1853 in search of a better life. Upon arriving in Victoria with his family, James obtained employment as a member of the Victorian public service, serving as a messenger and housekeeper in the office of the Master in Equity. Another maternal ancestor, Thomas Hoskin, and his future wife, Tryphena, emigrated from Cornwall to Melbourne in the 1850s in search of a new life. After marrying in Melbourne, the couple travelled to the country, where they helped pioneer the community of Violet Town in Victoria's north-east.

My maternal grandfather, Norman Tomkins, worked as a chauffeur for Sir Henry Wrixon at his property named Raheen in Kew. Sir Henry served as President in the Legislative Council. With the outbreak of war, Norman immediately enlisted for service. Serving with the 6th Battalion, my grandfather was a proud Anzac, having landed at Gallipoli on 25th April 1915. Upon returning to Australia after sustaining an injury at the front, Norman and his new wife, Elsie, raised four children during the height of the Depression. I am proud of their contribution and the manner in which the couple raised my mother, Jacqueline.

My paternal ancestors emigrated from England. John Layburn emigrated to Australia in the 19th century and took up residence in the rural New South Wales township of Carcoar. His son, John Joseph Layburn, later served his country on two occasions, as a member of the Bushmen's Regiment during the Boer War in South Africa.

Another paternal ancestor, George Alfred Wakeling, and his wife, Jane, moved to Manly, New South Wales, with their three children. George established a small business in Sydney. His son Reginald was passionate about political discussion and instilled in my father, Bill, and his three brothers the significance of political philosophy and debate.

I am proud to serve in this house as a member of the Liberal Party. The late Sir Robert Menzies, founder of this great party, developed the Liberal Party on a philosophy of smaller government and encouraging the right of the individual to grow and prosper. One only needs to look at the proposal by the then Chifley Labor government to nationalise the banking system. Menzies, as Leader of the Opposition, declared in the House of Representatives that such a move was:

> … a tremendous step towards the servile state, because it will set aside normal liberty of choice, and that is what competition means, and will forward the idea of the special supremacy of government. That is the antithesis of democracy. Democracy rests upon the view that the people are the rulers as well as the ruled; that the government has no

authority and no privilege beyond that granted by the people themselves; that while sovereignty attaches to the acts of Parliament, that sovereignty is derived from the people and has no other source.

It was this philosophy of free enterprise, small government and hard work that encouraged my father to join the Liberal Party at an early age and later serve as a ministerial adviser in the former Hamer government.

During my formative years I was taught about the Liberal philosophy around the family dinner table, a philosophy which supports the concept that wealth is created in the private sector and the health of the private sector determines the ultimate health of the economy. My philosophy was further developed through my experiences in both my education and employment.

My education at Haileybury College, my political studies at La Trobe University and my postgraduate studies in industrial relations at both RMIT and Monash universities, provided me with the opportunity to explore and debate a range of political philosophies. I can recall many passionate, philosophical debates with lecturers and fellow students during these formative years. I also look back with fondness on my time in student politics. As the new member for Malvern would recall, in the early 1990s spirited debate was led by Liberal students throughout university campuses regarding the need for voluntary student unionism, a dream finally realised with the recent passage of legislation through the Senate.

I bring to this house a range of business experiences in both the private and the public sectors that have enabled me to understand the impact of government regulation on Australian industry. Working in the industrial relations department of the Victorian Automobile Chamber of Commerce allowed me to understand the significance of the small business sector to the Victorian economy.

Small business is the engine room of the Victorian economy, and it is vital that the Victorian government develop the best mix of policies to encourage these businesses to prosper. Furthermore, my more recent role in a senior industrial relations position with the Adecco Group has provided me with a unique opportunity to understand the employment needs of many Australian businesses. Working for one of Australia's largest employers, those on-hires over 10,000 employees to thousands of businesses throughout Australia, has enabled me to develop a range of employment models with a large number of businesses throughout this nation.

Developing employment models on a national level has also demonstrated the disparity in legislation amongst the states in a range of portfolios. These experiences highlighted the need for greater harmonisation of government regulation throughout the Commonwealth. The former Kennett government should be commended for achieving harmonisation at a national level with respect to industrial relations. I believe it is incumbent on future governments to explore greater opportunity for harmonisation amongst the various legislators.

I have been provided with a wonderful opportunity to represent the needs and aspirations of my electorate. I remain steadfast in my desire to see the delivery of better services and infrastructure for the Knox community. I also commit myself to working for a better Victoria, a state in which business is encouraged to grow and prosper, to allow all Victorians the opportunity to achieve a better quality of life through the benefits of full-time employment.

I would like to take this opportunity to thank my wonderful campaign team and supporters for their hard work. I am indebted to the commitment of Liberal Party members in both the Rowville and Ferntree Gully branches, who committed many months to my campaign. I would also like to pay credit to my fantastic campaign committee, in particular Glynis Allen, Dawn Keast and former member Hurtle Lupton. I will always be sincerely grateful to my campaign chairman, Graeme McEwin, who is here today, for his commitment, drive and passion. Graeme is unswerving in his commitment to the Liberal Party in the Knox region. Graeme put his faith in me many years ago, and I am sincerely indebted to him.

I would like to thank my state colleague Kim Wells, the member for Scoresby, plus my federal colleagues, the Honourable Chris Pearce, the federal member for Aston, and Jason Wood, the federal member for La Trobe, for their support and counsel. The efforts of these members demonstrate the resolve of Liberal parliamentarians to assist their colleagues wherever possible.

I will always be proud of my parents, Bill and Jacqueline. I will always be very grateful to my mother, who put aside many issues to make sure that my education was the no.1 priority in her life whilst trying to cope on a single fixed income with the 17 per cent interest rates in the 1980s. I would like to pay credit to my brother, Tim, and my wonderful parents-in-law, Colin and Judy Golding, for being so giving of their time to my campaign.

I would like to thank my wonderful wife, Levili, and my two children, Thomas and Emily, who are not here today, for being such a fantastic family. Members in this house would know only too well the impact that an election campaign has on our immediate families, particularly those who fight an 18-month campaign.

I would also like to thank my work colleagues at Adecco who are here today for their support and friendship, and the many companies within the recruitment industry for their support.

Finally, I would like to acknowledge the contribution made to the electorate by the former member for Ferntree Gully, Ms Anne Eckstein. I wish her and her family well in the future and on behalf of the constituents of Ferntree Gully, thank her for the work she did during her term in office.

Foot note,

Nicholas Wakeling was the G.G.GSON of John Joseph Layburn who arrived in NSW in 1864. Although JJ Layburn never aspired to the Political arena, Nicholas was related to Sir William Mc Kell who was Premier of NSW and went on to be the Governor General of Australia.

His other GGGFATHER James Fines would be tickled green that his GGGSON had made it into parliament

The 2010 election
Nicholas had worked hard over the last four years and was returned with a big swing and the Liberal party was to form the new Govt. led By Ted Baillieu

Final Note

This book, 'Reluctant Heroes' touches on the men and women who made this country, Australia, what it is today.

Service men have gone to wars in the last 150 years and it is only now clear that they have returned with symptoms diagnosed as the Gulf War syndrome, before that Vietnam War related problems.

Jack Layburn came back from WW two with all types of medical problems that had never been seen until it was too late. His father John went to the Boer War and William Layburn was killed just a few weeks from the end of the Great War. Well, they were expected to give all for King and Country.

Women like Catherine Disney who battled heat and cold, lived in squalid and primitive conditions, raised ten children. We take our hats off to them all.

But as they say, "Life goes on."

The End

The Dying Soldier---
Written by my Grandfather during his time in the Boer War 1899 to 1901

The Tumult of the battle had ceased high in the air
The standard of Britain triumphantly waved;
And the remnant of foes had all but fled in despair,
Whom night intervening, from slaughter had saved;

When no veteran was seen by the light of his lamp
Slow pacing the bounds of the carcass strewn plain;
Not base his intent for he quitted his camp
To comfort the dying not plunder the slain

Though dauntless in awe, at a story of woe,
Down his age furrowed cheeks the warm tears often ran
Alike proud to conquer, or spare a brave foe

He fought like a hero but felt like a man

As he counted the slain "Are conquest," he cried
"Thou art glorious indeed, but how dearly thou'rt won."
Too dearly alas a voice faintly replied
It thrilled clearly his heart! twas the voice of his son.
As he counted the slain "Ah, conquest!"

John Joseph Layburn – Boer War

The Carcoar Lads – Prior to the Boer War

John Joseph Layburn (seated) and friend – Boer War

Australian Bushman's Contingent, Officers and men of "D" Squadron - Boer War

William Layburn – World War 1

Jack Layburn – World War 2

Jack Connelly and Hector Noel Spicer – World War 2
Both Jack and Noel were gunners in the Royal Australian Artillery in the defence of Darwin

Darwin life during World War 2

"I say old chap pass the soap"

"Pass the soap..." Livingstone airstrip, 457 Sqn. RAAF. 1943.

Occupation money to be used by the Japanese for the invasion of Australia and surrounding Islands – World War 2

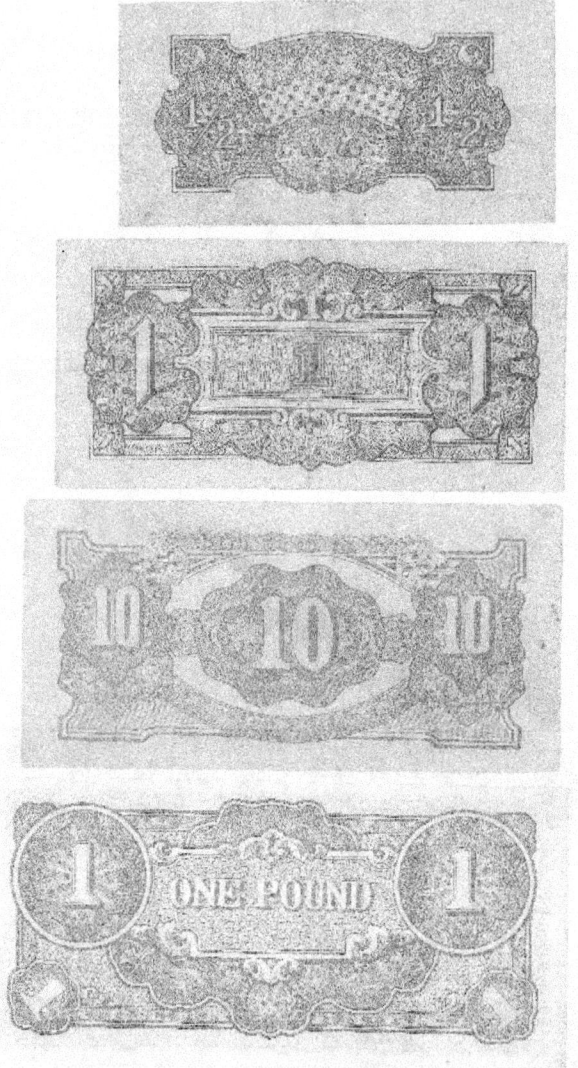

Early Settler's Cottage

Zig Zag Railway to Lithgow

Elands River – South Africa

Church ruins Taunagh Village, Sligo, Ireland

8 inch Disappearing Gun

Weatherboard Inn, Blue Mountains, NSW

Rising Star Hotel formerly known as Limekiln Hotel

Certificate of Freedom known as the Ticket of Leave

CERTIFICATE OF FREEDOM.

No. 30/288
Date, 11 May 1830

Prisoner's No. —
Name, — James Fines
Ship, — Medina
Master, — Brown
Year, — 1823
Native Place, — Kildare
Trade or Calling — Labourer
Offence, — Houserobbery
Place of Trial, — Dublin City
Date of Trial, — 1 April 1823
Sentence, — Seven years
Year of Birth, — 1799
Height, — 5 feet 3 1/2 Inches
Complexion, — Florid pockpitted
Hair, — Dark brown
Eyes, — Grey
General Remarks, Had a Ticket of Leave No 29/577 dated 5 Aug. 1829 Cancelled

Manly, NSW – 7 miles from Sydney – 1,000 miles from care

Carcoar Railway Station

Old Carcoar Railway Bridge

www.ingramcontent.com/pod-product-compliance
Lightning Source LLC
Chambersburg PA
CBHW080919180426
43192CB00040B/2470